QUESTIONS WRITERS ASK

Wise, Whimsical, and Witty Answers
from the Pros

Karen Speerstra

Robert D. Reed Publishers
P.O. Box 1992
Bandon, OR 97411
Phone: 541-347-9882; Fax: -9883
E-mail: 4bobreed@msn.com
Website: www.rdrpublishers.com

Author Photo © Ellen Donaldson Allen
Cover Photo "Research Paper" © Thomas Perkins at fotolia.com
Cover Design by Cleone L. Reed
Interior Design by Corryn Hurst

ISBN: 978-1-934759-32-5
ISBN 10: 1-934759-32-5

Library of Congress Control Number: 2009931932

Manufactured, Typeset, and Printed in the United States of America

Dedication

To John, the loving and supportive partner every writer deserves

Acknowledgments

Mange tusan takk as we say in my parents' native Norwegian language; many thousand thanks to all the writers whose work you find within these covers. Let's buy their books to show them we all care about what they've said.

I'd be remiss if I didn't thank Bob and Cleone Reed for their early vision for this book.

And to my friends who help me spread my written words around and who are there for me when I need inspiration, or a pick me up, a huge thank you!

A special hug to Anne Gilman who helped me retool this collection, early on.

Finally, to my family who supports me in all my writing efforts, listens to me go on and on…and on, and who even help edit and proofread from time to time. *Mange tusan takk!*

Table of Contents

Preface

Imagine conversations involving writers around the planet and across the centuries. They sit down to discuss common writing questions—twenty to be exact. That's what this book is about…the questions we ask as we attempt to place words on a blank page. Imagine what we'd hear if writers could magically join us in dialogue at a "common table."

For instance, imagine the thorny problem of turning a novel into a film or TV script:

> Never judge a book by its movie.
> - J. W. Eagan

> I can't think of any one film that improved on a good novel, but I can think of many good films that came from very bad novels.
> - Gabriel Garcia Marquez

> Turning one's novel into a movie script is rather like making a series of sketches for a painting that has long ago been finished and framed.
> - Vladimir Nabokov

> Reading a novelization of your own screenplay is like watching someone else kiss your girlfriend.
> - Don Marquis

> Having your book turned into a movie is like seeing your oxen turned into bouillon cubes.
> - John LeCarré

This collection attempts to offer advice from the "greats" and "near greats" but also puts in our hands a wonderful way to avoid writing for a few minutes. It's always more fun to read about how others do it than getting down to the nitty-gritty of doing it ourselves. But because we all need a break, these bits of wisdom and wit stand ready to cheer you and spur you on, to jump-start your own creativity.

In my research, I ran across a little book edited by James Charlton called *The Writer's Quotation Book: A Literary Companion*, first published by Pushcart Press, later by Penguin. The edition I found was published in 1985. Writers collect quotations, Charlton said, to create a "living place that conforms to their own sensibility and shape." Reason enough, I say.

As a free lance writer, author of several books, and former editor and publishing director, quotations have been spilling out of my own desk drawers and ever-expanding journals for decades. I index them so I later can find stuff. I have a notoriously bad memory. I thought I was being extraordinarily obsessive until I learned that Annie Dillard indexes her journals as well. So there.

How, you might ask, did I determine which quotations to include? I read. *A lot.* I visited many libraries. And wandered through Internet collections. But web sites can be slippery so I cross-checked and verified, corrected and sifted. One site, which I avoided, spelled one author's name John *Updyke*. An editor recently told me that quotations "float like viruses and morph around the web. You can't trust 'em." But there are some university sites that one would hope to be worthy of our trust. Maybe.

Furthermore, I was tired of reading many of the same old common writing quotations, and I was becoming more and more annoyed at not finding many women in most collections. So I set for myself the task of gathering some fresh thoughts, many of them from books recently published.

Thanks to my friend Orlo, I found quite a few in his basement office. There, I stumbled upon *Writing Life Stories*. It's a wonderful book by Bill Roorbach on how to take your memories and turn them into memoirs. His subtitle: "*How to make memories into memoirs, ideas into essays, and life into literature.*" That's *writing* in a nutshell.

About the structure of writing, Roorbach said: "*How to fashion the stone wall? And what kind will it be? How high? What shape? What length? Will it be primarily decorative? Will it serve a function? Is it part of a castle or only a cairn?*"

Why do we write? (Chapter 3) For our readers. They are the powerful ones!

Ursula K. Le Guin once said, "*As you read [a book] word by word and page by page, you participate in its creation, just as a cellist playing a Bach suite participates, note by note, in the creation, the coming-to-be, the existence of the music. And, as you read and re-read, the book of course participates in the creation of you, your thoughts and feelings, the size and temper of your soul.*"

That's what this collection attempts to do. It calls people together to participate, note-by-note, word-by-word, in our mutual *coming-to-be*. It is my hope that this collection will help all of us aspiring writers and creatives to better assess the size and temper of our own souls and help our readers better see their own.

So, build a few castles. Value your cairns. And have fun doing it.

1.

How do I get started?

In the primal beginning was the Word.
- Above the library in Ephesus

The journey of a thousand miles begins with one step.
- Lao-Tsu

With the possible exception of the equator, everything begins somewhere.
- Peter Robert Fleming

All serious daring starts within.
- Eudora Welty

In every phenomenon the beginning remains always the most notable moment.
- Thomas Carlyle

The world is round and the place which may seem like the end may also be only the beginning.
- Ivy Baker

Begin anywhere but the beginning.
- Marshall Cook, *Freeing Your Creativity*

...nothing starts at the beginning, at least not since the time of Adam and Eve. Everything starts in the middle of something else, and that's where it ends, as well.
- Terry Brooks, *Sometimes the Magic Works*

First sentences are doors to the world.
- Ursula K. Le Guin

If you can't catch the reader's attention at the start and hold it, there's no use going on.
- Marianne Moore

The first moments are critical. You can sit there, tense and worried, freezing the creative energies, or you can start writing *something*, perhaps something silly. It simply doesn't matter *what* you write; it only matters *that* you write. In five or ten minutes the imagination will heat, the tightness will fade, and a certain spirit and rhythm will take over.
- Leonard Bernstein

The great majority of men are bundles of beginnings.
- Ralph Waldo Emerson

I always write a good first line, but I have trouble in writing the others.
- Molière

In our openings we are most likely to lie.
- Anton Chekhov

I cannot start a story or chapter without knowing how it ends…Of course, it rarely ends that way.
- Kashua Ishigura

A beginning is that which is not itself necessarily after anything else, and which has naturally something else after it…
- Aristotle, *On the Art of Poetry*

Bring all your intelligence to bear on your beginning.
- Elizabeth Bowen

The only right way of telling a story is to begin at the beginning—at the beginning of the world. Therefore all books have to be begun in the wrong way for the sake of brevity.
- G.K. Chesterton

A bad beginning makes a bad ending.
- Euripides

What we call results are beginnings.
- Ralph Waldo Emerson

We are forever in the midst of beginnings and arrivals…Sometimes for years we seem to be nothing but middle. Middle and muddle…But the illusion of middle is comfort; middle can be wonderful insulation; middle is good—until it comes to an end, which is always sooner than we had hoped.
- David Whyte, *Crossing the Unknown Sea*

Everything has been said before, but since nobody listens, we have to keep going back and beginning all over again.
- André Gide

There will come a time when you believe everything is finished. That will be the beginning.
- Louis L'Amour

You expect far too much of a first sentence. Think of it as analogous to a good country breakfast: what we want is something simple, but nourishing to the imagination. Hold the philosophy, hold the adjectives, just give us a plane subject and verb and perhaps a wholesome, nonfattening adverb or two.
- Larry McMurtry

As long as you can start, you are all right. The juice will come.
- Ernest Hemingway, *Writers at Work*

I always do the first line well, but I have trouble with the others.
- Molière

First, find out what your hero wants, then just follow him!
- Ray Bradbury

Start by doing what is necessary; then do what is possible; and suddenly you are doing the impossible.
- Francis of Assisi

All great deeds and all great thoughts have a ridiculous beginning. Great works are often born on a street corner or in a restaurant's revolving door.
- Albert Camus

I write the first sentence and trust in God for the next.
- Laurence Sterne

A book begins as a private excitement of the mind.
- E.L. Doctorow

One of the most difficult things is the first paragraph. I have spent many months on a first paragraph, and once I get it, the rest just comes out very easily.
- Gabriel Garcia Marquez

If you start well, you will write all your stories.
- Natalie Goldberg

Every beginning is a consequence. Every beginning ends something.
- Paul Valéry

Everybody who has any respect for painting, feels scared when he starts a new canvas.
- Robert Henri

A great thought begins by seeing something differently, with a shift of the mind's eye.
- Albert Einstein

What Kierkegaard said about love is also true of creativity: every person must start at the beginning.
- Rollo May

I love writing. It's getting started that I abhor.
- Gary Provost

The last thing that we find in making a book is to know what we must put first.
- Blaise Pascal

The truth is at the beginning of anything and its end are like touching.
- Yoshida Kenko

Here is a useful rule for beginning: Know the story—as much of the story as you can possibly know, if not the whole story—before you commit yourself to the first paragraph.
- John Irving, "Getting Started"

The first step...shall be to lose the way.
- Galway Kinnell

First thoughts have tremendous energy. It is the way the mind first flashes on something.
- Natalie Goldberg

Starting a novel isn't so different from starting a marriage. The dreams you pin on people are enormous.
- Ann Patchett, *Writers [on Writing] Vol. II*

A garden in the early stage is not a pleasant or compelling place: it's a lot of arduous, messy, noisome work—digging up the hard ground, putting in fertilizer, along with the seeds and seedlings. So with beginning a story or novel.
- Ted Solotaroff

Start where the backstory begins to be important. Start at the beginning of the conflict.
- Christopher Keesler

The hard part is getting to the top of page 1.
- Tom Stoppard

Shall I begin like the novelists, with my birth, or like the poets, in the midst of the action?
- David Liss, *A Conspiracy of Papers*

Beginning to write, you discover what you have to write about.
- Kit Reed

The pages are still blank, but there is a miraculous feeling of the words all being there, written in invisible ink and clamoring to become visible.
- Vladimir Nabokov

You begin by hard work and discipline, digging in the dirt until your fingers are bloody; and suddenly the characters find themselves. The setting is in place… At such moments you are in what August Wilson calls the "land of magic."
- Sophy Burnham, *For Writers Only*

The grace to be a beginner is always the best prayer for an artist. The beginner's humility and openness lead to exploration. Exploration leads to accomplishment. All of it begins at the beginning, with the first small and scary step.
- Julia Cameron

When does a novel begin? The question is almost as difficult to answer as the question, when does the human embryo become a person? Certainly the creation of a novel rarely begins with the penning or typing of its first words.
- David Lodge, *The Art of Fiction*

Start by believing that your writing is important.
> - Eric Maisel, *Deep Writing: 7 Principles That Bring Ideas to Life*

I type out beginnings and they're awful. I need something driving down the center of a book, a magnet to draw everything to it.
> - Philip Roth

Openings can be tough. Sometimes you can block yourself by trying too hard to get them right...A common sense tip: Begin late in the story, starting with a scene or idea you plan to introduce. Then, when you have a draft or when you're really cooking on the piece, come back to the opening.
> - Jack Heffron, *The Writer's Idea Book*

Meaning is not thought up and then written down. The act of writing is an act of thought. All writing is experimental in the beginning. It is an attempt to solve a problem, to find a meaning, to discover its own way towards a meaning.
> - Donald Murray

I'll write maybe one long paragraph describing the events, then a page or two breaking the events into chapters, and then reams of pages delving into my characters. After that, I'm ready to begin.
> - Anne Tyler

Many writers work their way into a paper, letter, or story as if they were feeling their way into a dark house.
> - Gary Provost, *100 Ways to Improve your Writing (Mentor)*

The scariest moment is always just before you start. After that, things can only get better.
> - Stephen King, *On Writing*

Every writer starts out as a beginner.
> - Scott Ederstein

You can lower your sights by writing not *the* beginning, but *a* beginning.
> - Bruce Holland Rogers, *Word Work*

Questions are more important than answers. I'm looking for openings, not closings.
> - Madeleine L'Engle

The last thing one discovers in writing a book is what to put first.
- Blaise Pascal

If you start with a bang, you won't end with a whimper.
- T.S. Eliot

…it's often on days when I thought nothing happened that I'll start writing and go on for pages, a single sound or sight recalled from the afternoon suddenly loosing a chain or thoughts.
- Thomas Mallon

As soon as a writer has his story beginning, he plans his ending. Writers who say they just sit down and write, not knowing where the story will go, generally find themselves with a story that goes nowhere.
- Isabelle Ziegler, *Creative Writing*

A book calls for pen, ink, and a writing desk; today the rule is that pen, ink and a writing desk call for a book.
- Friedrich Nietzche

To create is always to learn, to begin over, to begin at zero.
- Matthew Fox

What we call the beginning is often the end and to make an end is to make a beginning. The end is where we start from. And every phrase and sentence is right…every phrase and every sentence is an end and a beginning. Every poem an epitaph.
- T.S. Eliot

It is like fishing. But I do not wait very long, for there is always a nibble…To get started, I will accept anything that occurs to me. Something always occurs, of course, to any of us. We can't keep from thinking.
- William Stafford, *A Way of Writing*

If I didn't know the ending of a story, I wouldn't begin. I always write my last line, my last paragraph, my last page first.
- Katherine Anne Porter

Advice to writers: Sometimes you just have to stop writing. Even before you begin.
- Stanislaw J. Lec, "Unkempt Thoughts"

The White Rabbit put on his spectacles. "Where shall I begin, please your Majesty?" he asked. "Begin at the beginning," the King said, gravely "and go on till you come to the end; then stop."
- Lewis Carroll, *Alice in Wonderland*

I usually need a can of beer to prime me.
- Norman Mailer

2.

What do I do about writer's block?

There is no such thing as writer's block—just fear and insecurity.
- Jim Bishop

Any writer who doesn't ever face writer's block is lying to you. Poverty helps… When you have deadline, even writing for television, when you know at a certain point the cameras are going to roll or you're in a movie and you're in production and you're rewriting, it's always easier. You don't have the luxury of playing solitaire.
- Peter Lefcourt

[Writer's block] was invented by people in California who couldn't write,.
- Terry Pratchett

Block. What a nasty word, this combination of *blah* and *blechh*, this icky reminder of blocked bowels.
- Arthur Plotnik, *The Elements of Authorship*

If you think you can, you can. And if you think you think you can't, you're right.
- Mary Kay Ash

The child decides when it wants to be born—not its mother.
- György Kurtág

If you are in difficulties with a book, try the element of surprise; attack it at an hour when it isn't expecting it.
- H. G. Wells

When asked what do you do when you reach a block in your writing, he tersely replied: Start another paragraph.
- Rutherford Montgomery

Invention flags, his brain goes muddy, and black despair succeeds brown study.
- William Congreve

Playing the piano is for me a way of getting unstuck…What it does is break the barrier that comes between the conscious and the unconscious mind. The conscious mind wants to take over and refuses to let the subconscious mind work, the intuition. So if I can play the piano, that will break the block, and my intuition will be free to give things up to my mind, my intellect.
- Madeleine L'Engle in Mihaly Csikszentmihalyi, *Creativity*

The journal is often our best friend. Given the way we work—high expectations breed anxiety—it's not surprising that when the pressure to produce is lifted, we find we can write again.
- Marlene A. Schiwy, *A Voice of Her Own*

I think writer's block is God's way of telling you one of two things—that you failed to think your material through sufficiently before you started writing, or that you need a day or two off with your family and friends.
- Terry Brooks, *Sometimes the Magic Works*

When I'm stuck, I imagine my best friend in a tough situation. "You've got to help me," my friend (character) says. "I can't get out of this without you." "Sorry, I'm just not in the mood," is not an option. "I'd rather scrub the kitchen floor," is not an option. I have to help my friend. I probe, ask questions. How did you get where you are? Where would you like to be? What tools do you have to help you?
- Camille Minichino

All that is necessary to break the spell of inertia and frustration is this: Act as if it were impossible to fail.
- Dorthea Brande

The only way out is the way through, just as you cannot escape from death except by dying. Being unable to write, you must examine in writing this being unable, which becomes for the present—henceforth?—the subject to which you are condemned.
- Howard Nemerov

Writer's block is only a failure of the ego.
- Norman Mailer

Writer's block results from too much head. Cut off your head.
- Joseph Campbell

In a dark time, the eye begins to see.
- Theodore Roethke

The writing researcher Mike Rose argues that many cases of writer's block stem less from emotional problems than from deficits in cognitive skills: for instance, having overly rigid compositional strategies. Such as a rule against sentence fragments.
- Alice W. Flaherty, *The Midnight Disease*

Writers have two main problems. One is writer's block, when the words won't come at all, and the other is logorrhea, when the words come so fast that they can hardly get to the wastebasket in time.
- Cecelia Bartholomew

I never had writer's block. You have to pay the rent, the mortgage, the light bill…I'll go back and look at something—the characters, the dialogue, *Sunset Boulevard* or something—and that will give me a boost.
- James Mulholland, *Late Show with David Letterman*

When you are stuck in a book; when you are well into writing it, and know what comes next, and yet cannot go on; when every morning for a week or a month you enter its room and turn your back on it; then the trouble is either of two things. Either the structure has forked, so the narrative or the logic, has developed a hairline fracture that will shortly split it up the middle—or you are approaching a fatal mistake. What you had planned will not do. If you pursue your present course, the book will explode or collapse, and you do not know about it yet, quite.
- Annie Dillard, *The Writing Life*

There is a vitality, a life force, an energy, a quickening, that is translated through you into action, and because there is only one of you in all time, this expression is unique. And if you block it, it will never exist through any other medium and will be lost.
- Martha Graham

The problem is when you're not writing you don't know if you're lying fallow or if you'll never write again.
- Norman Mailer

Quite often, when I am living through one or another form of "hard times," I think…no, I don't want to be a writer anymore…no, I can't bear the isolation, the uncertainty, the financial insecurity, the constant wrestling with inner truths, the constant necessity for keeping my eyes open to life, the unabating pressure to push myself beyond what I have only just begun to master, the sense that there is, in this, the most unpredictable of professions, no resting place.
        - Ingrid Bengis, *The Writer on Her Work*

A writer should value his blockages. That means he's starting to scale down, to get close.
        - Robert Pirsig

Writer's resistance (a term I like better than "writer's block") is persistent, so we must be persistent…We need to recognize that it is not a personal demon, but one almost universal to writers.
        - Susan Shaughnessy, *Walking on Alligators*

Without resistance you can do nothing.
        - Jean Cocteau, interview, *Writers at Work*

June 7. Bad. Wrote nothing today. Tomorrow no time.
        - Franz Kafka, *Diaries*

Writers often describe writer's block or creative failure as analogous to losing grace or being abandoned by God…the "dark night of the soul," a reference to the book of that name by the sixteenth-century mystic Saint John of the Cross.
        - Alice W. Flaherty, *The Midnight Disease*

If you're not writing well, why continue it? I just don't think this grinding away is useful.
        - Edmund White

Try drawing or painting a scene you're working on. Often this will help free up your imagination.
        - Kevin Henkes

You can only go half way into the darkest forest, then you are coming out the other side.
        - Chinese proverb

Some writers experience a block the moment they receive a signed contract. Others block until they receive the contract. One of the biggest blocks is perfectionism—when a writer believes, for example, that he or she is doing highly important work and refuses to settle for less.
- Theodore Rubin

What happens when a writer doesn't want to write anymore? When the progression of fingers across the keyboard is like an old dry horse hitched to the millstone, blinders and yoke lashed, the only path between day and nightfall one's own scoured rut of circling footsteps?
- Rita Dove

A writer not writing is practically a maniac within himself,
- F. Scott Fitzgerald, *Letters*

Block is different from a dry period, when the writer has nothing to say. Block means sitting before a project that you know you want to create and being unable to find the words. Your hand stops. Your mind recoils…I sometimes think that block is caused by loss of concentration, which is a signal of lack of faith.
- Sophy Burnham, *For Writers Only*

They have cut off my head, and picked out all the letters of the alphabet—all the vowels and consonants—and brought them out through my ears; and they want me to write poetry! I can't do it.
- John Clare

I think writer's block is simply the dread that you are going to write something horrible. But as a writer, I believe that if you sit down at the keys long enough, sooner or later something will come out.
- Roy Blount, Jr.

Depression can cause block in any field of creativity. But some psychiatrists think that depression is especially intertwined with and harmful to language because of the way depression drains away meaning.
- Alice W. Flaherty, *The Midnight Disease*

Writers Block is a myth with zealous adherents.
- Bruce Holland Rogers, *Word Work*

Never sit down to write until you know what you're going to write.
- Bruce Holland Rogers, *Word Work*

This time I must not blot a line. No revision; no second thoughts. Down it shall go. Already I am terrified. I have none of the tools of my trade. No row of pencils, no pencil sharpener, no drink. The standing jump."
  - Jean Rhys, diary

Self-sabotage can take many subtle forms. If you have to work against chaos, that is a misfortune to overcome. If you create your own chaos, that is an adaptation to examine.
  - Susan Shaughnessy, *Walking on Alligators*

Writing at such a time [against one's inclinations] is like making love at such a time. It's hopeless, it desecrates one's future, but one does it anyway because at least it is an act.
  - Norman Mailer

Writer's block is not a passive condition. It is an aggressive reaction, a loud shout from your unconscious calling your attention to the fact that something is out of adjustment…When you experience writer's block, it means your creative child is throwing herself on the floor and refusing to cooperate…Do you send her to her room without dinner? Do you give her a number of logical reasons why she *ought* to cooperate? Or do you try to find out why she doesn't want to in the first place?
  - Victoria Nelson, *Writer's Block and How To Use It*

The cure for writer's cramp is writer's block.
  - Inigo DeLeon

To go in the dark with a light is to know the light. To know the dark, go dark. Go without sight, and find that the dark, too, blooms and sings, and is traveled by dark feet and dark wings.
  - Wendell Berry

Hypergraphia is neither painful nor common. Writer's block is both.
  - Alice W. Flaherty, *The Midnight Disease*

You must do the thing you think you cannot do.
  - Eleanor Roosevelt

People have writer's block not because they can't write, but because they despair of writing eloquently.
  - Anna Quindlen, *Writers [on Writing] Vol. II*

When you get into a tight place and everything goes against you until it seems that you cannot hold on for a minute longer, never give up then, for that is just the place and time when the tide will turn.
- Harriet Beecher Stowe

No coward soul is mine.
- Emily Brontë

Almost all good writing begins with terrible first efforts...the first draft is the down draft—you just get it down. The second draft is the up draft—you fix it up...Writing a first draft is very much like watching a Polaroid develop. You can't—and in fact, you're not supposed to—know exactly what the picture is going to look like.
- Anne Lamott, *Bird by Bird*

It had been a very long time, and for a writer who's not publishing...there's a hollow feeling under the breastbone that I can only call creative death.
- John Dunning, *Booked to Die*

The perfect pointed pencil—the paper persuasive—the fantastic chair and a good light and no writing.
- John Steinbeck, *Journal of a Novel*

The trouble with workshops is that they trivialize art by minimizing the terror.
- Donald Hall

I have forgotten the word I intended to say, and my thought, unembodied, returns to the realm of shadows.
- Osip Mandelstam

The only thing that makes life possible is permanent, intolerable uncertainty: not knowing what comes next.
- Ursula LeGuin

But that's the adventure...that I don't know what's around the corner or beyond the next rise. I don't need to be told, just encouraged to go on and find out for myself.
- Elizabeth Cunningham

The best way out is always through.
- Robert Frost

Good workshops can be both supportive and direct, as long as the author feels that the other workshop members have read his/her work with careful attention.
- Charles Baxter

Organizations for writers palliate the writer's loneliness, but I doubt if they improve his writing....For he does his work alone and if he is a good enough writer he must face eternity, or the lack of it, each day.
- Ernest Hemingway

A writing workshop, even the best, is wanton with energy and talent; it can crush the weak and empower the crass...It is where somehow you pick up the notion that what you're doing is a good and noble thing, and though you may not write as well as you'd like, it is enough and will suffice.
- John L'Heureux

They don't suit everyone, but they do have the bonus that you get a chance to criticize other people's stories as well and so hone your own analytical skills... it can also teach the writer how to accept criticism without being crushed or becoming hostile.
- Christopher Evans, *Writing Science Fiction*

Psychiatric hospitals are not terrible places to write—they bear certain similarities to writers' colonies like Yaddo, except that health insurance pays.
- Alice W. Flaherty, *The Midnight Disease*

A creative writing class may be one of the last places you can go where your life still matters.
- Richard Hugo

Too many writing instructors put you down. They make you feel that if you can't be a Tolstoy or a Flaubert or a Balzac there's no point in trying.
- Irving Wallace

If everyone in your workshop laughs a lot, then you're probably doing more good than harm.
- Bruce Holland Rogers, *Word Work*

The workshop system produces what I call workshop junkies: people who do not become original writers because they continue to be encouraged for everything they do...The workshop...allows [the student] to think that he's already a poet before he's even written 15 or 50 or 150 poems.
- Diane Wakoski

Some want to learn to write, or to write better. Others…want some feedback…A certain kind of person finds writing classes and workshops to be like camp, and just wants to hang out with all these other people…Some people want other people with whom to share the disappointments and rejection letters and doldrums. A lot of people like to work on other people's writing because it helps them figure out what they themselves love in the written word, as well as what doesn't work for them.

- Anne Lamott, *Bird by Bird*

To Edmund Bergler, the twentieth-century analyst who coined the term "writer's block," and once remarked that he had "never seen a 'normal' writer," I can honestly reply: That's all right. I am not certain I have ever seen a "normal" psychoanalyst.

- Kathleen Norris, Acedia & Me

3.

Why do writers write, anyway?

Coleridge was a drug addict. Poe was an alcoholic. Marlowe was stabbed by a man whom he was treacherously trying to stab. Pope took money to keep a woman's name out of a satire; then wrote a piece so that she could still be recognized anyhow. Chatterton killed himself. Byron was accused of incest. Do you still want to be a writer—and if so, why?
- Bennett Cerf

All writers are vain, selfish and lazy and at the very bottom of their motives lies a mystery. Writing a book is a long, exhausting struggle, like a long bout of some painful illness. One would never undertake such at thing if one were not driven by some demon whom one can neither resist nor understand.
- George Orwell

Go into yourself. Search for the reason that bids you write, find out whether it is spreading out its roots in the deepest place of your heart, acknowledge to yourself whether you would have to die if it were denied you to write.
- Rainer Maria Rilke, *Letters to a Young Poet*

Write to save yourself and someday you'll write because you've been saved.
- Anne Michaels, *Fugitive Pieces*

All that I hope to say in books, all that I ever hope to say, is that I love the world.
- E.B. White

I write because I hate. A lot. Hard.
- William Gass

I think in order to write really well and convincingly, one must be somewhat poisoned by emotion, dislike, displeasure, resentment, fault-finding, imagination, passionate remonstrance, a sense of injustice—they all make fine fuel.
- Edna Ferber

To the degree to which we are motivated by feelings of enthusiasm and pleasure in what we do—or even by an optimal degree of anxiety—they propel us to accomplishment…Optimism is the great motivator.
>   - Daniel Goleman, *Emotional Intelligence*

One writes to make a home for oneself, on paper, in time and in other's minds.
>   - Alfred Kazin

I always tell people that I became a writer not because I went to school but because my mother took me to the library. I wanted to become a writer so I could see my name in the card catalog.
>   - Sandra Cisneros

Writing a best-seller with conscious intent to do so is, after all, a state of mind that is not without comparison to the act of marrying for money only to discover that the absence of love is more onerous than anticipated.
>   - Norman Mailer, *The Spooky Art*

I wrote from a sense of need. I needed something to do. You can't sleep all day long.
>   - Snoopy, Charles Schultz

I write in order to shut my eyes.
>   - Franz Kafka

By writing our stories, we begin to understand what was formerly unclear.
>   - Louise DeSalvo, *Writing as a Way of Healing*

We are a species that needs and wants to understand who we are. Sheep lice do not seem to share this longing, which is one reason they write so little.
>   - Anne Lamott

I wrote my books because of a compulsion to make some record of a fascinating era in veterinary practice.
>   - James Herriot, in Richard Joseph, *Bestsellers: Top Writers Tell How*

The main thing is—father and mother must eat. Write.
>   - Anton Chekhov

The need to write comes from the need to make sense of one's life and discover one's usefulness.
>   - John Cheever, speech

The true function of a writer is to produce a masterpiece and…no other task is of any consequence.
- Cyril Connolly

If I don't write to empty my mind, I go mad.
- George Gordon (Lord) Byron

An artist is a creature driven by demons…He has a dream. It anguishes himself so much he must get rid of it.
- William Faulkner

You can't be afraid to deal with your demons. You've got to go there to be able to write.
- Lucinda Williams

The purpose of a writer is to keep civilization from destroying itself.
- Albert Camus

In this dark and wounded society, writing can give you the pleasures of the woodpecker, of hollowing out a hole in a tree where you can build your nest and say, "This is my niche, this is where I live now, this is where I belong."
- Anne Lamott, *Bird by Bird*

Every writing career starts as a personal quest for sainthood, for self-betterment. Sooner or later, and as a rule quite soon, a man discovers that his pen accomplishes a lot more than his soul.
- Joseph Brodsky

People say I'm compulsive and ambitious, but…I don't think of myself as either. But the record of that constant series of big books, all of which have been widely received all around the world, must show some motive.
- James Michener, in Richard Joseph, *Bestsellers: Top Writers Tell How*

He [Michener] was forty when he wrote *Tales of the South Pacific*. His motivation had been boredom, though he thought that an honest record of what had actually happened would be of value, as he put it, to "a few people."
- Richard Joseph, *Bestsellers: Top Writers Tell How*

You're a writer. And that's something better than being a millionaire. Because it's something holy.
- Harlan Ellison, *On Being a Writer*

I should write this so as to never forget it.
    - Anaïs Nin

Every word written is a victory against death.
    - Michel Butor

I don't want to be a doctor, and live by men's diseases; nor a minister to live by their sins; nor a lawyer to live by their quarrels. So I don't see there's anything left for me but to be an author.
    - Nathaniel Hawthorne

The thrill of seeing oneself in print…provides some sort of primal verification: you're in print; therefore you exist.
    - Anne Lamott, *Bird by Bird*

And the day came when the risk to remain tight in a bud was more painful than the risk it took to blossom.
    - Anaïs Nin

Graphomania, the desire to be published…is merely an excessive desire to write.
    - Alice W. Flaherty, *The Midnight Disease*

Everyone thinks writers know more about the inside of the human head, but that is wrong. They know less, that's why they write. Trying to find out what everyone else takes for granted.
    - Margaret Atwood

Every writing career starts as a personal quest for sainthood, for self-betterment. Sooner or later, and as a rule quite soon, a man discovers that his pen accomplished a lot more than his soul.
    - Joseph Brodsky

To write is to note down the music of the world.
    - Hélène Cixous, Rootprints, *Memory and Life Writing*

Writing is my form of celebration and prayer, but it is also the way in which I organize and inquire about the world.
    - Diane Ackerman, *An Alchemy of Mind*

I am not a writer except when I write.
    - Juan Carlos Onetti

A writer strives to express a universal truth in the way that rings the most bells in the shortest amount of time.
  - William Faulkner, *On Being a Writer*

A writer is like a bag lady going through life with a sack and a pointed stick collecting stuff.
  - Tony Hillerman

Young writers should be encouraged to write, and discouraged from thinking they are writers.
  - Wallace Stegner

I knew I was supposed to be a writer; I had made that declaration in the closet of my soul.
  - Padgett Powell

What do prisoners do? Write, of course; even if they have to use blood as ink, as the Marquis de Sade did.
  - Alice W. Flaherty, *The Midnight Disease*

I'm the kind of writer that people think other people are reading.
  - V.S. Naipaul, *Radio Times*

Writers aren't people exactly. Or if they're any good, they're a whole *lot* of people trying so hard to be one person…Writers are children—even in normal times they can't keep their minds on their work.
  - F. Scott Fitzgerald, *The Last Tycoon*

The work is hard, the perks are few, the pay is terrible, and the product, when it's finally finished, is pure joy.
  - Mary Lee Settle

You're gambling with something vital. Most writers get smashed egos.
  - Norman Mailer

I love being a writer. What I can't stand is the paperwork.
  - Peter De Vries, *It Takes a Certain Type to Be a Writer* [Erin Barret and Jack Mingo]

People become writers because they can't do things that bosses tell them to do.
  - Les Whitten

You're all alone when you're a writer. Sometimes you just feel you need a humanity bath. Even a ride on a subway will do that.
- Saul Bellow

A writer lives, at least, in a state of astonishment. Beneath any feeling he has of good or evil of the world lies a deeper one of wonder at it all. To transmit that feeling, he writes.
- William Sansom

Yes, it's hard to write, but it's harder not to.
- Carl Van Doren

Not to repeat oneself is every writer's obsession. Not to slide into sentimentality, not to imitate, not to spread oneself too thin.
- Elie Wiesel, *Writers [on Writing]*

The role of the writer is not to say what we can all say but what we are unable to say.
- Anaïs Nin

Part of becoming a writer is the desire to have everything mean something.
- Louise Erdrich

A writer is somebody for whom writing is more difficult than it is for other people.
- Thomas Mann, *Essays of Three Decades*

The task of the writer is to seize the reader by the back of the neck and force him to love life.
- Leo Nikolayevich Tolstoy

Every writer is a frustrated actor who recites his lines in the hidden auditorium of his skull.
- Rod Serling

Every writer, without exception, is a masochist, a sadist, a peeping Tom, an exhibitionist, a narcissist, an "injustice collector" and a depressed person constantly haunted by fears of unproductivity.
- Edmund Bergler

A writer is a controlled schizophrenic.
- Edward Albee

A pathological business, writing, don't you think? Just look at what a writer actually does: all that unnatural tense squatting and hunching, all those rituals: pathological!
- Hans Magnus Enzensberger

Every writer is turning one's worst moments into money.
- J.P. Donleavy

Writers, like teeth, are divided into incisors and grinders.
- Walter Bagehot

Fine writers should split hairs together, and sit side by side, like friendly apes, to pick the fleas from each other's fur.
- Logan Pearsall Smith

When I was a young boy they called me a liar. Now that I'm all grown up, they call me a writer.
- Isaac Bashevis Singer

It is splendid to be a writer, to put men into the frying pan of your words and make them pop like chestnuts.
- Gustave Flaubert, letter to Louise Colet

Writers are the most important people in American today, doing the most crucial work, bearing a heavy responsibility as the last exemplars of American entrepreneurship and cussedness. It takes brains to write, and you can't fake it. Anybody who can turn out a good story is probably smarter than half the corporation executives in America and a good deal more honest.
- Garrison Keillor

A serious writer is not to be confounded with a solemn writer. A serious writer may be a hawk or a buzzard or even a popinjay, but a solemn writer is always a bloody owl.
- Ernest Hemingway

There are two literary maladies—writer's cramp and swelled head.
- Coulson Kernahan

Someone once asked Margaret Mitchell what she was "doing" and she replied, "Doing? It's a full-time job to be the author of *Gone With the Wind*."
- E.B. White, *The Points of My Compass*

American writers want to be not good but great; and so are neither.
- Gore Vidal

The faults of great writers are generally excellencies carried to excess.
- Samuel Taylor Coleridge

Only a mediocre writer is always at his best.
- W. Somerset Maugham

Victor Hugo was a madman who thought he was Victor Hugo.
- Jean Cocteau

Writing is more than anything a compulsion, like some people wash their hands thirty times a day for fear of awful consequences if they do not. It pays a whole lot better than this type of compulsion, but it is no more heroic.
- Julie Burchill

The art of writing, like the art of love, runs all the way from a kind of routine hard to distinguish from piling bricks to a kind of frenzy closely related to delirium tremens.
- H.L. Menken, *Minority Report*

Writing may be either the record of the deed or a deed. It is nobler when it is a deed...
- Henry David Thoreau, *Journal*, 1844

For me, writing something down was the only road out.
- Anne Tyler

Writing is both mask and unveiling.
- E.B. White

If you do not breathe through writing, if you do not cry out in writing, or sing in writing, then don't write, because our culture has no use for it.
- Anaïs Nin

Writing is just having a sheet of paper, a pen, and not a shadow of an idea of what you are going to say.
- Francoise Sagan

Either write something worth reading or do something worth writing.
- Benjamin Franklin

A writer strives to express a universal truth in the way that rings the most bells in the shortest amount of time.
- William Faulkner

A good writer possesses not only his own spirit but also the spirit of his friends.
- Friedrich Nietzsche

A great writer creates a world of his own and his readers are proud to live in it. A lesser writer may entice them in for moment, but soon he will watch them filing out.
- Cyril Connolly

As a writer one must be invisible, yet everywhere, as God in His heaven is.
- Gustave Flaubert

How vain it is to sit down to write when you have not stood up to live.
- Henry David Thoreau

Writing is an act of faith, and nothing else.
- E.B. White

When the wings of my mind are beating, I've got to go ahead!
- Anton Chekhov

Writing is like prostitution. First you do it for love. Then you do it for a few friends. Finally you do it for money.
- Jean-Baptiste Molière

Writing gives you the illusion of control, and then you realize it's just an illusion, that people are going to bring their own stuff into it.
- David Sedaris

Writing is the best way to talk without being interrupted.
- Jules Renard

In the end, all books are written for your friends.
- Gabriel Garcia Marquey

When we write, we command the attention of other members of our tribe. Therefore, we assert that what we have to say is valuable...it had better be.
- Richard Mitchell, *Less Than Words Can Say*

…writing on a page reminds us that it is not the same thing as life on either side of it—life before anyone looks at the writing and after anyone stops looking at it.
  - Richard Poirier, *The Renewal of Literature*

If I let my fingers wander idly over the keys of a typewriter it *might* happen that my screed made an intelligible sentence. If an army of monkeys were strumming on typewriters they *might* write all the books in the British Museum.
  - Arthur S. Eddington, *The Nature of the Physical World*

What is writing, if it is not the countenance of our daily experience: sensuous, contemplative, imaginary, what we see and hear, dream of, how it strikes us, how it comes into us, travels through us, and emerges in some language hopefully useful to others.
  - M.C. Richards, *Poetry, Pottery, and the Person*

I must write it all out, at any cost. Writing is thinking. It is more than living, for it is being conscious of living.
  - Anne Morrow Lindbergh

It is as if the life lived has not been lived until it is set down in this unconscious sequence of words.
  - Edna O'Brien

Writing a long and substantial book is like having a friend and companion at your side, to whom you can always turn for comfort and amusement, and whose society becomes more attractive as a new and widening field of interest.
  - Winston Churchill, *A Churchill Reader*

Communication is never easy, as we discovered at Babel.
  - Madeleine L'Engle, *The Summer of the Great Grandmother*

You're given the form, but you have to write the sonnet yourself. What you say is completely up to you.
  - [Mrs. Whatsit] Madeleine L'Engle, *Wrinkle In Time*

There's a great power in words, if you don't hitch too many of them together.
  - Josh Billings

Cooking and writing require the perfect balance of letting go and sticking to your plan.
  - Nancy Slonim Aronie, *Writing From the Heart*

People do not deserve to have good writing, they are so pleased with bad.
- Ralph Waldo Emerson

It's a bad business, this writing. No marks on paper can ever measure up to the world's music in the mind, to the purity of the image before its ambush by language.
- Mary Gorden, *Writers on Writing*

Writing is a solitary occupation. Family, friends, and society are the natural enemies of the writer. He must be alone, uninterrupted, and slightly savage if he is to sustain and complete an undertaking.
- Jessamyn West

Writing is not necessarily something to be ashamed of, but do it in private and wash your hands afterwards.
- Robert Heinlein

The act of putting pen to paper encourages pause for thoughts; this in turn makes us think more deeply about life, which helps us regain our equilibrium.
- Norbet Platt

All writing is a form of prayer.
- John Keats

Here, write it, or it will be erased by the wind.
- Isabel Allende

Writing keeps me from believing everything I read.
- Gloria Steinem

Writing is a lonely job unless you're a drinker, in which case you always have a friend within reach.
- Emilio Estevez

Writing is as habit-forming as tobacco.
- Erskine Caldwell

You have to throw yourself away when you write.
- Max Perkins, [A. Scott Berg, *Max Perkins—Editor of Genius*]

Writing is the act of burning through the fog.
- Natalie Goldberg, *Writing Down the Bones*

What writing is…Telepathy.
- Stephen King, *On Writing*

It is through writing that you come to clarity about the time you live in, its problems. It is through writing that you take the reality all the way into yourself and live into it. Writing is not an escape.
- Jens Bjørneboe, Interview, *Bindestreken*, 1970

Writing introduces division and alienation, but a higher unity as well. It intensifies the sense of self and fosters more conscious interaction between persons. Writing is consciousness-raising.
- Walter J. Ong, *Orality and Literacy*

All of writing is a huge lake. There are great rivers that feed the lake, like Tolstoi and Dostoevski. And there are trickles, like Jean Rhys. All that matters is feeding the lake. I don't matter. The lake matters. You must keep feeding the lake.
- Jean Rhys

In the sense that there was nothing before it, all writing is writing against the void.
- Mark Strand

Writing is really a way of thinking—not just feeling but thinking about things that are dis-parate, unresolved, mysterious, problematic or just sweet.
- Toni Morrison [from Judith Viorst, *Necessary Losses*]

Life can't ever really defeat a writer who is in love with writing, for life itself is a writer's lover until death—fascinating, cruel, lavish, warm, cold, treacherous, constant.
- Edna Ferber

Writing is thinking on paper.
- William Zinsser

Writing is life. Breathe deeply of it.
- Terry Brooks, *Sometimes the Magic Works*

Life is what happens to a writer between drafts.
- Dennis Miller

He writes so well, he makes me feel like putting my quill back into my goose.
- Fred Allen

You may be able to take a break from writing, but you won't be able to take a break from being a writer.
- Stephen Leigh

Writers are not just people who sit down and write. They hazard themselves. Every time you compose a book your composition of yourself is at stake.
- E.L. Doctorow

Hardly anybody ever writes anything nice about introverts. Extroverts rule. This is rather odd when you realize that about nineteen writers out of twenty are introverts…a writer's job is ingoing.
- Ursula K. Le Guin

With a common strangeness [Scott] Momaday scallops thin, hesitant lines, poised for revelation, surviving on small truths.
- Vine Deloria in Kenneth Lincoln, *Native American Truths*

The way you write reflects the way you think and the way you think is the mark of the kind of person you are.
- William Saffire

Writing is not chewing your nails and picking your teeth, but a matter of public interest.
- Alfred Döblin

Writing is a hellish task, best snuck up on, whacked on the head, robbed and left for dead.
- Ann-Marie MacDonald

What makes writing good? That's easy: the lyrical description, the arresting metaphor, the dialogue that falls so true on the ear that it breaks the heart, the plot that winds up exactly where it should.
- Barbara Kingsolver, *Small Wonders*

Writing is a socially acceptable form of schizophrenia.
- E.L. Doctorow

Writing is a craft consisting of pen, paper and whiskey.
- William Faulkner

The writing process is made up of mess and mystery.
- Susan R. Horton, *Thinking Through Writing*

To write is to sow and to reap at the same time
> - Elie Wiesel

Writing is not a performance but a generosity.
> - Brenda Uland

Writing teaches us our mysteries.
> - Marie De L'Incarnation

It's a very excruciating life facing that blank piece of paper every day and having to reach up somewhere into the clouds and bring something down out of them.
> - Truman Capote

No doubt I shall go on writing, stumbling across tundras of unmeaning, planting words like bloody flags in my wake. Loose ends, things unrelated, shifts, nightmare journeys, cities arrived at and left, meetings, desertions, betrayals, all manner of unions, adulteries, triumphs, defeats…these are the facts.
> - Alexander Trocchi

If writing is thinking and discovery and selection and order and meaning, it is also awe and reverence and mystery and magic.
> - Toni Morrison

Meaning is not thought up and then written down. The act of writing is an act of thought. All writing is experimental in the beginning. It is an attempt to solve a problem, to find a meaning, to discover its own way towards a meaning.
> - Donald Murray

Being a writer is like having homework every night for the rest of your life.
> - Lawrence Kasdan

Good writing is, among many other things, an illusion. The primary illusion is of ease.
> - Bill Roorbach, *Writing Life Stories*

Is it constantly on my mind when I'm going clickety-clack on the machine that this is somehow going to enlarge the scope of human comprehension? I would have to say no, that's not what I'm thinking about. I'm trying to get the line done.
> - Robert Stone

I was standing in the schoolyard waiting for a child when another mother came up to me. "Have you found work yet?" she asked. "Or are you still writing?"
- Anne Tyler

…it's often on days when I thought nothing happened that I'll start writing and go on for pages, a single sound or sight recalled from the afternoon suddenly loosing a chain of thoughts.
- Thomas Mallon

Writing is the hardest way of earning a living with the possible exception of wrestling alligators.
- William Saroyan

Writing is a cop-out. An excuse to live perpetually in fantasy land, where you can create, direct and watch the products of your own head. Very selfish.
- Monica Dickens

No one is able to enjoy such feast than the one who throws a party in his own mind.
- Selma Lagerlöf

The only end of writing is to enable the readers better to enjoy life, or better to endure it.
- Samuel Johnson

Good writing is a kind of skating which carries off the performer where he could not go.
- Ralph Waldo Emerson

Sometimes I have good luck and write better than I can.
- Ernest Hemingway

Writing is not a profession, occupation or job; it is not a way of life: it is a comprehensive response to life.
- Gregory McDonald

Writing is like any other profession—break dancing, ninth grade, doctor of philosophy—it's what I do to justify the air I breathe, the food I ingest, the time I take up on earth.
- Nikki Giovanni, "Writers on the Writing Process," *The Norton Sampler*, ed. Thomas Cooley

Writing is not a profession but a vocation of unhappiness.
- Georges Simenon

Writing isn't hard. It isn't any harder than ditch-digging.
- Patrick Dennis

Write only if you cannot live without writing. Write only what you alone can write.
- Elie Wiesel

The pen is mightier than the sword.
- Edward Bulwer-Lytton

His father ground his ink blacker and blacker. The blacker the ink, the more patient the man.
- Maxine Hong Kingston, *China Men*

The pen is the tongue of the mind.
- Miguel de Cervantes

One ought to write only when one leaves a piece of one's flesh in the inkpot each time one dips one's pen.
- Leo Nikolayevich Tolstoy

The palest ink is better than the most retentive memory.
- Chinese proverb

The game of golf would lose a good deal if croquet mallets and billiard cues were allowed on the putting green. You ought to be able to show that you can do it a good deal better than anyone else with the regular tools before you have a license to bring in your own improvements.
- Ernest Hemingway

The most essential gift for a good writer is a built-in, shock-proof shit detector.
- Ernest Hemingway

John Updike set the standard for writers to aspire to: it is "to work steadily, even shyly, in the spirit of those medieval carvers who so fondly sculpted the undersides of choir seats."
- James J. Kilpatrick, *The Writer's Art*

No one is asking, let alone demanding, that you write. The world is not waiting with bated breath for your article or book. Whether or not you get a single word on paper, the sun will rise, the earth will spin, the universe will expand. Writing is forever and always a choice—your choice.
- Beth Mende Conny

Writing is so difficult that I often feel that writers, having had their hell on earth, will escape all punishment hereafter.
- Jessamyn West

It's nervous work. The state you need to write in is the state that others are paying large sums to get rid of.
- Shirley Hazzard

I am convinced that all writers are optimists…How otherwise could any human being sit down to a pile of blank sheets and decide to write, say two hundred thousand words on a given theme?
- Thomas Costain

Let us dare to read, think, speak, write. Let every sluice of knowledge be open and set flowing.
- John Adams

All writing is communication; creative writing is communication through revelation—it is the Self escaping into the open.
- E.B. White

If you're trying to write, you have to let your attention drop. You can't maintain an interest in anything else.
- Barbara Tuchman

Writing is not a genteel profession. It's quite nasty and tough and kind of dirty.
- Rosemary Mahoney

Look carefully. Record what you see. Find a way to make beauty necessary; find a way to make necessity beautiful.
- Anne Michaels, *Fugitive Pieces*

Writing practice softens the heart and mind, helps to keep us flexible so that rigid distinctions between apples and milk, tigers and celery disappear.
- Natalie Goldberg, *Writing Down the Bones*

Writing is a struggle against silence.
- Carlos Fuentes

Every noble work is at first impossible.
- Thomas Carlyle

Ride the whirlwind. That's the most we can do.
- Arthur Clarke

Writing books is the only thing I know how to do really. I'm like Paul, the hero in *Misery*, in that way. I lead a fairly boring life, except when I write. And when I write, man, I have wonderful adventures.
- Stephen King, *Secret Windows*

In the spent of one night he wrote three propositions:
That nothing lasts. That hell is the denial of the ordinary.
That clean white paper waiting under pen is the gift beyond
History and hurt and heaven.
- John Ciardi, *The Gift*

To me, writing is a horseback ride into heaven and hell and back. I am grateful if I can crawl back alive.
- Thomas Sanchez

Writers break black letters out of lead and line them up on white sheets of paper and ask others to read the sentences we have created for ourselves.
- Terry Tempest Williams, *Finding Beauty in a Broken World*

The pages are still blank, but there's a miraculous feeling of the words being there, written in invisible ink and clamoring to become visible.
- Vladimir Nabokov

Nothing stinks like a pile of unpublished writing.
- Sylvia Plath

It is not study alone that produces a writer; it is intensity.
- Edward G. Bulwer Lytton

If you do not breathe through your writing, if you do not cry out in writing, or sing in writing, then don't write, because our culture has no use for it.
- Anaïs Nin

A writer arrives to express a universal truth in the way that rings the most bells in the shortest amount of time.
  - William Faulkner, *On Being a Writer*

I must be private, secret, as anonymous and submerged as possible in order to write.
  - Virginia Woolf

The important thing in writing is the capacity to astonish. Not shock—shock is a worn-out word—but astonish.
  - Terry Southern

Most writers regard truth as their most valuable possession, and therefore are most economical in its use.
  - Mark Twain

The process of writing has something infinite about it. Even though it is interrupted each night, it is one single notation.
  - Elias Canetti

My whole theory of writing I can sum up in one sentence: An author ought to write for the youth of his own generation, the critics of the next, and the schoolmasters of ever afterward.
  - F. Scott Fitzgerald

Love the writing, love the writing, love the writing…the rest will follow.
  - Jane Yolen

Once writing has become your major vice and greatest pleasure only death can stop it.
  - Ernest Hemingway

I must write it all out, at any cost. Writing is thinking. It is more than living, for it is being conscious of living.
  - Anne Morrow Lindbergh

Anybody can become a writer, but the trick is to STAY a writer.
  - Harlan Ellison

The act of writing requires a constant plunging back into the shadow of the past where time hovers ghostlike.
  - Ralph Ellison

Once I begin the act of writing, it all falls away—the view from the window, the tools, the talismans, and I am unconscious of myself...one's carping inner critics are silenced for a time...there is always a surprise, a revelation. During the act of writing, I have told myself something that I didn't know I knew.
- Gail Godwin

Writing is one of the few professions in which you can psychoanalyze yourself, get rid of hostilities and frustrations in public and get paid for it.
- Octavia Butler

Writing is a form of therapy; sometimes I wonder how all those, who do not write, compose, or paint can manage to escape the madness, the melancholia, the panic fear, which is inherent in a human condition.
- Graham Greene

It's very strange, but the mere act of writing anything is a help. It seems to speed one on one's way.
- Katherine Mansfield

A writer needs loneliness, and he gets his share of it. He needs love, and he gets shared and also unshared love. He needs friendship. In fact, he needs the universe. To be a writer is, in a sense, to be a daydreamer—to be living a kind of double life.
- Jorge Luis Borges

A writer has the duty to be good, not lousy; true, not false; lively, not dull; accurate, not full of error. He should tend to lift people up, not lower them down.
- E.B. White

The writer, like the bee, gathers honey from whatever circumstances he happens to be in. And had I done that it would not have mattered...
- [Antoine de St. Exupery] Anne Morrow Lindbergh, *War Without and War Within*

The writer, like everyone else, is equipped in infancy with a thick padding of things he believes to be true, but which aren't.
- Jon Franklin, *Writing for Story*

If you are a writer, you are a writer always, not just while you are writing. Your imagining ear is turned on twenty-four hours a day.
- Gail Sher, *The Intuitive Writer*

Among Tibetan lamas, there is a hearing hierarchy (differing levels of ability to hear mystical forces) based on differing levels of self-discipline. Writers too are pedigreed human beings. Our ears are sharp, finely honed, and exquisitely sensitive…we pick up sounds other people miss.
> - Gail Sher, *The Intuitive Writer*

A writer is someone who is enormously taken by things anyone else would walk by.
> - James Dickey

The role of a writer is not to say what we all can say, but what we are unable to say.
> - Anaïs Nin

He is a man of thirty-five, but looks fifty. He is bald, has varicose veins and wears spectacles, or would wear them if his only pair were not chronically lost. If things are normal for him, he will be suffering from malnutrition, but if he has recently had a lucky streak, he will be suffering from a hangover. At present it is half past eleven in the morning, and according to his schedule he should have started work two hours ago; but even if he had made any serious effort to start he would have been frustrated by the almost continuous ringing of the telephone bell, the yells of the baby, the rattle of an electric drill out in the street, and the heavy boots of his creditors clumping up the stairs. The most recent interruption was the arrival of the second post, which brought him two circulars and an income tax demand printed in red. Needless to say, this person is a writer.
> - George Orwell

Practically everybody in New York has half a mind to write a book, and does.
> - Groucho Marx

Writers are a little below the clowns and a little above the trained seals.
> - John Steinbeck

The vital difference between a writer and someone who merely is published is that the writer seems always to be saying to himself, as Stendhal actually did, "If I am not clear, the world around me collapses.
> - Alfred Kazin, "The Language of Pundits," *Atlantic Monthly*, July, 1961

Nowadays three witty turns of phase and a lie make a writer.
> - Georg C. Lichtenberg

I avoided writers very carefully because they can perpetuate trouble as no one else can…
> - F. Scott Fitzgerald, *The Crack-up*

I don't know why people would want to have lunch with writers. I've eaten with writers. We have appalling table manners and rarely say anything other than "Pass the salt" or "If you're not going to eat that, can I have it?"
> - Neil Gaiman

The only good writer was a dead writer. Then he couldn't surprise anyone any more, couldn't hurt anyone any more.
> - John Steinbeck, *Travels with Charley*

One reason the human race has such a low opinion of itself is that it gets so much of its wisdom from writers.
> - Wilfrid Sheed

Do you want to be a writer just a little bit? Do you want just a little bit to be a writer? I didn't think so. Don't hold back. Be all of a writer. Don't save any for next time. Write it all, every time. There will always be more.
> - Marshall Cook, *Freeing Your Creativity*

If you are a writer you locate yourself behind a wall of silence and no matter what you are doing, driving a car or walking or doing housework…you can still be writing, because you have that space.
> - Joyce Carol Oates

Writers are not just people who sit down and write. They hazard themselves. Every time you compose a book your composition of yourself is at stake.
> - E. L. Doctorow

For the writer there is no oblivion. Only endless memory.
> - Anita Brookner

The writer places himself in a condition of silent receptivity. He begins by pushing aside all impediments, tries to rid himself of extraneous stimuli. Only then, then, when the way is clear, do the fine hair-top extensions of the inner senses begin their tracking process.
> - Sven Birkerts, *The Gutenberg Elegies*

A writer is like a bean plant—he has his day, and then he gets stringy.
> - E.B. White, letter

Unprovided with original learning, unformed in the habits of thinking, unskilled in the arts of composition, I resolved to write a book.
- Edward Gibbon

He [the writer] must teach himself that the basest of all things is to be afraid; and teaching himself that, forget it forever, leaving no room in his workshop for anything but the old verities and truths of the heart...
- William Faulkner, Dec. 1950, receiving the Nobel Prize

A writer writes not because he is educated but because he is driven by the need to communicate. Behind the need to communicate is the need to share. Behind the need to share is the need to be understood. The writer wants to be understood much more than he wants to be respected or praised or even loved. And that perhaps, is what makes him different from others.
- Leo Rosten

I do not so much write a book as sit up with it, as with a dying friend. During visiting hours, I enter its room with dread and sympathy for its many disorders I hold its hand and hope it will get better.
- Annie Dillard, *The Writing Life*

Each of us is like a desert, and a literary work is like a cry from the desert, or like a pigeon let loose with a message in its claws, or like a bottle thrown into the sea. The point is: to be heard—even if by one single person.
- Francois Mauriac

Good writers define reality; bad ones merely restate it. A good writer turns fact into truth; a bad writer will, more often than not, accomplish the opposite.
- Edward Albee

Good writers have two things in common: they would rather be understood than admired, and they do not write for hairsplitting and hypercritical readers.
- Friedrich Nietzsche

Writers are as jealous as pigeons.
- Anton Chekhov

Writers seldom choose as friends those self-contained characters who are never in trouble, never unhappy or ill, never make mistakes, and always count their change when it is handed to them.
- Catherine Drinker Bowen

I have yet to meet a writer who could change water into wine, and we have a tendency to treat them like that.
    - Michael Tolkin

The responsibility of a writer is to excavate the experience of the people who produced him.
    - James Baldwin

When writers meet they are truculent, indifferent, or over-polite. Then comes the inevitable moment. A shows B that he has read something of B's. Will B show A? If not, then A hates B; if yes, then all is well. The only other way for writers to meet is to share a quick pee over a common lamppost.
    - Cyril Connolly

Writers are vacuum cleaners who suck up other people's lives and weave them into stories like a sparrow builds a nest from scraps.
    - Garrison Keillor

It's not often that someone comes along who is a true friend and a good writer. Charlotte was both.
    - E.W. White, *Charlotte's Web*

Writers seldom write the things they think. They simply write the things they think folks think they think.
    - Ethan Hubbard

A born writer is born scrofulous; his career is an accident dictated by physical or circumstantial disabilities.
    - Dylan Thomas, *The Collected Letters of Dylan Thomas*

Every writer is a narcissist. This does not mean that he is vain; it only means that he is hopelessly self-absorbed.
    - Leo Rosten

Writers are forged in injustice as a sword is forged.
    - Max Perkins, A Scott Berg, *Max Perkins: Editor of Genius*

If I could live as a tree, as a river, as the moon, as the sun, as a star, as the earth, as a rock, I would…Writing permits me to experience life as any number of strange creations.
    - Alice Walker

The world needs writers. We will always be necessary. There are few professions that can claim that distinction.
- Rod McKuen

The only reason for being a professional writer is that you can't help it.
- Leo Rosten

As a writer you are free. You are about the freest person that ever was. Your freedom is what you have bought with your solitude, your loneliness.
- Ursula K. Le Guin

Writers must fortify themselves with pride and egotism as best they can. The process is analogous to using sandbags and loose timbers to protect a house against flood. Writers are vulnerable creatures like anyone else. For what do they have in reality? Not sandbags, not timbers. Just a flimsy reputation and a name.
- Brian Aldiss

A writer needs three things, experience, observation, and imagination, any two of which, at times any one of which, can supply the lack of the others.
- William Faulkner

It's easy, after all, not to be a writer. Most people aren't writers, and very little harm comes to them.
- Julian Barnes, *Flaubert's Parrot*

It's rarely that you see an American writer who is not hopelessly sane.
- Margaret Anderson

If a young writer can refrain from writing, he shouldn't hesitate to do so.
- André Gide

If I had to give young writers advice, I would say don't listen to writers talking about writing or themselves.
- Lillian Hellman

All a writer has to do to get a woman is to say he's a writer. It's an aphrodisiac.
- Saul Bellow

Every book has been written with guilt, powered by pain. Every book has been a baby I did not bear, 10,000 meals I did not cook, 10,000 beds I did not make.
- Erica Jong

In a sense the world dies every time a writer dies, because, if he is any good, he has been a wet nurse to humanity during his entire existence and has held earth close around him, like the little obstetrical toad that goes about with a cluster of eggs attached to his legs.
>   - E. B. White

To write is a humiliation.
>   - Edward Dahlberg

No one asked you to be a writer.
>   - Sherwood Anderson

A writer is not a confectioner, a cosmetic dealer, or an entertainer. He is a man who has signed a contract with his conscience and his sense of duty.
>   - Anton Chekhov

How do you know if you're a writer? Write something every day for two weeks, then stop, if you can. If you can't, you're a writer.
>   - Charles Ghigna

The Writer's Oath: I promise solemnly: 1) to write as much and as often as I can; 2) to respect my writing self; 3) to nurture the writing of others.
>   - Gail Carson Levine, *Writing Magic: Creating Stories That Fly*

Writing is conscience, scruple and the farming of our ancestors.
>   - Edward Dahlberg

If you haven't always been doing it, you haven't always wanted to do it.
>   - George V. Higgins, *On Writing*

Writers have a rare power not given to anyone else; we can bore people long after we are dead.
>   - Sinclair Lewis

Writing is the incurable itch that possesses many.
>   - Juvenal

Writing is the spirit's manual labor par excellence.
>   - James J. O'Connell, *Avatars of the Word*

What is written without effort is in general read without pleasure.
>   - Samuel Johnson

The moving finger writes, and having written moves on. Nor all thy piety nor all thy wit, can cancel half a line of it.
- Omar Khayyam

For even the most childish intoxication with progress will soon be forced to recognize that writing and books have a function that is eternal. It will become evident that formulations in words and the handing on of these formulations through writing are not only important aids but actually the only means by which humanity can have a history and continuing consciousness of itself.
- Hermann Hesse, *Reading in Bed*, ed. Steven Gilbar

I want to write, but more than that, I want to bring out all kinds of things that lie buried deep in my heart.
- Anne Frank

When I'm writing I enjoy it and I enjoy reading my proofs. But the minute it comes out I detest it;...I'm vexed and sick at heart about it.
- Anton Chekhov, *The Seagull*

All good writing is *swimming under water* and holding your breath.
- F. Scott Fitzgerald, *The Crack-up*

Writing is manual labor of the mind: a job, like laying pipe.
- John Gregory Dunne, *Esquire*, Oct '86

Writing must always have intention because words have power.
- Suheir Hammad

Good writing differs from drivel in how much the writer has agonized over the words and how little the agonizing shows.
- Arthur Plotnik, *The Elements of Authorship*

Writing comes more easily if you have something to say.
- Sholem Asch

That's not writing, that's typing.
- Truman Capote of Jack Kerouac

The expression "to write something down" suggests a descent of thought to the fingers whose movements immediately falsify it.
- William Gass, "Habitations of the Word," *Kenyon Review*

You can only write what you need to write.
> - P. D. James

All writing slants the way a writer leans and no man is born perpendicular although many men are born upright.
> - E.B. White, *The New Yorker*, Feb. 18, 1956

Writing, which is my form of celebration and prayer, is also my form of inquiry.
> - Diane Ackerman

I think all writing is a disease.
> - William Carlos Williams, *Newsweek*, 7 Jan '57

Writing a book was an adventure. To begin with, it was a toy, an amusement; then it became a mistress, then a master, and then a tyrant.
> - Winston Churchill

I certainly don't enjoy writing. I get a fine warm feeling when I'm doing well, but that pleasure is pretty much negated by the pain of getting started each day. Let's face it, writing is hell.
> - William Styron

Writing is an occupation in which you have to keep proving your talent to those who have none.
> - Jules Renard

Writing is putting words on paper until the voices in your head shut up.
> - Frank Fradella

Writing is like walking in a deserted street. Out of the dust in the street you make a mud pie.
> - John Le Carré

Writing means revealing yourself to excess.
> - Franz Kafka

Don't you wish you had a job like mine? All you have to do is think up a certain number of words! Plus, you can repeat words! And they don't even have to be true!
> - Dave Barry

Writing is the only thing that…when I'm doing it, I don't feel that I should be doing something else.
- Gloria Steinem

To write weekly, to write daily, to write shortly, to write for busy people catching trains in the morning or for tired people coming home in the evening, is a heartbreaking task for men who know good writing from bad. They do it, but instinctively draw out of harm's way anything precious that might be damaged by contact with the public, or anything sharp that might irritate its skin.
- Virginia Woolf, *The Common Reader*

It is necessary to write, if the days are not to slip emptily by. How else, indeed, to clap the net over the butterfly of the moment? For the moment passes, it is forgotten; the mood is gone; life itself is gone. That is where the writer scores over his fellows: he catches the changes of his mind on the hop.
- Vita Sackville-West

I have to constantly balance "being a writer" with being a wife and mother. It's a matter of putting two different things first, simultaneously.
- Madeleine L'Engle

I had more free time with my sons than other fathers, though I wonder when I was with them, was I entirely free? A writer's working day is a strange, diffuse thing that never really ends and gives him a double focus much of the time.
- John Updike, *Living With a Writer*

When I'm writing, the darkness is always there. I go where the pain is.
- Anne Rice

Against the disease of writing one must take special precautions, for it is a dangerous and a contagious disease.
- Peter Abelard, letter

The trade of authorship is a violent and indestructible obsession.
- George Sand

The sensation of writing is the sensation of spinning, blinded by love and daring. It is the sensation of a stunt pilot's turning barrel rolls, or an inchworm's blind rearing from a stem in search of a route. At its worst, it feels like an alligator wrestling. At its best, the sensation of writing is that of any unmerited grace. It is handed to you, but only if you look for it.
- Annie Dillard, Laura Cerwinski, *Writing as a Healing Art*

Writing, I explained, was mainly an attempt to out-argue one's past; to present events in such a light that battles lost in life were either won on paper or held to a draw.
- Jules Feiffer, *Ackroyd*

I shall live badly if I do not write, and I shall write badly if I do not live.
- Françoise Sagan

Once in seven years I burn all my sermons, for it is a shame if I cannot write better sermons now than I did seven years ago.
- John Wesley

Good writing is always religious. Joyce was religious. He may have been profane, but he was religious. Beckett is religious. Dostoevsky. Tolstoy.
- Edna O'Brien

To write is to remember. Even when you write an editorial about an issue of the moment, you ransack your mind for details—out of experience, out of reading and thinking—to support your argument. I saw ransack, using a dead metaphor on purpose...ransack as with a duffel bag? attic? junkyard or dump? filing cabinet? If a filing cabinet is to be ransacked, it probably resembles a duffle bag.
- Donald Hall, *The Contemporary Essay*

Writing is an act of mischief.
- Theodore Roethke

To write is to descend, to excavate, to go underground.
- Anaïs Nin, *The Diary of Anaïs Nin*

The solitude of writing is also quite frightening. It's quite close to madness, one just disappears for a day and loses touch.
- Nadine Gordimer

Watch children at play. They are terribly serious. The same is true with writing. You get caught up in the rhythm. That's when it really gets to be complete play.
- Madeleine L'Engle, *On Being a Writer*

There it is on paper, you say, plainly to be read, so it couldn't have been so unendurable.
- Edna Ferber

And above all, never forget that the pen is mightier than the plow-share. By this I mean that writing, all in all, is a hell of a lot more fun than farming. For one thing, writers seldom, if ever, have to get up at five o'clock in the morning and shovel manure. As far as I am concerned, that gives them the edge right there.
    - Willa Cather

...and if I have not written words upon paper as I should like to have done, I have written large upon the page of life that was left open for me.
    - Louis L'Amour

The work of writing goes on inside you all the time. And to dodge this enormously difficult work is to be lazy, and to be lazy is to be dull. To be dull is to be unread.
    - William Sloane, *The Craft of Writing*

Not writing would be like going the rest of your life without having dreams.
    - Stephen King

Writing is making sense of life. You work your whole life and perhaps you've made sense of one small area.
    - Nadine Gordimer

The truth is this: Writing is a bumper-to-bumper crawl through hell with an occasional jolt to the next level of anguish.
    - Arthur Plotnik, *The Elements of Authorship*

Writers don't write from experience, though many are resistant to admit that they don't. I want to be clear about this. If you wrote from experience, you'd get maybe one book, maybe three poems. Writers write from empathy.
    - Nadine Gordimer

To write is to write is to write is to write is to write is to write is to write.
    - Gertrude Stein

Writing is a legitimate way, an important way, to participate in the empowerment of the community that names me.
    - Toni Cade Bambara

Writing, whether it be a grocery list or *The Brothers Karamazov* freezes the words of the mind into a permanent and public form.
    - Richard Mitchell, *Less Than Words Can Say*

Teaching and writing are separate, but serve/feed one another in so many ways. Writing travels the road inward, teaching, the road out—helping OTHERS move inward. It is an honor to be with others in the spirit of writing and encouragement.
- Naomi Shihab Nye

How can I know what I think, till I see what I say?
- E.M. Forster

What an occupation! To sit and flay your fellow men and then offer their skins for sale and expect them to buy them.
- August J. Strindberg

You have to throw yourself away when you write.
- Max Perkins, A Scott Berg, *Max Perkins: Editor of Genius*

Writing a thing down fixes it in place as surely as a rattlesnake skin stripped from the meat and stretched and tacked to a barn wall. Every bit as stationary, and every bit as false to the original thing. Flat and still and harmless.
- Charles Frazier, *Thirteen Moons*

Writing is to descend like a miner to the depths of the mine with a lamp on your forehead, a light whose dubious brightness falsifies everything, whose wick is in permanent danger of explosion, whose blinking illumination in the coal dust exhausts and corrodes your eyes.
- Blaise Cendrars

The profession of book-writing makes horse racing seem like a solid, stable business.
- John Steinbeck

Every secret of a writer's soul, every experience of his life, every quality of his mind is written large in his works.
- Virginia Woolf

In a very real sense, the writer writes in order to teach himself, to understand himself; the publishing of his ideas, though it brings satisfaction, is a curious anticlimax.
- Alfred Kazin

A professional writer is an amateur who didn't quit.
- Richard Bach

Every writer is a frustrated actor who recites his lines in the auditorium of his mind.
- George Bernard Shaw

Those of us who write are responsible for the effect of our books…Like it or not, we either add to the darkness of indifference and out-and-out evil which surrounds us or we light a candle to see by.
- Madeleine L'Engle, *The Summer of the Great Grandmother*

Writers spend far too much time recording when they should be brooding.
- Kenneth Atchity, *A Writer's Time*

The writer is a person who is standing apart, like the cheese in "The Farmer in the Dell" standing there alone but deciding to take a few notes.
- Anne Lamott, *Bird by Bird*

There are two kinds of writers; the great ones who can give you truths, and the lesser ones, who can only give you themselves.
- Clifton Fadiman

I don't really think that writers, even great writers, are prophets, or sages, or Messiah-like figures; writing is a lonely, sedentary occupation and a touch of megalomania can be comforting around five on a November afternoon when you haven't seen anybody all day.
- Angela Carter

Only amateurs say that they write for their own amusement. Writing is not an amusing occupation. It is a combination of ditch-digging, mountain-climbing, treadmill and childbirth. Writing may be interesting, absorbing, exhilarating, racking, relieving. But amusing? Never!
- Edna Ferber

It is necessary to write, if the days are not to slip emptily by.
- Vita Sackville-West

We do not write in order to be understood, we write in order to understand.
- Cecil Day-Lewis

In an odd way, writing is a testament to my lack of imagination. I can't picture what another kind of life would look like.
- Hari Kunzru

One who can handle a pen will never have to beg.
- Chinese proverb

I write to correct life's unfairness.
- Verandah Porche

I write to unearth all those things that scare me, to reach those places in my soul that may seem remote and dark to others I write to preserve my sanity and to honor the sacrifices made by all those who came before me. The way I figure, it's a privilege just to be given a voice to speak and to be heard. God and the universe will take care of the rest.
- Edwidge Danticat, *Essence*, May, 1996

Picture me sitting at breakfast in the morning. As I sip my coffee, my wife glances down at the floor and observes, "Bruce, we really need a new dining room rug. This one is wearing out." Right there I have the inspiration to write another article.
- Bruce Barton

The best emotions to write out of are anger and fear or dread...The least energizing emotions to write out of is admiration. It is very difficult to write out of because the basic feeling that goes with admiration is a passive contemplative mood.
- Susan Sontag

All great things are done for their own sake.
- Robert Frost

A writer ought to comfort the afflicted, and afflict the comfortable.
- Mark Twain

I like to write when I feel spiteful: it's like having a good sneeze.
- D.H. Lawrence, letter

If you can't annoy somebody with what you write, I think there's little point in writing.
- Robert Benchley, *Chips off the Old Benchley*

The aim, if reached or not, makes great the life: try to be Shakespeare, leave the rest to fate!
- Robert Browning

I write to make people anxious and miserable and to worsen their indigestion.
- Wendy Cope

You ask me why I do not write something…I think one's feelings waste themselves in words, they ought all to be distilled into actions and into actions which bring results.
- Florence Nightingale, *Florence Nightingale*

I just write when fear overtakes me.
- Fran Liebowitz

I feel more alive when I'm writing than I do at any other time—except when I'm making love. Two things when you forget time, when nothing exists except the moment—the moment of writing, the moment of love. That perfect concentration is bliss.
- May Sarton

I write to discover what I think. After all, the bars aren't open that early.
- Daniel J. Boorstin

Write to keep in contact with our ancestors and to spread truth to people.
- Sonia Sanchez

I want to write books that unlock the traffic jam in everybody's head.
- John Updike

I write to bring back what is gone, to relive what is lost, to make a mosaic out of fragments.
- Minfong Ho

I write for the same reason I breathe—because if I didn't, I would die.
- Isaac Asimov

When I wrote Dr. Zhivago I had the feeling of an immense debt toward my contemporaries. It was an attempt to repay it.
- Boris Pasternak, *Writers at Work*

People want to write. The desire to express is relentless. People want others to know what they hold to be truthful. They need the sense of authority that goes with authorship.
- Donald H. Graves, *Papers on Research About Learning*

One of my motivating forces has been to recreate the world I know into a world I wish I could be in. Hence my optimism and happy endings. But I've never dreamed I could actually reshape the real world.
- Kristin Hunter

Striving for excellence motivates you; striving for perfection is demoralizing.
- Harriet Braiker

No one does anything from a single motive.
- Samuel Taylor Coleridge

Writing has so much to give, so much to teach, so many surprises…It's like discovering that while you thought you needed the tea ceremony for the caffeine, what you really needed was the tea ceremony. The act of writing turns out to be its own reward.
- Anne Lamott, *Bird by Bird*

People write for two primary reasons: to be read and to make money.
- Isabelle Ziegler, *Creative Writing*

I write because I'm afraid to say some things out loud.
- Real Live Preacher, *Real Live Preacher,* weblog

Why do most writers write? Because it isn't there.
- Thomas Berger

I hold a beast, an angel, and a madman in me, and my enquiry is as to their working, and my problem is their subjugation and victory, down throw and upheaval and my effort is their self-expression.
- Dylan Thomas

Some writers are only born to help another writer to write one sentence.
- Ernest Hemingway, *Green Hills of Africa*

You do it for personal satisfaction, for the challenge, for the creative process. If you don't get happiness from those three areas, and you don't make any money, you've wasted a lot of time creating your book.
- Rollin Riggs, [Judy Mandell, *Book Editors Talk to Writers*]

Any writer overwhelmingly honest about pleasing himself is almost sure to please others.
- Marianne Moore

I write what I would like to read—what I think other women would like to read. If what I write makes a woman in the Canadian mountains cry and she writes and tells me about it, especially if she says, "I read it to Tom when he came in from work and he cried too," I feel I have succeeded.
- Kathleen Norris

Why Write? The reason is perfectly simple: to live…because it is an endless beginning, a constantly new first time, like intercourse or pain. As long as one writes, ruin is averted, it doesn't slip away; and that's why I write: to bear the world as it steadily crumbles into nothingness.
- Günter Kunert, *The Poet's Work*

My sole literary ambition is to write one good novel, then retire to my hut in the desert, assume the lotus position, compose my mind and senses, and sink into mediation, contemplating my novel.
- Edward Abbey

Anything that is written to please the author is worthless.
- Blaise Pascal

There is no pleasure in the world like writing well and going fast. It's like nothing else. It's like a love affair, it goes on and on, and doesn't end in marriage. It's all courtship.
- Tennessee Williams

All writers are vain, selfish, and lazy, and at the very bottom of their motives there lies a mystery.
- George Orwell

Writers, if they are worthy of that jealous designation, do not write for other writers. They write to give reality to experience.
- Archibald Macleish

I always write about my own experiences, whether I've had them or not.
- Ron Carlson

We are the species that clamors to be lied to.
- Joyce Carol Oates

In Sri Lanka a well-told lie is worth a thousand facts.
- Michael Ondaatje

We write, we make music, we draw pictures, because we are listening for meaning, feeling for healing. And during the writing of the story, or the painting, or the composing or singing or playing, we are returned to that open creativity which was ours when we were children.
- Madeleine L'Engle, *Walking on Water*

A bird doesn't sing because it has an answer, it sings because it has a song.
- Maya Angelou

I have no idea how people who don't write endure their lives…Some of the things that happen to us in life seem to have no meaning, but when you write them down you find the meanings for them; or you translate life into worlds, you force a meaning.
- Maxine Hong Kingston

With a pencil and a paper, I could revise the world.
- Alison Lurie

Our final wish is to have scribbled on the wall our "Kilroy was here."
- William Faulkner

We write to taste life twice, in the moment and in retrospection.
- Anaïs Nin, *Vol V, Diary*

I write the way I write because I am the kind of person I am…I am a woman and I write from that experience. I am a black woman and I write from that experienced.
- Lucille Clifton

The responsibility of a writer is to excavate the experience of the people who produced him.
- James Baldwin

Go into yourself. Search for the reason that bids you write; find out if it is spreading out its roots in the deepest places of your heart, acknowledge to yourself whether you would have to die if it were denied you to write."
- Rainer Maria Rilke, *Letters to a Young Poet*

Writing is not about making a buck, not about publishers and agents. Writing is not about feeling good. Writing is about pain, suffering, hard work, risk and fear.
- Sue Grafton

The tears had turned to ink.
- Dawna Markova

Nothing like bereavement to keep the heart porous. It's hardness of the heart that can close down a writer.
- Bono

One writes not to be read, but to breathe—one writes to think, to pray, to analyze. One writes to clear one's mind, to dissipate one's fears, to face one's doubts, to look at one's mistakes—in order to retrieve them. One writes to capture and crystallize one's joy, but also to analyze and disperse one's gloom.
- Anne Morrow Lindbergh, *War Without and War Within*

I write because I don't know what I think until I read what I say.
- Flannery O'Connor

One never knows, one just endures, keeps the faith, burrows through the muck and tries to appreciate every sunset. And, if one must, one writes.
- Frank Cotolo

I have written every poem, every novel, for the same purpose—to find out what I think, to know where I stand.
- May Sarton

I like to think of the world I created as being a kind of keystone in the universe; that, small as the keystone is, if it were ever taken away the universe itself would collapse.
- William Faulkner

Two hundred years ago Johann Sebastian Bach was writing the rules of harmony for all time. Why did he do it? Pride of workmanship.
- W. Edwards Deming

…prestige. The chief glory of every people arises from its authors.
- Samuel Johnson

A curious itch for scribbling takes possession of many and grows inveterate in their insane hearts.
- Juvenal

No man but a blockhead ever wrote, except for money.
- Samuel Johnson, Boswell's *The Life of Johnson*

We should write because it is human nature to write. Writing claims our world. It makes it directly and specifically our own.

>   - Julia Cameron, *The Right to Write*

If you would not be forgotten
As soon as your are dead and rotten
Either write things worth reading
Or do things worth the writing.

>   - Benjamin Franklin, *Poor Richard's Almanac*

I started to write out of my own insecurity and woundedness and inner struggles that became my source. I started to write where I was nervous, where I felt anxious, lonely. I started to express those things that most people don't dare to express.

>   - Henri J. M. Nouwen, *Publisher's Weekly*, Oct. 2, 1981

To live, to err, to fall, to triumph, to recreate life out of life!…On and on and on and on!

>   - James Joyce

I'm someone who writes to save her life…I can't imagine what I would do if I didn't write. I would be dead or I would be in jail…

>   - Jamaica Kincaid, [Donald McQuade, Robert Atwan, *The Writer's Presence*]

Dollars damn me; and the malicious Devil is forever grinning in upon me, holding the door ajar…What I feel most moved to write, that is banned—it will not pay. Yet, altogether, write the other way I cannot. So the product is a final hash, and all my books are botches.

>   - Herman Melville

Writing is a form of therapy; sometimes I wonder how all those who do not write, compose or paint can manage to escape the madness, the melancholia, the panic fear which is inherent in a human situation.

>   - Graham Greene

We do not write in order to be understood; we write in order to understand.

>   - C. Day Lewis, *The Poetic Image*

I write to understand.

>   - Eli Wiesel

Many people hear voices when no one is there. Some of them are called mad and are shut up in rooms where they stare at the walls all day. Others are called writers and they do pretty much the same thing.
- Meg Chittenden

Clearly, many writers write for reasons other than a desire to produce great literature for others' benefit. They write for therapy. They write (queasily) to "express" themselves. They write to give organization to, or to escape from, their long, long days. They write for money, or because they are obsessive. They write as a shout for help, or as an act of family revenge. La, la, la. There are a lot of reasons to write a lot. Sometimes it works out OK.
- Richard Ford, *Writers on Writing*

Why did I write? Because I found life unsatisfactory.
- Tennessee Williams

The purpose of writing is to make your mother and father drop dead with shame.
- J. P. Donleavy

One writes to make a home for oneself, on paper, in time, in others' minds.
- Alfred Kazin

I knew that when I grew up I should be a writer...Looking back through my work, I see it is invariably when I lacked a political purpose that I wrote lifeless books.
- George Orwell, "Why I Write"

I think the whole glory of writing lies in the fact that it forces us out of ourselves and into the lives of others.
- Sherwood Anderson

I believe in not quite knowing. A writer needs to be doubtful, questioning. I write out of curiosity and bewilderment.
- William Trevor

I write entirely to find out what I'm thinking, what I'm looking at, what I see and what it means.
- Joan Didion

You don't write a novel out of sheer pity any more than you blow a safe out of a vague longing to be rich. A certain ruthlessness and a sense of alienation from society is as essential to creative writing as it is to armed robbery.
- Nelson Algren

There are three reasons for becoming a writer: the first is that you need the money; the second, that you have something to say that you think the world should know; the third is that you can't think what to do with the long winter evenings.
- Quentin Crisp

The sole excuse which a man can have for writing is to unveil for others the sort of world which mirrors itself in his individual glass.
- Rémy de Gourmont

You do have a boss, although it's not a person; it's a deadline. You keep pretty regular hours—that is, if you want to get anything done. (I take Christmas, my birthday, Easter and the Fourth of July off and write the other 361 days each year.)
- Stephen King, *Secret Windows*

The only sensible ends of literature are, first, the pleasurable toil of writing; second, the gratification of one's family and friends; and lastly, the solid cash. (And not necessarily in that order.)
- Nathaniel Hawthorne

Above all, love is the main generator of all good writing. Love, passion, compassion are all welded together.
- Carson McCullers

Any woman who writes is a survivor.
- Tillie Olsen

We write to expose the unexposed.
- Anne Lamott, *Bird by Bird*

What greater delight and wonder can there be than to leave the straight lines of personality and deviate into those footpaths that lead beneath brambles and thick tree trunks into the heart of the forest where lie those wild beasts, our fellow men.
- Virginia Woolf, *Street Haunting*

One must avoid ambition in order to write. Otherwise something else is the goal: some kind of power beyond the power of language. And the power of language, it seems to me, is the only kind of power a writer is entitled to.
- Cynthia Ozick, interview, *Paris Review*

There is no perfect time to write. There is only now.
- Barbara Kingsolver, *The Poisonwood Bible*

You may write for the joy of it, but the act of writing is not complete in itself. It has its end in its audience.
- Flannery O'Connor

This work is in the invisible realm. When you work in the territory of mind, you see nothing…you need great patience and self-trust to sense the invisible harvest in the territory of the mind. You need to train the inner eye for the invisible realms where thoughts can grow, and where feelings put down their roots.
- John O'Donohue, *Anam Cara*

Our obligation is to give meaning to life and in doing so, to overcome the passive, indifferent life.
- Elie Wiesel

I write entirely to find out what I'm thinking, what I'm looking at, what I see and what it means. What I want and what I fear…In many ways writing is the act of saying **I,** of imposing oneself on people, of saying listen to me, see it my way, change your mind.
- Joan Didion, "Why I Write."

Unconsciously perhaps from the beginning, and more and more consciously during the last…years, my work has been motivated by a desire to make myself responsibly at home in this world and in my native and chosen place.
- Wendell Berry, *Home Economics*

I set myself on fire and people come to watch me burn.
- John Wesley

People want to know why I do this, why I write such gross stuff. I like to tell them that I have the heart of a small boy –and I keep it in a jar on my desk.
- Stephen King

I want to write, but more than that, I want to bring out all kinds of things that lie buried deep in my heart.
- Anne Frank

Some of us are like wheelbarrows, only useful when pushed and easily upset.
- Jack Herbert

Why do I write? The truth, the unvarnished truth, is that I haven't a clue.
- Gloria Naylor, *Writer's Home Companion*

Writers need to write. That's why you panic at the completion of a play or a novel. When you aren't writing you aren't certain you exist.
      - Sophy Burnham, *For Writers Only*

Motivation is what gets you started. Habit is what keeps you going.
      - Jim Ryun

People often say that motivation doesn't last long. Well, neither does bathing— that's why we recommend it daily.
      - Zig Ziglar

You shall know the truth, and it will make you odd.
      - Flannery O'Connor

All writers are vain, selfish and lazy, and at the very bottom of their motives lies a mystery. Writing a book is a long, exhausting struggle, like a long bout of some painful illness. One would never undertake such a thing if one were not driven by some demon whom one can neither resist nor understand.
      - George Orwell, "Why I Write"

And if I have to be a thieving, immoral crow in order to write a book, then by God, I'll grow black feathers on my fanny and croak as loud as I can.
      - Pasi Jääskeläinen

4.

How should I create and handle my characters?

I always begin with a character or characters, and then try to think up as much action for them as possible.
- John Irving

Actions both constitute the person and reveal him...The term character itself, we note, is part of the history of writing, first referring in Greek to a tool for marking or engraving and then subsequently to the "characters" of writing—the letters that were engraved; then moving to "the hand," and finally to the person.
- Frederick Buechner, *The Sacred Journey*

Faulkner claimed he ran along behind his characters with pencil in hand, trying to keep up with what they are saying and doing.
- Flannery O'Connor, *The Nature and Aim of Fiction*

Each character deserves a name that meets the needs of the story and evokes the desired response from the readers.
- Arthur Plotnik

I let my characters express themselves through dreams because that will give a side to them that you couldn't get any other way.
- Gail Godwin [Mickey Pearlman and Katherine Usher Henderson, *A Voice of One's Own*]

But then there are moments when the characters seem to speak to you. They start to...connect the dots.
- Robert Hicks

Characters are the beating heart of any story.
- Kim Edwards, *Creating Fiction*

I feel at times that I'm making up these little people and I've lost my mind.
    - Carolyn Chute

Characters must not brood too long. They must not waste time running up and down ladders in their own insides.
    - E.M. Forster

Graham Greene once said that there were certain characters who took care of themselves. He never had to bother about them in the writing. Others, he had to go to great pains with.
    - Norman Mailer, *The Spooky Art*

I tell my students you have an absolute right to write about people you know and love. You do. But the kicker is you have a responsibility to make the characters large enough that you will not have sinned against them.
    - Dorothy Allison

This thing happens, where the characters take over and you almost want to look behind you to see who's writing your story.
    - Joseph Wambaugh

The test of a round character is whether it is capable of surprising in a convincing way. If it never surprises it is flat. If it does not convince, it is a flat pretending to be round.
    - E.M. Forster

The creative act is an act of schizophrenia. I must be both the character and at the same time be able to observe the character completely objectively and from outside of him. If you're only inside of him you cannot exert artistic control. If you're only outside, you have all the control, but there's nothing worth saying.
    - Edward Albee [in an interview with Sigmund Koch]

I quit writing about Tom and Huck because they were ready to grow up and become liars.
    - Mark Twain

J.R.R. Tolkien has confessed that about a third of the way through *The Fellowship of the Ring*, some ruffian named Strider confronted the hobbits in an inn, and Tolkien was in despair. He didn't know who Strider was, where the book was going or what to write next.
    - Ansen Dibell, *The Elements of Fiction Writing: Plot*

Often I'll find clues to where the story might go by figuring out where the characters would rather not go.
- Doug Lawson

The characters in a novel are made out of the sentences. That's what their substance is.
- Jonathan Miller

People change and forget to tell each other.
- Lillian Hellman

The creations of a great writer are little more than the moods and passions of his own heart, given surnames and Christian names, and sent to walk the earth.
- William Butler Yeats

Fancy names are of course out. They belong primarily in soap operas, where the viewer must make quick identification of the characters so hastily dramatized before him…Scorn it or not, one way to find a name is to read your telephone book, especially if you are in another town or country.
- Hallie Burnett, *On Writing the Short Story*

I became, and remain, my characters' close and intent watcher: their director, never. Their creator I cannot feel that I was or am.
- Elizabeth Bowen

The most common source of inspiration for creating characters is your own life. No problem there. You already know a lot about yourself and the people around you…go ahead and put all your pals in your books…Characters aren't real people, but like real people they are in a constant state of development.
- Donna Levin, *Get That Novel Written!*

I have found my hero and he is me.
- George Sheridan

I would never write about anyone who is not at the end of his rope.
- Stanley Elkin

We walk through ourselves, meeting robbers, ghosts, giants, old men, young men, wives, widows, brothers-in-love. But always meeting ourselves.
- Stephen Dedalus, James Joyce's *Ulysses*

I try to create sympathy for my characters, then turn the monsters loose.
      - Stephen King

Imagine that! You know, he used to have the most extraordinary interest in the people here in Kentucky. He could never get enough of my tales of Kentucky folk. He used to make me repeat family names like Barefoot and Boffin and Baggins and good country names like that...Practically all the names of Tolkien's hobbits are listed in the Lexington, Kentucky phone book.
      - A former Oxford classmate of Tolkein's from Kentucky, Guy Davenport, *The Geography of the Imagination*

Using stereotyped characters is the timid writer's approach.
      - Isabelle Ziegler, *Creative Writing*

Find out what your hero or heroine wants, and when he or she wakes up in the morning, just follow him or her all day.
      - Ray Bradbury

You try to create characters who invite a strong reaction from readers, whether pity, contempt, empathy, whatever.
      - Tony Hillerman

The reader wants to see something happen between pages one and four hundred, and nothing happens if the characters don't change.
      - Terry Brooks, *Sometimes the Magic Works*

People are the story, and the whole story.
      - William Sloane

No one wants to see the village of the happy people.
      - Lew Hunter

My mind is a world in itself, which I have peopled with my own creatures.
      - Lady Caroline Lamb

If your deepest beliefs drive your writing, they will not only keep your work from being contrived but will help you discover what drives your characters.
      - Anne Lamott, *Bird by Bird*

Your characters should be as smart as you are, if not smarter.
      - Tina Fey

Contemporary modernist writers flatten their characters by handling them at a great distance, as if with tongs.
- Annie Dillard, *Living by Fiction*

If you are writing stories, you must never be an advocate of your characters. Never be saying (in so many words), "See what a fascinating heroine this is, how adorable; how fine and brace the hero!"…if they were fascinating and adorable it would show.
- Brenda Ueland, *If You Want to Write*

I spend a lot of time working on characters. I start off with a resume—a job application form that I have extended a little bit. I fill that out and sort of forced myself to think about the characters. Then, if I am lucky, I will find a picture of my character in a magazine. I will go through hundreds of pictures to find pictures of my characters and pictures of their houses.
- Walter Dean Myers

[D. H. Lawrence's characters] don't really speak their words—not conversationally, not to one another—they are *not* speaking on the street, but are playing like fountains or radiating like the moon or storming like the sea, or their silence is the silence of wicked rocks.
- Eudora Welty

A writer begins by breathing life into his characters. But if you are very lucky, they breathe life into you.
- Caryl Phillips

If your story actors become real people to you, with human qualities, emotions and desires—whatever their age—they'll help you devise the plot.
- Lee Wyndham, *Writing for Children & Teenagers*

To explain the inner life of your characters, at length, is to cheat readers of their own intelligence and experience. Show them people as they would meet them if the reader were in the book…Let your readers figure out the character… Never…take away the joy of discovery.
- Rita Mae Brown, *Starting from Scratch*

Most bad books get that way because their authors are engaged in trying to justify themselves. If a vain author is alcoholic, then the most sympathetically portrayed character in the book will be an alcoholic. This sort of thing is very boring for outsiders.
- Stephen Vizinczey

I try to think of characters who on the surface of their actions are deeply unsympathetic. It's the writer's job to make them sympathetic, in spite of themselves.

- John Irving

The characters, the situation, which strike one as real will be those that touch and interest one most, but the measure of reality is very difficult to fix.

- Henry James

The characters of my stories *are* family for me, and that is why many of them appear in more than one book. I don't want to leave them at the end of the book. I want to find out what happens to them.

- Madeleine L'Engle, *The Rock That Is Higher*

What I want to do when I write is to contemplate character—either by inventing my own in novels and short stories based on my own experience, or by studying character and history.

- Rebecca West

The characters in the story seem to lead another life, not even remotely like mine. It's sort of magic and sort of like dreaming.

- R.D. Larson

The business of a novelist is, in my opinion, to create characters first and foremost, and then to set them in the snarl of the human currents of his time, so that there results an accurate permanent record of a phase of human history.

- John Dos Passos

My characters talk to one another, and when it reaches a certain pitch of excitement I jump out of bed and run and trap them before they are gone.

- Ray Bradbury

When I have a chance to write about a period of my life, an experience, and I can rework it into the life of my hero, then everything changes and I can no longer remember what happened in reality. That is why when I am not writing, I am suffering because I remember too much of concrete life. I have to destroy my past in order to win my own freedom.

- Andrei Bitov

You build a character by asking yourself questions about the person to which only you know the answers.

- Oscar Collier, *How to Write & Sell Your First Novel*

No one can create a character from pure observation; if it is to have life it must be at least in some degree a representation of himself.
- Somerset Maugham

I start with a tingle, a kind of feeling of the story I will write. Then come the characters, and they take over, they make the story.
- Isak Dinesen

It is in their "good" characters that novelists make, unawares, the most shocking self-revelations.
- C.S. Lewis

We are nauseated by the sight of trivial personalities decomposing in the eternity of print.
- Virginia Woolf

Never be afraid to kill off your characters.
- Brendan Gill

When writing a novel a writer should create living people; people not characters. A character is a caricature.
- Ernest Hemingway

Every human being has hundreds of separate people living under his skin. The talent of a writer is his ability to give them their separate names, identities, personalities and have them relate to the other characters living with him.
- Mel Brooks

Writing fiction is a solitary occupation but not really a lonely one. The writer's head is mobbed with characters, images and language.
- Hilma Wolitzer

Start out with an individual and you find that you have created a type—start out with a type and you find that you have created nothing.
- F. Scott Fitzgerald, *In His Own Time*

If you're going to have a character appear in a story long enough to sell a newspaper, he'd better be real enough that you can smell his breath.
- Ford Maddox Ford

Show me a character totally without anxieties and I will show you a boring book.
- Margaret Atwood

Writers seldom choose as friends those self-contained characters who are never in trouble, never unhappy or ill, never make mistakes, and always count their change when it is handed to them.
- Catherine Drinker Bowen

What is character but the determination of incident? What is incident but the illustration of character?
- Henry James

Whoever has the luck to be born a character can laugh even at death. Because a character will never die! A man will die, a writer, the instrument of creation: but what he has created will never die.
- Luigi Pirandello

The characters in my novels are my own unrealized possibilities. That is why I am equally fond of them all and equally horrified by them. Each one has crossed a border that I myself have circumvented. It is that crossed border (the border beyond which my own "I" ends) which attracts me most. For beyond that border begins the secret the novel asks about. This novel is not the author's confession; it is an investigation of human life in the trap the world has become.
- Milan Kundera, *The Unbearable Lightness of Being*

Characters take on life sometimes by luck, but I suspect it is when you can write most entirely out of yourself, inside the skin, heart, mind and soul of a person who is not yourself, that a character becomes in his own right another human being on the page.
- Eudora Welty

I can do to him whatever I like. I'm allowed to torture him as much as I want. He's mine.
- J.K. Rowling

You can't make the Duchess of Windsor into Rebecca of Sunnybrook Farm.
- Cleveland Amory

I collect lines and snippets of things somebody might say—things I overhear, things I see in the newspaper, things I think up, dream up, wake up with in the middle of the night. I write a line down in my notebook. If I can get enough of those things, then characters begin to emerge.
- Richard Ford

I act all these characters. If I don't cry about them, if I don't laugh at their jokes, if I don't lose my temper and if I don't swear, it doesn't seem that I am writing them; someone else is. I act all these characters; I live these characters.
- Catherine Cookson, in Richard Joseph, *Bestsellers: Top Writers Tell How*

Get so well acquainted with your characters that they live and grow in your imagination exactly as if you saw them in the flesh; and finally tell their story with all the truth and tenderness and severity you are capable of.
- Katherine Anne Porter

Would you not like to try all sorts of lives—one is so very small—but that is the satisfaction of writing—one can impersonate so many people.
- Katherine Mansfield

A writer's knowledge of himself, realistic and unromantic, is like a store of energy on which he must draw for a lifetime; one volt of it properly directed will bring a character alive.
- Graham Greene

You need to find out as much as possible about the interior life of the people you are working with…One way to do this is to look within your own heart, at the different facets of your personality…Just don't pretend you know more about your characters than they do, because you don't…It's teatime and all the dolls are at the table. Listen. It's that simple.
- Anne Lamott, *Bird by Bird*

Often I'll find clues to where the story might go by figuring out where the characters would rather not go.
- Doug Lawson

We ourselves are characters within a huge story that is visibly unfolding all around us, participants within the vast imagination, or Dreaming, of the world.
- David Abram

Each writer is born with a repertory company in his head. Shakespeare has perhaps 20 players, and Tennessee William has about 5, and Samuel Beckett one—and maybe a clone of that one. I have 10 or so, and that's a lot. As you get older, you become more skillful at casting them.
- Gore Vidal

I expect any day now, I will have said all I have to say; I'll have used up all my characters, and then I'll be free to get on with my real life.
- Anne Tyler

You can never know enough about your characters.
- W. Somerset Maugham

Try to make the characters you don't like at least as plausible as the characters you do.
- Steven Vincent Benét, *Stephen Vincent Benét on Writing*, ed. George Abbe

I often think about rewriting or continuing the life of particular characters in subsequent books, but I have found that it's a kind of trap because you never really go on to another topic.
- Toni Morrison, *Time*, Jan 21, 1998

You are going to love some of your characters because they are you or some facet of you, and you are going to hate some of your characters for the same reason.
- Anne Lamott

The writer should be not the judge of his characters and their conversations, but only an unbiased witness.
- Anton Chekhov

Action is character.
- F. Scott Fitzgerald, *The Last Tycoon*

Characterization is an accident that flows out of action and dialogue.
- Jack Woodford

[on Virginia Woolf's *To the Lighthouse*]…there is an interior with not very much happening. Just that rush, it's almost just a breathless rush of images and yet that control is just so absolute, it's fabulous. I think that the insides of her characters are so wonderfully revealed; they just seem to creep up on you.
- Alice McDermott [Mickey Pearlman and Katherine Usher Henderson, *A Voice of One's Own*]

Dialogue is the poetry in the prose. It gives air to the narrative.
- Lynn Freed, *Reading, Writing and Leaving Home*

Dialogue is the audio portion of the program.
> - Stephen King, *On Writing: A Memoir of the Craft*

Dialogue looks lovely on the page.
> - Gail Carson Levine, *Writing Magic: Creating Stories That Fly*

Dialogue must appear realistic without being so…Dialogue in fiction is what characters do to one another.
> - Elizabeth Bowen

I notice particularly the cadence of their voices, the sort of phrases they'll use, and that's what I'm all the time trying to hear in my head, how people word things—because everybody speaks an entirely different language.
> - Frank O'Connor, *Writers at Work: The Paris Review Interviews*

Dialogue achieves its power in the dynamics of a fleeting moment of sight, sound, smell, and touch.
> - Gloria Naylor, *"A Question of Language"*

Speak your dialogue out loud. If it sounds like the way people talk, then write it down.
> - Tom Clancy

You should let dialogue get as nearly out of control as you can. Characters should say what they say to each other instead of what they mean to say.
> - Robert Stone

Dialogue is the yeast that lightens the bread and should be paid for at double rate—whereas by the word-system it counts the same as the dough.
> - Mark Twain, letter

If you were to make little fishes talk, they would talk like whales.
> - Oliver Goldsmith to Dr. Johnson

Dialogue—two people conversing—often portrays the conflicting desires, needs, wishes, or perception of the participants. There is also an inherent tension in the format of statement/response.
> - Gabriele Lusser Rico, *Writing the Natural Way*

In what we think of as bad dialogue, the characters talk directly to each other.
> - Diane Johnson

One line of dialogue that rings true reveals character in a way that pages of description can't.
- Anne Lamatt

Dialogue is the thin bridge which must, from time to time, carry the entire weight of the novel.
- Elizabeth Bowen

Dialogue is not just quotation. It is grimaces, pauses, adjustments of blouse buttons, doodles on a napkin, and crossings of legs…Conversations are like icebergs—only the very tops are visible. Most of their weight, their mass, their meanings are under the surface. Make your readers feel the tension between what is above and what's below, and you'll have a story.
- Jerry Stern

Dialogue is *the* way to nail character, so you have to work on getting the voice right…Dialogue that is written in dialect is very tiring to read…It makes our necks feel funny.
- Anne Lamott, *Bird by Bird*

Try and write straight English; never using slang except in dialogue and then only when unavoidable. Because all slang goes sour in a short time. I only use swear words, for example, that have lasted at least a thousand years for fear of getting stuff that will be simply timely and then go sour.
- Ernest Hemingway

Writing dialogue is simply giving voice to the characters that live inside of us. When you're in control of your dialogue, you can release and tighten the tension at will.
- Gloria Kempton, *Dialogue*

It's a crazy business, anyway, locking yourself in a room and inventing conversations, no way for a grown-up to behave.
- John Leonard

5.

What can you tell me about plots and settings?

Plot does not simply move with time, but spreads out conceptually in metaphorical space.
- John L.'Heureux

Story: The King died and then the queen died.
Plot: The King died and then the queen died of grief.
- E.M Forster

[A writer] must remind himself that the story of Romeo and Juliet had been told by an Italian writer of novellas—but that Shakespeare told it better, and that the same plot was retold later in the form of *Abie's Irish Rose* and, more recently, in *West Side Story*.
- Isabelle Ziegler, *Creative Writing*

There are no new plots, there are only new people, new treatment, new reactions, new locations, new times.
- Adele Rogers St. Johns

Plot—any plot—is merely the development of your characters through a consecutive series of situations.
- Steven Vincent Benét, *Stephen Vincent Benét on Writing*, ed. George Abbe

Plotting is like sex. Plotting is about desire and satisfaction, anticipation and release You have to arouse your reader's desire to know what happens, to unravel the mystery, to see good triumph. You have to sustain it, keep it warm, feed it, just a little bit, not too much at a time, as your story goes on. That's called suspense. It can bring desire to a frenzy, in which case you are in a good position to bring off a wonderful climax.
- Colin Greenland

Plots are what a writer sees with.
> -Eudora Welty

Somebody wants something and it's hard for them to get it.
> - Todd Strasser

Sometimes a plot triumphs too completely. The characters have to suspend their natures at every turn, or else are so swept away by the course of Fate that our sense of their reality is weakened.
> - E.M. Forster

I don't praise plots as accurate representations of life, but as ways to keep readers reading.
> - Kurt Vonnegut

Trying to explain in rational, analytical fashion how we come up with our plots and our thematic structures threatens in an odd sort of way to reveal that we are all just humbugs hiding behind a velvet curtain.
> - Terry Brooks, *Sometimes the Magic Works*

The main plot line is simple: Getting your character to the foot of the tree, getting him up the tree, and then figuring out how to get him down again.
> - Jane Yolen

Plot is about many things—character, imagination, irony, logic, and nearly always about the unexpected.
> - Hallie Burnett, *On Writing the Short Story*

Commit the following definition to memory and never allow yourself to forget it: Plot is a plan of action devised to achieve a definite and much desired end— through cause and effect...Don't let an accident or coincidence or someone else step in and solve everything.
> - Lee Wyndham, *Writing for Children & Teenagers*

The author makes a tacit deal with the reader. You hand them a backpack. You ask them to places certain things in it—to remember, to keep in mind—as they make their way up the hill...If you hand them a yellow Volkswagen and they have to haul this to the top of the mountain—to the end of the story—and they find that this Volkswagen has nothing whatsoever to do with your story, you're going to have a very irritated reader on your hands.
> - Frank Conroy

The quality of this novel is the way the plot is treated and not the plot itself.
- Vladimir Nabokov

Sometimes I say a little prayer, and I know you won't believe this, but a plot comes, just like that. Then I know I have to read about twenty or thirty historical books. I do like to get the background right.
- Barbara Cartland, in Richard Joseph, *Bestsellers: Top Writers Tell How*

Drama is the way of holding the reader's attention. The basic formula for drama is setup, buildup, payoff—just like a joke.
- Anne Lamott, *Bird by Bird*

One of the writer's corollaries to Murphy's Law should read: Every Plot Starts to Go Wrong Just After the First Big Scene.
- Ansen Dibell, *The Elements of Fiction: Plot*

I began plotting novels at about the time I learned to read.
- James Baldwin

Make everyone fall out of the plane first, and then explain who they were and why they were in the plane to begin with.
- Nancy Ann Dibble

Plot springs from character...I've always sort of believed that these people inside me—these characters—know who they are and what they're about and what happens, and they need me to help get it down on paper because they don't type.
- Anne Lamott

Your plot will fall into place as, one day at a time, you listen to your characters carefully, and watch them move around doing and saying things and bumping into each other.
- Anne Lamott, *Bird by Bird*

A plot is a thousand times more unsettling than an argument, which may be answered.
- Eudora Welty, *The Atlantic Monthly*, October 1965

The heroine's journey begins with "separation from the feminine," and ends with "integration of masculine and feminine."
- Maureen Murdock

Plot is built of significant events in a given story—significant because they have important consequences. Taking a shower isn't necessarily plot…Plot is the things characters do, feel, think, or say, that make a difference to what comes next…Plot is a verb.
>   - Ansen Dibell, *The Elements of Fiction: Plot*

Good old script, which connects this letter to that, and this line to that—well, that's how good plots work, right? When this loops around and connects to that…
>   - John Barth

The beauty of word processing, God bless my word processor, is that it keeps the plotting very fluid. The prose becomes like a liquid that you can manipulate at will. In the old days, when I typed, every piece of typing paper was like cased in concrete.
>   - Sue Grafton

It signifies both what happens in story—and what does not.
>   - Jane Yolen, *Take Joy*

Plot might seem to be a matter of choice. It is not. The particular plot is something the novelist is driven to. It is what is left after the whittling-away of alternatives.
>   - Elizabeth Bowen

A line to direct the reader's interest.
>   - W. Somerset Maughm

I do not write and never have written to an arranged plot. The book is composed at once, like a picture, and may start anywhere, in the middle or at the end. I may go from the end to the beginning in the same day, and then from the beginning to the middle.
>   - Joyce Cary

When in doubt have a man come through a door with a gun in his hand.
>   - Raymond Chandler

Nothing can happen nowhere.
>   - Elizabeth Bowen

Place remembers events.
>   - James Joyce, *Notebooks*

I always try to make the setting fit the story I have in mind...I have always felt that making the reader aware of the vast emptiness of our high desert is important to making the story work.
- Tony Hillerman

Setting exists so that the character has someplace to stand, something that can help define him, something he can pick up and throw, if necessary, or eat, or give to his girlfriend.
- John Gardner

There are...places where one breathes in spirit, places where a man can steep himself in it, or if you prefer, where he quickens the sense of the divine in himself. This is the greatest gift of Earth and Heaven to man.
- Louis Charpentier, *The Mysteries of Chartres Cathedral*

There is always in life a place to leave and a new place to find, and in between a zone of hesitation and uncertainty tinged with more or less intense anxiety.
- Paul Tournier, *A Place for You*

You can fall in love at first sight with a place as with a person.
- Alec Waugh

Every place is given its character by certain patterns of events that keep on happening there. These patterns are always interlocked with certain geometric patterns...they may be dead or alive...when they are dead, they keep us locked in inner conflict.
- Christopher Alexander, *The Timeless Way of Building*

Place is something the soul makes for storing images.
- Albert Magnus

We continue to displace ourselves—no longer with unity of direction, like a migrant flock, but more like the refugees from a broken ant hill.
- Wendell Berry, *The Unsettling of America*

The place God calls you to is the place where your deep gladness and the world's deep hunger meet.
- E. B. McNeil, *The Psychology of Being Human*

To be rooted is perhaps the most important and least recognized need of the human soul.
- Simone Weil, *The Need for Roots*

The question of questions for mankind—the problem which underlies all others, and which is more deeply interesting than any other—is the ascertainment of the place which Man occupies in nature and of his relations to the universe of things.

- Thomas Huxley

Each blade of grass has its spot on earth whence it draws its life, its strength, and so is man rooted to the land from which he draws his faith together with his life.

- Joseph Conrad

The soul of landscape, the spirits of the elements, the genius of every place will be revealed to a loving view of nature.

- Karl Jaspers, *Philosophy*

People give pain, are callous and insensitive, empty and cruel...but place heals the hurt, soothes the outrage, fills the terrible vacuum that these human beings make.

- Eudora Welty

The holes and tunnels of an old warren become smooth, reassuring and comfortable with use. There are no snags or rough corners...All the faults have been put right and everything in use is of proved value.

- Richard Adams, *Watership Down*

Wisdom sits in places.

- Apache Proverb

An author knows his landscape best; he can stand around, smell the wind, get a feel for his place.

- Tony Hillerman

Tell me the landscape. Never write about a place until you're away from it, because that gives you perspective.

- Ernest Hemingway

Tell me the landscape in which you live and I will tell you who you are.

- José Ortega y Gasset

Poets need not go to Niagara to write about the force of falling water.

- Robert Frost

Odysseus never did sail "beyond the sunset." He eventually made his way back to Ithaca, his old home and kingdom, which he found to be in a dreadful mess, usurped by rogues. He set to, and sorted it out. It was there, where he had come from, that he made his "newer world." There is no escaping. The future for us, too, is in our own place, if we can learn to see it differently, and are "strong in will" to change it.

- Charles Handy, *The Relevance of a Decade*

Some places speak distinctly. Certain dank gardens cry aloud for a murder; certain old houses demand to be haunted; certain coasts are set apart for shipwrecks.

- Robert Louis Stevenson

The worst part of a modern stylish mansion is that it has no place for ghosts.
- Oliver Wendell Holmes, *The Poet at the Breakfast Table*

Here I am, where I ought to be. A writer must have a place where he or she feels this, a place to love and be irritated with.

- Louise Erdrich, *NY Times*, 28 Jul '85

Write about winter in the summer. Describe Norway as Ibsen did, from a desk in Italy; describe Dublin as James Joyce did, from a desk in Paris. Willa Cather wrote her prairie novels in New York City; Mark Twain wrote *Huckleberry Finn* in Hartford, Connecticut. Recently, scholars learned that Walt Whitman rarely left his room.

- Annie Dillard, *The Writing Life*

An individual is not distinct from his place; he is that place.
- Gabriel Marcel

Most of us have to be transplanted before we blossom.
- Louise Nevelson

How hard it is to escape from places. However carefully one goes they hold you—you leave little bits of yourself fluttering on the fences—like rags and shreds of your very life.

- Katherine Mansfield

Fiction depends for its life on place. Place is the crossroads of circumstance, the proving ground of, What happened? Who's here? Who's coming?
- Eudora Welty

France is a land, England is a people, and America is a willingness of heart.
    - F. Scott Fitzgerald

The attributes you need to be a travel writer are somewhat contradictory. For travel you need to be tough and resilient and to write you must be sensitive and sympathetic.
    - Colin Thubron

Under the Tuscan Sun brought more tourists than ever to Italy's fertile and sundrenched Tuscany region, while *Sideways* gave Santa Barbara wine country a welcome PR boost.
    - Ty Treadwell

Las Vegas: all the amenities of modern society in a habitat unfit to grow a tomato.
    - Jason Love

Oakland: There is no there there.
    - Gertrude Stein

New York has a trip-hammer vitality which drives you insane with restlessness if you have no inner stabilizer.
    - Henry Miller

New York, the nation's thyroid gland.
    - Christopher Morley, *Shore Leave*

I wonder what it is in the New York air that enables me to sit up till all hours of the night in an atmosphere which in London would make a horse dizzy, but here merely clears the brain.
    - James Agate

New York is to the nation what the white church spire is to the village—the visible symbol of aspiration and faith, the white plume saying the way is up!
    - E.B. White

The final story, the final chapter of western man, I believe, lies in Los Angeles.
    - Phil Ochs

Venice is like eating an entire box of chocolate liqueurs in one go.
    - Truman Capote

Let the site tell you its secrets.
> - Christopher Alexander, *A Pattern Language*

When a man leaves home, he leaves behind some scrap of his heart…it's the same with a place a man is going to. Only then he sends a scrap of his heart ahead.
> - Frederick Buechner, *Godric*

The writer operates at a peculiar crossroads where time and place and eternity somehow meet. His problem is to find that location.
> - Flannery O'Connor

Place is something the soul makes for storing images.
> - Albert Magnus

It's not down on any map; true places never are.
> - Herman Melville

An individual is not distinct from his place; he is that place.
> - Gabriel Marcel

The human's persistent effort to anchor meaning in place expresses itself in endless variations…That's why Luther happened to remember that it was on the privy in the monastery in Wittenberg where he was struck in 1512 by the freeing words of justification by faith in Romans 1:17.
> - Belden C. Lane, *Landscape of the Sacred*

Is there a spiritual geography; are there certain places upon the earth which are more, or less, attuned to certain modes of consciousness? And if so, do such qualities belong to the earth itself, to certain qualities of light, or sound, or scent or rock formation?
> - Kathleen Raine, *The Lion's Mouth*

The memories in things speak reciprocally with people, where the very earth remembers the imprints of history…The specific place-names should be spoken aloud upon arriving at each one. This way you bring alive what happened and still happens there.
> - Kenneth Lincoln, *Native America Renaissance*

Places remember events.
> - James Joyce, *Notebook*

They [Lummi Tribal Council] say that logging these trees will destroy sacred places which collectively contribute to the most precious thing of all—that which in the Salish language is called *skalalitude* or "a sacred state of mind where magic and beauty are everywhere.
- James A. Swan, *Sacred Places*

Most of us have to be transplanted before we blossom.
- Louise Nevelson

There is always in life a place to leave and a new place to find, and in between a zone of hesitation and uncertainty tinged with more or less intense anxiety.
- Paul Tournier, *A Place for You*

We continue to displace ourselves—no longer with unity of direction, like a migrant flock, but more like the refugees from a broken ant hill.
- Wendell Berry, *The Unsettling of America*

People give pain, are callous and insensitive, empty and cruel...but place heals the hurt, soothes the outrage, fills the terrible vacuum that these human beings make.
- Eudora Welty

The most gifted travel writers—from Lawrence Durrell to Peter Matthiesen—have all performed the impossible task of affording entry to the landscape and consciousness of another world.
- Belden C. Lane, *Landscapes of the Sacred*

My wound is geography. It is also my anchorage, my port of call.
- Pat Conroy, *The Prince of Tides*

Of course Nebraska is a storehouse of literary material. Everywhere is a storehouse of literary material. If a true artist were born in a pigpen and raised in a sty, he would still find plenty of inspiration for his work. The only need is the eye to see.
- Willa Cather

Nothing has really happened until it's been described.
- Virginia Woolf

Geomancy is commonly known as the "art of harmonious placement," for it has been used to find the right time and place for all human activities.
- Richard Feather Anderson, *The Power of Place*

I grew up in this town [Temuco, Argentina], my poetry was born between the hill and the river, it took its voice from the rain, and like the timber, it steeped itself in the forests.
- Pablo Neruda, *Wall St. Journal* 14 Nov '85

Every place is given its character by certain patterns of events that keep on happening there. These patterns are always interlocked with certain geometric patterns…they may be dead or alive…when they are dead, they keep us locked in inner conflict.
- Christopher Alexander, *The Timeless Way of Building*

The sorghum-sweet serenity of the place skewered me squarely for an instant on a knifeblade of nostalgia for the rural South.
- William Styron, *Sophie's Choice*

If you describe things as better than they are, you are considered to be a romantic; if you describe things as worse than they are, you will be called a realist; and if you describe things exactly as they are, you will be thought of as a satirist.
- Quentin Crisp

You don't write about the horrors of war. No. You write about a kid's burnt socks lying in the road.
- Richard Price

Caress the detail, the divine detail.
- Vladimir Nabokov

Name names. Make your writing physical. Use lots of nouns. "Food" is an idea; "black-bean soup" is a thing.
- David Long

Load every rift with ore.
- John Keats

Even the tiniest object in your fiction—a pink ribbon, a cricket, a needle and thread—can carry a lot of weight.
- Stephen Delaney

Details are electric.
- Bonnie Goldberg

A significant detail is something that has push or is a symbol of push. By push I mean possessing a force that drives a person.
  - Larry Reinhart, *How to Write a Mystery*

Details make stories human, and the more human a story can be, the better.
  - V.S. Pritchett

Give one vivid detail, and readers will build the rest.
  - Jerome Stern, *Making Shapely Fiction*

Detail makes the difference between boring and terrific writing. It's the difference between a pencil sketch and a lush oil painting. As a writer, words are your paint. Use all the colors.
  - Rhys Alexander

Some say God is in the details; some say the Devil is in the details. Both are correct…Tactically speaking, I'd say go ahead and crowd in the first draft—put everything in. Then in revising decide what counts, what tells; and cut and recombine till what's left is what counts. Leap boldly.
  - Ursula Le Guin

The right details plunk us down inside a story and put us in our character's shoes.
  - Gail Carson Levine, *Writing Magic: Creating Stories That Fly*

Love is the hardest thing in the world to write about. So simple. You've got to catch it through details, like the early morning sunlight hitting the gray tin of the rainspout in front of her house. The ringing of a telephone that sounds like Beethoven's "Pastoral." A letter scribbled on her office stationery that you carry around in your pocket because it smells of all the lilacs in Ohio.
  - Billy Wilder

When we write best we dig up mysteries and each new detail is a new shovel.
  - Barry Lane, *Writing as a Road to Self-Discovery*

Don't tell me the moon is shining; show me the glint of light on broken glass.
  - Anton Chekhov

6.

Where do you get your ideas?

Ideas, like children, do not come from nowhere. But they seem to have their own gestation period, collecting themselves up in bits and pieces, forcing one to wait for them.
- Mary Catherine Bateson, *Peripheral Visions*

You get very gaudy ideas at night but they don't stand up.,
- Raymond Chandler

Einstein didn't go around wracking his brain, muttering to himself, "How, oh how, can I come up with a Great Idea?" You just do what comes naturally... Mozart said things should "flow like oil." Trying harder is not the trick. The trick is getting the right concept to begin with and then make variations.
- Douglas R. Hofstadter, *Metamagical Themas*

If I'm trying to sleep, the ideas won't stop. If I'm trying to write, there appears a barren nothingness.
- Carrie Latet

Great ideas originate in the muscles.
- Thomas A. Edison

Labor gives birth to ideas.
- Jim Rohn

Ideas come from the imagination, and that imagination is in turn the product of the sum total of an individual's life experiences...A common fallacy is that writers should lead exciting and colorful lives, joining safaris or taking canoes up the Kimpopo...*All* experiences, however outwardly dull, may stimulate the mind.
- Christopher Evans, *Writing Science Fiction*

Serious people have few ideas. People with ideas are never serious.
- Paul Valery

Our concepts are like a thread made of fibers. The solidity of the thread is not due to the presence of a single fiber running its full length, but to the intertwining of a large number of fibers.
- Ludwig Josef Johan Wittgenstein, *Philosophical Investigations*

This is the way to get ideas: Never to let adverse circumstances discourage you, but to believe there is a way out of every difficulty, which may be found by earnest thoughts.
- L. Frank Baum

Ideas are like rabbits. You get a couple and learn how to handle them, and pretty soon you have a dozen.
- John Steinbeck

If an idea doesn't stick with me for more than twenty-four hours, it probably wasn't all that hot in the first place.
- Terry Brooks, *Sometimes the Magic Works*

When I am, as it were, completely myself, entirely alone, and of good cheer, it is on such occasions that my ideas flow best and most abundantly. Whence and how they come, I know not; nor can I force them…When I proceed to write down my ideas, I take out of the bag of my memory…what has been previously collected…For this reason the committing to paper is done quickly enough, for everything is…already finished; and it rarely differs on paper from what was in my imagination.
- Wolfgang Amadeus Mozart, Holmes, *The Life of Mozart*

Ideas do not belong to people. Ideas live in the world as we do. We discover certain ideas at certain times.
- Mary Caroline (M.C.) Richards, *Centering*

It's easy to come up with new ideas; the hard part is letting go of what worked for you two years ago, but will soon be out of date.
- Roger Van Oech

Frequently schoolchildren ask me, "Where do you get your ideas from?" The answer, which always puzzles them is, "I don't get my ideas, they get me."
- Robertson Davies

I am suggesting that your best idea for a business will be something that is deep within you, something that can't be stolen because it is uniquely yours, and anyone else trying to execute it without the (perhaps unconscious) thought you have given the subject will fail. It's not basically different from writing a novel. A good business and a good novel are faithful and uncluttered expressions of yourself.
- Paul Hawken, *Growing a Business*

At first people refuse to believe that a strange new thing can be done, then they begin to hope it can't be done, then they see it can be done—then it is done and all the world wonders why it was not done centuries before.
- Frances Hodgson Burnett, *The Secret Garden*

Great ideas come into the world as gently as doves.
- Albert Camus

All there is to writing is having ideas. To learn to write is to learn to have ideas.
- Robert Frost

Any powerful idea is absolutely fascinating and absolutely useless until we choose to use it.
- Richard Bach, *One*

It was at Rome, on the 15th of October, 1764, as I sat musing amidst the ruins of the Capitol, while the barefoot friars were singing vespers in the Temple of Jupiter, that the idea of writing the decline and fall of the city first started to my mind.
- Edward Gibbon

If you haven't got an idea, start a story anyway. You can always throw it away, and maybe by the time you get to the fourth page you *will* have an idea, and you'll only have to throw away the first three pages.
- William Campbell Gault

If you have an apple and I have an apple and we exchange these apples then you and I will still each have one apple. But if you have an idea and I have an idea and we exchange these ideas, then each of us will have two ideas.
- George Bernard Shaw

Ideas can no more flow backward than can a river.
- Victor Hugo

Every morning between 9 and 12 I go to my room and sit before a piece of paper. Many times, I just sit for three hours with no ideas coming to me. But I know one thing. If an idea does come between 9 and 12 I am there ready for it.
- Flannery O'Connor

The human race is divided into two sharply differentiated and mutually antagonistic classes: a small minority that plays with ideas and is capable of taking them in, and vast majority that finds them painful, and is thus arrayed against them, and against all who have traffic with them.
- H.L. Menchken

Like a mutation, an idea may be recorded in the wrong time, to lie latent like a recessive gene and spring once more to life in an auspicious era.
- Loren Eiseley

If at first the idea is not absurd, then there is no hope for it.
- Albert Einstein

Every composer knows the anguish and despair occasioned by forgetting ideas which one had no time to write down.
- Hector Berlioz

All the good ideas I ever had came to me while I was milking a cow.
- Grant Wood

If you have the same ideas as everyone else but have them one week earlier than everyone else then you will be hailed as a visionary. But if you have them five years earlier you will be named a lunatic.
- Barry Jones

Every book is the wreck of a perfect idea.
- Iris Murdoch

The idea that is not dangerous is not worthy of being called an idea at all.
- Elbert Hubbard

To get the right word in the right place is a rare achievement. To condense the diffused light of a page of thought into the luminous flash of a single sentence, is worthy to rank as a prize composition just by itself…Anybody can have ideas—the difficulty is to express them without squandering a quire of paper on an idea that ought to be reduced to one glittering paragraph.
- Mark Twain

An idea, to be suggestive, must come to the individual with the force of revelation.

- William James

Daring ideas are like chessmen moved foreword; they may be beaten but they may start a winning game.

- Johann Wolfgang von Goethe

To swear off making mistakes is very easy. All you have to do is swear off having ideas.

- Leo Burnett

I carry my ideas about me for a long time, often a very long time, before I commit them to writing.

- Ludwig van Beethoven

Don't worry about people stealing your ideas. If your ideas are any good, you'll have to ram them down people's throats.

- Howard Aiken

Great people talk about ideas. Small people talk about other people.

- Tobias S. Gibson

Ideas lose themselves as quickly as quail, and one must wing them the minute they rise out of the grass, or they are gone.

- Thomas F. Kennedy

You have to have an idea of what you are going to do, but it should be a vague idea.

- Pablo Picasso

Drawing is putting a line around an idea.

- Henri Matisse

There is one thing stronger than all the armies in the world; and that is an idea whose time has come.

- Victor Hugo

Ideas not coupled with action never become bigger than the brain cells they occupied.

- Arnold H. Glasgow

When an idea reaches critical mass there is no stopping the shift its presence will induce.
  - Marianne Williamson

An idea is putting truth in check-mate.
  - Jose Orgtega Y Gasset

I can't understand why people are frightened of new ideas. I'm frightened of old ones.
  - John Cage

…just when ideas fail, a word comes in to save the situation.
  - Johann Wolfgang von Goethe

My writing comes from ideas that make a sound in my heart.
  - Katherine Patterson

Writing is no trouble: you just jot down ideas as they occur to you. The jotting is simplicity itself—it is the occurring which is difficult.
  - Stephen Leacock

Ideas have come from strange places…I remember I had this kind of dream or image of a walled garden and there was a baby in a cradle, and it was something like a legend or a fairy tale…eventually that turned into my novel *Bellefleur*. Where it came from I have no idea. It's just the unconscious, I guess, or a dream.
  - Joyce Carol Oates

Night time is really the best time to work. All the ideas are there to be yours because everyone else is asleep.
  - Catherine O'Hara

Everybody walks past a thousand story ideas every day. The good writers are the ones who see five or six of them. Most people don't see any.
  - Orson Scott Card

Why is it I get my best ideas in the morning while shaving?
  - Albert Einstein

When I'm looking for an idea, I'll do anything—clean the closet, mow the lawn, work in the garden.
  - Kevin Henkes

Everyone who has ever taken a shower has had an idea. It's the person who gets out of the shower, dries off, and does something about it that makes a difference.
- Nolan Bushnell

Joseph Heller described the conception of Catch-22 this way: "I was lying in bed when suddenly this line came to me: 'It was love at first sight. The first time he saw the chaplain X fell madly in love with him.'" The "X" turned out to be Yossarain, but Heller didn't have the name, didn't even know that this "X" was in the army.
- Joan Didion, "Making Up Stories"

You look out the window, and you see the tip of a tiger outside, and you know there's a whole tiger attached to that tip, and you wonder about the tiger.
- Mekeel McBride

The material's out there, a calm lake waiting for us to dive in.
- Beverly Lowry

Ideas are the cheapest part of writing. They are free. The hard part is what you do with ideas you've gathered.
- Jane Yolen

Every new idea is an impossibility until it is born.
- Ron Brown

Nothing is more dangerous than an idea when you have only one.
- Alain Chartier

The art of writing has for backbone some fierce attachment to an idea.
- Virginia Woolf

Ideas won't keep. Something must be done about them.
- Alfred North Whitehead

Ideas move fast when their time comes.
- Carolyn Heilbrun

Many ideas grow better when transplanted into another mind than in the one where they sprung up.
- Oliver Wendell Holmes

I am suggesting that your best ideas for a business will be something that is deep within you, something that can't be. If you want to get an idea across, wrap it up in a person.
- Ralph Bunche

People will accept your ideas much more readily if you tell them Benjamin Franklin said it first.
- David H. Comins

It's useless to send armies against ideas.
- George Brandes

An idea not coupled with action will never get any bigger than the brain cell it occupied.
- Arnold H. Glasgow

Many ideas grow better when they are transplanted into another mind than the one where they sprang up.
- Oliver Wendell Holmes

Style and structure are the essence of a book; great ideas are hogwash.
- Vladimir Nabokov, *Writers at Work*

Hang ideas! They are tramps, vagabonds, knocking at the back-door of your mind, each taking a little of your substance, each carrying away some crumb of that belief in a few simple notions you must cling to if you want to live decently and would like to die easy!
- Joseph Conrad

The ideas I stand for are not mine I borrowed them from Socrates. I swiped them from Chesterfield. I stole them from Jesus. And I put them in a book. If you don't like their rules, whose would you use?
- Dale Carnegie

I'm looking for something to write about, waiting for something to happen. I'm waiting patiently like a hunter in a duck blind, waiting for the ducks to fly over.
- Joseph Wambaugh

If you have a skeleton in your closet, take it out and dance with it.
- Carolyn MacKenzie

If you can't explain your theory to a bartender, it's probably no good.
- Ernest Rutherford

Even if my marriage is falling apart and my children are unhappy, there is still a part of me that says, "God! This is fascinating!"
- Jane Smiley

An original idea. That can't be too hard. The library must be full of them.
- Stephen Fry

An idea is a feat of association, and the height of it is a good metaphor.
- Robert Frost

In every great time there is some one idea at work which is more powerful than any other, and which shapes the events of the time and determines their ultimate shape.
- Francis Bacon

Ideas control the world.
- James A. Garfield

Getting an idea should be like sitting down on a pin. It should make you jump up and do something.
- E.L. Simpson

Everything has been thought of before, but the difficulty is to think of it again.
- Johann Wolfgang von Goethe

Man's fear of ideas is probably the greatest dike holding back human knowledge and happiness.
- Morris L. Ernst

The value of an idea lies in the using of it.
- Thomas A. Edison

You have to hatch ideas—and then hitch them.
- Ray D. Everson

A new idea is like a child. It's easier to conceive than to deliver.
- Ted Koysis

Ideas are fatal to caste.
>   - E.M. Forster

Writing about an idea frees me of it. Thinking about it is a circle of repetitions.
>   - Mason Cooley

Like a mutation, an idea may be recorded in the wrong time, to lie latent like a recessive gene and spring once more to life in an auspicious era.
>   - Loren Eiseley

The great truths are too important to be new.
>   - W. Somerset Maugham

In oneself lies the whole world and if you know how to look and learn, then the door is there and the key is in your hand. Nobody on earth can give you either the key or the door to open, except yourself.
>   - Jiddu Krishnamurti

When writing poetry, it is not inspiration that produces a bright idea, but the bright idea that kindles the fire of inspiration.
>   - Cesare Pavese

When I get an idea I start at once building it up in my imagination. I change the construction, make improvements and operate the device in my mind.
>   - Nikola Tesla [Dorothy and Jerome Singer, *Imagination and Play in the Electronic Age*]

The generation of ideas involves factors that are not exclusively cerebral, factors that include the physiology, the emotions, the outer world.
>   - Robert Grudin, *The Grace of Great Things*

Ideas without action are worthless.
>   - Harvey MacKay

A good idea will keep you awake during the morning, but a great idea will keep you awake during the night.
>   - Marilyn Vos Savant

Adults are always asking little kids what they want to be when they grow up because they're looking for ideas.
>   - Paula Poundstone

The test of a first-rate intelligence is the ability to hold two opposed ideas in the mind at the same time and still retain the ability to function.
- F. Scott Fitzgerald

There is nothing so dangerous as an idea—when it's the only one you've got.
- Emile Chartier

The questions which one asks oneself begin, at last, to illuminate the world, and become one's key to the experiences of others.
- James Baldwin

The writer with a fixed idea is like a goose laying a stone.
- Nancy Willard

Ideas are diamonds, and they are stocked and stored in the great structure that we call our mind-body system. Beneath the surface crust of ordinary consciousness, we are all filled with ideas and associations linking with other ideas—the very stuff of evolution moving in us to emerge as innovation.
- Jean Houston, *A Passion for the Possible*

Nothing you write, if you hope to be good, will ever come out as you first hoped.
- Lillian Hellman

The world is a warehouse of forms which the writer raids: this is a stickup.
- Annie Dillard, *Living by Fiction*

Some poems come entire, bless them, dictated by the muse or *ha-Shem* or the tooth fairy.
- Marge Piercy, *Writers [On Writing]*

Little words hurt big ideas.
- Howard W. Newton

A man is a poet if the difficulties inherent in his art provide him with ideas; he is not a poet if they deprive him of ideas.
- Paul Valéry

So where do the ideas—the salable ideas—come from?…They come from my nightmares…A good assumption is what scares you will scare someone else.
- Stephen King, *Secret Windows*

[with fiction] Ideas for what I am working on come in the night, in the tub, on planes, in the middle of supper. I keep a notebook on the night table, so that when an idea bombs in at 2 A.M., I will not get up and turn on the computer. One reason I learned to meditate was to control my fictional imagination and not let the characters take me over.

    - Marge Piercy, *Writers [on Writing]*

Any powerful idea is absolutely fascinating and absolutely useless until we choose to use it.

    - Richard Bach, *One*

There is no idea so brilliant or original that a sufficiently untalented writer can't screw it up.

    - Raymond Feist

There is no idea so stupid or hackneyed that a sufficiently talented writer can't get a good story out of it.

    - Lawrence Watt-Evans

A crank is someone with a new idea—until it catches on.

    - Mark Twain

Inspiration is the art of breathing in.

    - Marcus Bach, *The Power of Perception*

There was never a great soul that did not have some divine inspiration.

    - Marcus Tullius Cicero

The glow of inspiration warms us; it is a holy rapture.

    - Ovid

[It is] the Alka-Seltzer moment, the moment when the tablet hits the water and begins to fizz.

    - Trevor Baylis

Inspiration may be a form of super-consciousness, or perhaps of subconsciousness—I wouldn't know. But I am sure it is the antithesis of self-consciousness.

    - Aaron Copland

Inspiration is a farce that poets have invented to give themselves importance.

    - Jean Anouilh

Whatever inspiration is, it's born from a continuous "I don't know."
- Wislawa Szymborska

And Archimedes, as he was washing, thought of a manner of computing the proportion of gold in King Hiero's crown by seeing the water flowing over the bathing-stool. He leaped up as one possessed or inspired, crying "I have found it! Eureka!"
- Plutarch

When you are born in Ireland you are given a ready-made world. Someone, a Rumanian, I think, called it "the coherent miseries of an oppressed, small place." But it is a surface world, and it is not enough. You have to nest upon it, incubate it into something greater, to release something unusual from it. Like ancient bodies from a bog.
- Seamus Heaney [David W. McCullough, *People Books, Book People*]

The greatest inspiration is often born of desperation.
- Comer Cotrell

Chance furnishes me what I need. I am like a man who stumbles along; my foot strikes something, I bend over and it is exactly what I want.
- James Joyce, Brenda Maddox, *The Real Life Molly Bloom*

I write for a couple of hours every day, even if I only get a couple of sentences. I put in that time. You do that every day, and inspiration will come along. I don't allow myself not to keep trying. It's not fun, but if you wait until you want to write, you'll never do it.
- Dave Barry

We are both earthly beings, with our feet on the ground, and beings of inspiration and imagination and weightlessness. We're both. That's our genius, and we must not be talked out of us.
- Mary C. Richards

It's all about technique. The great mistake of this century is to put inspiration and creativity first.
- Vivienne Westwood

Better beware of notions like genius and inspiration; they are a sort of magic wand and should be used sparingly by anybody who wants to see things clearly.
- José Ortega Y Gassett

Inspiration seeks the artist as the artist seeks inspiration.
  - Jane Roberts, *The World View of Paul Cezanne*

If I spend a long time in silence, which I really love, that's very good for my writing. The main thing is just to live intensely and to feel. If there's the slightest little bubble from the spring coming up, I try to go with the bubble until it gets to the top of the water and then try to be there for it so that I can begin to understand what is happening down in the depths.
  - Alice Walker, [Donald McQuade, Robert Atwan, *The Writer's Presence*]

You can't wait for inspiration. You have to go after it with a club.
  - Jack London

Write while the heat is in you. The writer who postpones the recording of his thoughts uses an iron which has cooled to burn a hole with. He cannot inflame the minds of his audience.
  - Henry David Thoreau

They [*Sonnets to Orpheus*] are perhaps the most mysterious, even to me, in their way of arising and imposing themselves on me, the most enigmatical dictation I have ever sustained and achieved.
  - Rainer Maria Rilke, letter to Xavier von Moos

Writing everyday as one practices the piano everyday keeps one nimble and then when the great moments of inspiration come, one is in good form, supple and smooth.
  - Anäis Nin

Just as appetite comes by eating, so work brings inspiration, if inspiration is not discernable at the beginning.
  - Igor Stravinsky

A deadline is negative inspiration. Still, it's better than no inspiration at all.
  - Rita Mae Brown

My sole inspiration is a telephone call from a director.
  - Cole Porter

I know writers who write only when inspiration comes. How would Isaac Stern play if he played the violin only when he felt like it? He would be lousy.
  - Madeleine L'Engle

Inspiration comes from working everyday.
- Charles Beaudelaire

Inspiration is a guest that does not willingly visit the lazy.
- Pyotr Tchaikovsky

The ultimate inspiration is the deadline.
- Nolan Bushnell

When inspiration does not come to meet me, I go halfway to meet it.
- Sigmund Freud

It isn't that inspiration doesn't exist, but it comes only with writing.
- John Braine

Inspiration is wonderful when it happens, but the writer must develop an approach for the rest of the time…The wait is simply too long.
- Leonard S. Bernstein

A moment's insight is sometimes worth a life's experience.
- Oliver Wendell Holmes

I didn't have to think up so much as a comma or a semicolon; it was all given, straight from the celestial recording room. Weary, I would beg for a break, an intermission, time enough, let's say, to go to the toilet or take a breath of fresh air on the balcony. Nothing doing!
- Henry Miller

You must never lose the awareness that in yourself you are nothing; you are only an instrument. An instrument is nothing until it is lifted.
- Kathryn Hulme

When I'm inspired, I get excited because I can't wait to see what I'll come up with next.
- Dolly Parton

When we hear the word "inspiration" we imagine something that comes like a bolt of lightning, and at once with a rapt flashing of the eyes, tossed hair and feverish excitement, a poet or artist begins furiously to paint or write…But this isn't so. Inspiration comes very slowly and quietly.
- Brenda Ueland, *If You Want to Write*

Isaiah (or was it Elisha?) was caught up into Heaven in a chariot of fire once. But when the weather is divine and I am free to work, such a journey is positively nothing.
- Katherine Mansfield

Far away in the sunshine are my highest aspirations. I may not reach them, but I can look up and see their beauty, believe in them, and try to follow where they lead.
- Louisa May Alcott

State your intentions, Muse. I know you're there.
Dead bards who pined for you have said
You're bright as flame, but fickle as air.
My pen and I, submerged in liquid hade,
Much dark can spread, on days and over reams
But without you, no radiance can shed.
Why rustle in the dark, when fledged with fire?
Craze the night with flails of light. Reave
Your turbid shroud. Bestow what I require.

But you're not in the dark. I do believe
I swim, like squid, in clouds of my own make,
To you, offensive. To us both, opaque.
What's constituted so, open a pen
Can penetrate. I have one here, let's go.
- Neal Stephenson, Invocation, *Quicksilver*

The muse whispers to you when she chooses, and you can't tell her to come back later, because you quickly learn in this business that she might not come back at all.
- Terry Brooks, *Sometimes the Magic Works*

True artists, true poets, generate and give birth today, tomorrow, ever. From this habit of labor results a ceaseless comprehension of difficulties which keep them in communion with the muse and her creative forces.
- Honoré de Balzac

It was this. My father had left a small collection of books in a little room upstairs, to which I had access (for it adjoined my own) and which nobody else in our house ever troubled.
- Charles Dickens, *David Copperfield*

I think you need to get to a point where writing is something you can do on demand instead of waiting for a muse.
- Jodi Picoult

In the power and splendor of the universe, inspiration waits for millions to come. Man has only to strive for it. Poems greater than the *Iliad*, plays greater than *Macbeth*, stories more engaging than *Don Quixote* await their seeker and finder.
- John Masefield, NY *Times*, 1 Jun '58

You're going to be unemployed if you really think you just have to sit around and wait for the muse to land on your shoulder.
- Nora Roberts

Every writer scrounges for inspiration in different places, and there's no shame in raiding the headlines. It's necessary, in fact, when attempting contemporary satire.
- Carl Hiaasen, *Writers [on Writing]*

I write when I'm inspired, and I see to it that I'm inspired at nine o'clock every morning.
- Peter de Vries

Out of the closets and into the museums, libraries, architectural monuments, concert halls, bookstores, recording studios and film studios of the world. Everything belongs to the inspired and dedicated thief.
- William S. Burroughs

A writer writes, and if he begins by remembering a tree in the backyard, that is solely to permit him gradually to reach the piano in the parlor upon which rests the photograph of the kid brother killed in the war.
- William Saroyan, *Writers [on Writing]*

It has a lot to do with where I grew up. I set myself back in that pure, empty landscape whenever I am working on something…[because] there's nothing like it…It's the place where everything comes from.
- Louise Erdrich [Mickey Pearlman and Katherine Usher Henderson *A Voice of One's Own]*

Images provide messages that are understood by the immune system. They link conscious thoughts with the white blood cells in such a way that the appropriate combinations and numbers come rushing forth to perform in ways that not even the most knowledgeable immunologist could command.
- Jeanne Achterberg, *Imagery in Healing*

I woke up the other morning with a complete story in my mind—a story I'd never even dreamt of writing, never even thought of before. That can happen to anybody. You have to give yourself material, though. You've got to treat the human mind constantly with ideas. The human mind, itself, will make the comparisons, the connections, and the adjustments.
- Louis L'Amour

I felt, I knew, that I had hit it. I walked around and I wept; and I knelt down—I always do that after I've written what I know is a good piece. But at the same time I had, as God is my witness, the actual sense of a Presence—as if Yeats himself were *in* that room. The experience was in a way terrifying, for it lasted at least half an hour. That house, I repeat, was charged with a psychic presence: the very walls seemed to shimmer. I wept for joy.
- Theodore Roethke, after writing "The Dance," Lewis Hyde, *The Gift.*

The soul thinks in images.
- Aristotle

A daydream is a meal at which images are eaten. Some of us are gourmets, some gourmands, and a good many of us take their images precooked out of a can and swallow them down whole, absent-mindedly and with little relish.
- Richard M. Restak, *The Brain*

All images have meaning because they contain a spiritual element.
- Sandra G. Shuman, *Source Imagery*

Imagery is always dancing with the sheer delight of an imagination at play because it originates in instincts.
- Robert Bly and Marion Woodman, *The Maiden King*

A picture is a poem without words.
- Horace

Man lives by images. Only images can set verbs in motion again.
- Gaston Bachelard

John Fowles remarked that his novel *The French Lieutenant's Woman* sprang from a single image he saw for ten seconds in a dream. A woman appeared, her face partially concealed by a scarf, standing at the end of a dock in a storm.
- Robert Bly, *Iron John*

Imagery is the universal language of the unconscious. Thinking in pictures precedes thinking in words.
- Frances E. Vaughan, *Awakening Intuition*

We live immediately only in the world of images.
- Carl G. Jung

We read five words on the first page of a really good novel and we begin to forget that we are reading printed words on a page; we begin to see images.
- John Gardner

Everything you can imagine is real.
- Pablo Picasso

Follow your image as far as you can no matter how useless you think it is. Push yourself.
- Nikki Giovanni

A rock pile ceases to be a rock pile the moment a single man contemplates it, bearing within him the image of a cathedral.
- Antoine de Saint-Exupéry, *Flight to Arras*

Images haunt. There is a whole mythology built on this fact: Cezanne painting until his eyes bled. Wordsworth wandering the Lake Country hills in an impassioned daze. Blake describes it very well, and so did a colleague of Tu Fu who said to him, "It is like being alive twice." Images are not quite ideas, they are stiller than that, with less implications outside themselves. And they are not myth, they do not have that explanatory power; they are nearer to pure story. Nor are they always metaphors; they do not say this is that, they say this is.
- Robert Hass, *Twentieth Century Pleasures*

You must give birth to your images. They are the future waiting to be born... fear not the strangeness you feel. The future must enter into you long before it happens.
- Rainer Maria Rilke, *Letter to a Young Poet*

One of the problems in writing a parable is finding images which will be devoid of any too specific historical or geographical associations for the reader, but at the same time be concrete enough to hold his interest.
- W.H. Auden, *A Change of Air*

Imagination is real because every perception of the world around us is absolutely colored by the narrative or image-filled lens through which we perceive. We are all poets and artists as we live our daily lives, whether or not we recognize this role and whether or not we believe it.
        - Thomas Moore, *Original Self*

In reality, Kundalini is the power of imagination, the power of fantasy, which takes the place of a real function. When a man dreams instead of acting, when his dreams take the place of reality, when a man dreams himself to be an eagle, a lion, or a magician, it is the force of Kundalini acting in him. Kundalini can be acting in all the centers and with its help all the centers can be satisfied with the imaginary instead of the real.
        - G.I. Gurdjieff and P.D. Ouspensky, *In Search of the Miraculous*

Logic can take you from A to B, but imagination encircles the world.
        - Keith Critchlow, *Time Stands Still*

Because your imagination transcends time, it is one of your greatest touchstones to your own identity.
        - Jane Roberts, *The Nature of Personal Reality*

Imagination has brought mankind through the dark ages to its present state of civilization. Imagination led Columbus to discover America. Imagination led Franklin to discover electricity.
        - L. Frank Baum

What is now proved was once only imagin'd.
        - William Blake

Reason can answer questions, but imagination has to ask them.
        - Ralph Gerard

I believe that creative imagination is a common factor for all mankind, but held in diminishing degrees of consciousness and strength. Children, scientists, artists and mystics hold it with strength, and use it with freedom and faith.
        - Ruth Sawyer, *The Way of the Storyteller*

The world is but a canvas to our imaginations.
        - Henry David Thoreau

Imagination is the air of the mind.
        - Philip James Bailey

This world is but a canvas to our imagination.
- Henry David Thoreau

Imagination is the highest kite one can fly.
- Lauren Bacall

What if imagination and art are not frosting at all, but the foundation of human experience?
- Rollo May

You learn from the imaginative what the real world is.
- Bernard Malamud

Imagination is a divine gift.
- Madeleine L'Engle

Man's imaginative inventions must originate with God and must in consequence reflect something of eternal truths.
- J. R. R. Tolkein

For in the imagination is contained all the positive and the highest good; all the negative and the deepest evil.
- Harold Stone, Introduction, *Sand Play*

Imagination…is the picture-forming power of the mind. It is the quality that helps us to see the rainbow in a muddy pool, pictures in clouds, wings on a caterpillar.
- Nina Willis Walter, *Let Them Write Poetry*

Reason is the natural order of truth; but imagination is the organ of meaning.
- C.S. Lewis

Imagination is the voice of daring. If there is anything Godlike about God it is that. He dared to imagine everything.
- Henry Miller

The imagination may be compared to Adam's dream—he awoke and found it truth.
- John Keats, letter

The world is but a canvas to our imagination.
- Henry David Thoreau

The road to Xanadu is a long road, and much of it goes on in the unconscious and subliminal mind.
    - William Sloane, *The Craft of Writing*

The imagination is the creative force of the individual. It always negotiates different thresholds and releases possibilities of recognition and creativity that the linear, controlling, eternal mind will never even glimpse. The imagination works on the threshold that runs between light and dark, visible and invisible, quest and question, possibility and fact...Where the imagination is awake and alive, fact never hardens or closes but remains open, inviting you to new thresholds of possibility and creativity.
    - John O'Donohue, *Anam Cara*

The imagination is not, as its etymology suggests, the faculty for forming images of reality; it is the faculty for forming images which go beyond reality, which sing reality. It is a superhuman faculty.
    - Gaston Bachelard, *Water and Dreams*

...I will set sail to places I now only imagine. There I will be blessed with new visions and new magic. I will feel once again like a creative contributor to this mysterious world. But for now, I wait. An act of faith. Land ho.
    - Margaret Wheatly, Myron Kellner-Rogers, *A Simpler Way*

The imagination can cross thousands of miles and can make an impression thousands of miles away, too.
    - Paracelsus

The imagination is like a lantern. It illuminates the inner landscapes of our life and helps us discover their secret archaeologies.
    - John O'Donohue, *Beauty: The Invisible Embrace*

The imagination is not subject to the will of the artist. To accept the fruits as gifts is to acknowledge that we are not their owners or masters, that we are, if anything, their servants, their ministers.
    - Lewis Hyde

I think the imagination is the single most powerful tool humankind possesses. It beats the opposable thumb.
    - Ursula K. Le Guin, *The Wave in the Mind*

We are condemned to live out what we cannot imagine.
    - Thomas Moore, *Care of the Soul*

Teaching English to adolescents for twenty years gives me the authority to say, kill the imagination and you kill the soul. Kill the soul and you're left with a listless apathetic creature who can become hopeless or brutal or both. Kill the metaphors and you kill desire; the image magnetizes the movement of the energy.
     - Marion Woodman, *Bones*

I doubt that the imagination can be suppressed. If you truly eradicated it in a child, he would grow up to be an eggplant.
     - Ursula K. Le Guin, *The Language of the Night*

Without imagination of the one kind or of the other, moral existence is indeed a dreary and prosaic business…Illumined by the imagination, or life—whatever its defeats—is a never-ending unforeseen strangeness and adventure and mystery.
     - Walter De La Mare

A writer's job is to imagine everything so personally that the fiction is as vivid as memories.
     - John Irving

Take the obvious, add a cupful of brains, a generous pinch of imagination, a bucketful of courage and daring, stir well and bring to a boil.
     - Bernard M. Baruch

Trust that little voice in your head that says, "Wouldn't it be interesting if…" And then do it.
     - Duane Michals, *More Joy of Photography*

You must give birth to your images. They are the future waiting to be born…
     - Rainer Maria Rilke

The quality of the imagination is to flow, and not to freeze.
     - Ralph Waldo Emerson, *The Portable Emerson*

N.C. Wyeth once said to me that a born writer, encountering a squall in a rowboat, could there derive all the imaginative essentials of being in a ship beset by a great storm at sea.
     - Paul Horgan, *Approaches to Writing*

Sometimes imagination pounces; mostly it sleeps soundly in the corner, purring.
     - Leslie Grimutter

Having imagination, it takes you an hour to write a paragraph that, if you were unimaginative, would take you only a minute. Or you might not write the paragraph at all.
- Franklin P. Adams, *Half a Loaf*

We are what we imagine. Our very existence consists of our imagination of ourselves…The greatest tragedy that can befall us is to go unimagined.
- N. Scott Momaday

The kind of imagination I use in writing, when I try to lose control of consciousness, works very much like dreams. The subconscious takes over and it's fun…I do feel if ever I was looking for a source of material, all I would have to do is go back to my dreams.
- Amy Tan

He who has imagination without learning has wings but no feet.
- Joseph Joubert

You can't depend on your judgment when your imagination is out of focus.
- Mark Twain, *Notebook*

Imagination was given to man to compensate for what he is not; a sense of humor to console him for what he is.
- Francis Bacon

I am certain of nothing but the holiness of the heart's affections and the truth of imagination.
- John Keats

What I tend to do is to wake about five in the morning—this happens quite often—think about the invention, and then image it in my mind in 3D, as a kind of construct. Then I do experiments with the image—sort of rotate it, and say, "Well, what'll happen if one does this?" And by the time I get up for breakfast I can usually go to the bench and make a string and sealing wax model that works straight off, because I've done most of the experiments already.
- James Lovelock

When I get an idea I start at once building it up in my imagination. I change the construction, make improvements and operate the device in my mind. It is absolutely immaterial to me whether I run my turbine in my thought or test it in my shop. I even note if it is out of balance.
- Nikola Tesla

Whatever one man is capable of imagining, other men will prove themselves capable of realizing.
    - Jules Verne

An ulcer is an unkissed imagination taking its revenge for having been jilted. It is an undanced dance, an unpainted watercolor, an unwritten poem.
    - John Ciardi

Imagination is not to be divorced from the facts. It is a way of illuminating the facts.
    - Alfred North Whitehead

Consistency is the last refuge of the unimaginative.
    - Oscar Wilde

Writing is a cop-out. An excuse to live perpetually in fantasy land, where you can create, direct and watch the products of your own head.
    - Monica Dickens

The way a long work is completed is by daily tapping the first imaginative impulse. That's got to be so strong that it never dies in the course of the whole performance.
    - Paul Horgan

Perhaps the most important thing we can ever do in our lives is find a way to keep the wild—both the wild inside and the wild outside us—and to tap into it.
    - Anne Rivers Siddons

Imagination and fiction make up more than three quarters of our real life.
    - Simone Weil

The imagination has resources and intimations we don't ever know about.
    - Cynthia Ozick

The imagination is committed to the justice of wholeness. It will not choose one side in an inner conflict and repress or banish the other; it will endeavor to initiate a profound conversation between them in order that something original can be born.
    - John O'Donohue, *Anam Cara*

Live out of your imagination, not your history.
    - Steven Covey

For the imagination thrives on ignorance and on the moist moral impress it takes from new pressures of experiences.
        - W.S. Di Piero, *Shooting the Works*

In a poet an act of the imagination is an act of faith. If he loses this faith he too is lost…Go back to childhood as much as you need but not to your days before toilet training. And don't leave your toys on the stairs.
        - David Greenhood, *The Writer on His Own*

By the time the imagination is finished with a fact, believe me, it bears no resemblance to a fact.
        - Philip Roth

Imagination grows by exercise, and contrary to popular belief, is more powerful in the mature than in the young.
        - William Somerset Maugham

To be willing to live within the imagination is to commit oneself to the gathering together of the pieces that might begin to form a self.
        - Deena Metzger

Appealing workplaces are to be avoided. One wants a room with no view, so imagination can meet memory in the dark.
        - Annie Dillard, *The Writing Life*

As much as I dislike the actual process of writing, there's always a point, after a half hour, that I really love it. There's a real lightness of imagination that you let happen when you're writing.
        - Ethan Canin

We spend most of our time and energy in a kind of horizontal thinking. We move along the surface of things going from one quick base to another, often with a frenzy that wears us out. We collect data, things, people, ideas, "profound experiences," never penetrating any of them…But…there are times when we stop. We sit still. We lose ourselves in a pile of leaves or its memory. We listen and breezes from a whole other world begin to whisper. Then we begin our "going down."
        - James Carroll

What I give form to in daylight is only one per cent of what I have seen in darkness.
        - M.C. Escher

A treasure-trove of imaginative powers lies within us all. These powers often lie stunned and dormant, yet to awaken the pictures that live in our story-imagination is to become more fully and radiantly alive.
- Nancy Mellon

Imagination is a good horse to carry you over the ground—not a flying carpet to set you free from probability.
- Robertson Davies

If you have built castles in the air, your work need not be lost; that is where they should be. Now put the foundations under them.
- Henry David Thoreau

The faculty of imagination is both the rudder and the bridle of the senses.
- Leonardo Da Vinci

Imagination will often carry us to worlds that never were. But without it we go nowhere.
- Carl Sagan

Great imaginations are apt to work from hints and suggestions, and a single moment of emotion is sometimes sufficient to create a masterpiece.
- Margaret Sackville

Microsoft is a company that manages imagination.
- Bill Gates

Accept offerings of your imagination as you accept the shell your eye spots on the beach. Some you just glance at. Others you pick up and examine a bit. Some you take home and keep around for a few weeks. Some you want to polish, frame, or put into a necklace and keep forever.
- Wayne Dyer, *The Sky's the Limit*

A daydream is a meal at which images are eaten. Some of us are gourmets, some gourmands, and a good many take their images pre-cooked out of a can and swallow them down whole, absent-mindedly and with little relish.
- Richard M. Restak, *The Brain*

The imagination is an eye, a marvelous third eye that floats free. In the child, that eye sees with 20/20 clarity; with age, its vision dims...The job of the fantasy-horror writer is to make you, for a little while, a child again.
- Stephen King, *Notes On Horror*

St. Thomas noted the word "phantasy," "phantosia," gets its name from light, *phos*. Without light nothing can be seen. Without imagination (traces of sensation) nothing is seen (known) by internal sight. Imagination helps us deal more effectively with both the present and the future.

    - Marlene Halpin, *Imagine That*

Where the writer and the reader collaborate to make the work of fiction is perhaps, above all, in the imagination. In the joint creation of the fictive world.

    - Ursula K. LeGuin, *Dancing at the Edge of the World*

I feel more and more every day, as my imagination strengthens, that I do not live in this world alone but in a thousand worlds.

    - John Keats, letter

…imagination needs moodling—long, inefficient, happy idling, dawdling and puttering.

    - Brenda Ueland, *If You Want to Write*

Imagination is the key to my lyrics. The rest is painted with a little science fiction.

    - Jimi Hendrix

He who has imagination without learning has wings but no feet.

    - Joseph Jourbert

Imagination, producing new metaphors or revivifying old, is not the cause of truth, but its condition.

    - C.S. Lewis

The world of reality has its limits; the world of imagination is boundless.

    - Jean-Jacques Rouseau

Imagination is the beginning of creation. You imagine what you desire, you will what you imagine, and at last you create what you will.

    - George Bernard Shaw

I saw the angel in the marble and carved until I set him free.

    - Michelangelo

Among Celts "imagination" means soul…The imagination operates at a threshold where light and dark, visible and invisible, possibility and fact come together.

    - Matthew Fox, *Creativity*

The imagination is grounded in the energy of the organs of the body, which is to say it has a biological source.
- Joseph Campbell

My imagination makes me human and makes me a fool; it gives me all the world and exiles me from it.
- Ursula Le Guin

Gaining access to that interior life is a kind of…archaeology: on the basis of some information and a little bit of guesswork you journey to a site to see what remains were left behind and you reconstruct the world.
- Toni Morrison

It is the imagination that gives shape to the universe.
- Barry Lopez

We have a duty towards music; namely to invent it…Invention presupposes imagination but should not be confused with it. For the act of invention implies the necessity of a lucky find and of achieving realization of this find. What we imagine does not necessarily take on concrete form and may remain in a state of virtuality; whereas invention is not conceivable apart from its actually being worked out.
- Igor Stravinsky, *Poetics of Music*

A lady's imagination is very rapid: it jumps from admiration to love, from love to matrimony in a moment.
- Jane Austen

You cannot trust your eyes when your imagination is out of focus.
- Mark Twain

Uttering a word is like striking a note on the keyboard of the imagination.
- Ludwig Wittgenstein, *Philosophical Investigations*

Imagination means singing to a wide invisible audience…It makes erotic philosophers of us, as we imagine the world in images that make whole. To imagine is to give birth to—to embody the Spirit in word and picture and behavior. The world will change when we can imagine it different and, like artists, do the work of creating new social forms."
- Mary C. Richards, *Imagine Inventing Yellow*

What I sought in books was imagination. It was depth, depth of thought and feeling, some sort of extreme of subject matter; some nearness to death, some call to courage…I wanted wildness, originality, genius, rapture, hope. I wanted strength, not tea parties.
     - Annie Dillard, *An American Childhood*

I've got a sort of idea, but I don't suppose it's a very good one.
     - A.A. Milne, *Winnie the Pooh*

7.

What can you tell me about writing a novel?

Novel, n. A short story padded.
- Ambrose Bierce, *The Devil's Dictionary*

Every true novel is a historical novel.
- Paul Horgan, *Approaches to Writing*

Writing a novel is actually searching for victims. As I write I keep looking for casualties. The stories uncover the casualties.
- John Irving

When does a novel end? It ends when it has consumed its own material, the actions terminated, the tensions resolved...In any novel, the end is implicit in the beginning and the beginning validates the end.
- William Sloane, *The Craft of Writing*

This [*To the Lighthouse*] is going to be fairly short; to have father's character done complete in it; and mother's; and St. Ives; and childhood; and all the usual things I try to put in—life, death, etc. But the centre is father's character, sitting in a boat, reciting, "We perished, each alone, while he crushes a dying mackerel."
- Virginia Woolf, *Diary*, Thursday, May 14, 1925

People without hope not only don't write novels, but what is more to the point, they don't read them. They don't take a long look at anything, because they lack the courage.
- Flannery O'Connor, *The Nature and Aim of Fiction*

Anybody can write a short story—a bad one, I mean—who has industry and paper and time enough; but not everyone may hope to write even a bad novel. It is the length that kills.
- Robert Louis Stevenson

Every novel is an attempt to capture time, to weave something solid out of air. The author knows it is an impossible task—that is why he keeps on trying.
- David Beaty

The final test for a novel will be our affection for it, as it is the test of our friends, and of anything else which we cannot define.
- E. M Forster

Novelists are an enviable lot...When they sit down to uncover and expose the processes of life, they can use the whole inventory of their own autobiographical experience with impunity while, at one and the same time, shamelessly filling in all its deficits by the exercise of fictive imagination. Not so for poor fools like me who, unable to escape the call of the writing life, spend all our careers laboring in the fields of nonfiction.
- Phyllis Tickle, *The Shaping of Life: A Spiritual Landscape*

A novel is a story. It's just a story. It has a beginning, a middle and an end. That's all there is and you can handle it.
- Oscar Collier, *How to Write and Sell Your First Novel*

A novel ought to at least start out by being able to stump us.
- Eudora Welty, *The Eye of the Story*

There is no such thing as a secure writer; every novel is an impossible mountain.
- John le Carré, *Writer's Mentor*

The novel is the easiest and the most difficult of literary genres...the form offers no resistance; anything goes, so long as it isn't boring.
- Jens Bjørneboe, "Alone with the Paper"

Name any great novel that didn't weary you first time through,
- Norman Mailer, *The Spooky Art*

The novel is the affliction for which only the novel is the cure.
- Joyce Carol Oates

Good novels are not written by orthodoxy-sniffers, nor by people who are conscience-stricken about their own orthodoxy. Good novels are written by people who are not frightened.
- George Orwell

Writing novels preserves you in a state of innocence—a lot passes you by—simply because your attention is otherwise diverted.
- Anita Brookner

The institution of writing and reading novels is like a grand old Middle American city gutted and drained by superhighways. Ringing the depressed inner city of serious work are prosperous clonal suburbs of mass entertainment: techno and legal thrillers, novels of sex and vampires, of murder and mysticism.
- Jonathan Franzen

I suppose that every novelist has something in common with a spy; he watches, he overhears, he seeks motives and analyses characters, and in his attempt to serve literature he is unscrupulous.
- Graham Greene, "A Sort of Life"

We are all like Scheherazade's husband, in that we want to know what happens next. That is universal and that is why the backbone of a novel has to be the story.
- E.M Forster, *Aspects of the Novel*

A novel is balanced between a few true impressions and the multitude of false ones that make us most of what we call life.
- Saul Bellow, Nobel Prize Speech

The novel is likely, if the best literary brains cannot be induced to return to it, to survive in some perfunctory, despised and hopeless degenerate form, like modern tombstones, or the Punch and Judy show.
- George Orwell

The first thing you have to consider when writing a novel is your story, and then your story—and then your story!
- Ford Maddox Ford

There are three rules for writing the novel. Unfortunately, no one knows what they are.
- W. Somerset Maugham

A beginning, a muddle and an end.
- Philip Larkin, *New Fiction*

There are no laws for the novel. There never have been, nor can there ever be.
- Doris Lessing

Write a novel not a research paper.
> - Stephen King, *On Writing: A Memoir of the Craft*

Render, do not report.
> - Henry James

All middle-class novels are about the trials of three, all upper-class novels about mass fornication, all revolutionary novels about a bad man turned good by a tractor.
> - Christina Stead

Sometimes a novel emerges simply as a voice, saying something that sounds almost silly at first.
> - Thomas Fleming, *Writers on Writing*

Ulysses defines the modern novel. Almost anything that looks new is in *Ulysses* somewhere.
> - Martin Amis

Every novel is a debtor to Homer.
> - Ralph Waldo Emerson

A good novel tells us the truth about its hero; but a bad novel tells us the truth about its author.
> - G.K. Chesterton

A novelist is a man who doesn't like his mother.
> - Georges Simenon

Every fiction since Homer has taught friendship, patriotism, generosity, contempt of death. These are the highest virtues; and the fictions which taught them were therefore of the highest, though not of unmixed, utility.
> - James Mackintosh

Writing a novel is like driving a car at night. You can see only as far as the headlights, but you can make the whole trip that way.
> - E.L. Doctorow

Writing a novel is a terrible experience, during which the hair often falls out and the teeth decay.
> - Flannery O'Connor

A novelist has two lives—a reading and writing life, and a lived life. He or she cannot be understood at all apart from this…The desire to write a novel is the single required prerequisite for writing a novel.
- Jane Smiley, *Thirteen Ways of Looking at the Novel*

The really great novel tends to be the exact negative of its author's life.
- Andre Maurois

The only reason for the existence of a novel is that it does attempt to represent life.
- Henry James

Being a novelist, I want to know every world.
- Norman Mailer, *The Spooky Art*

A novelist is a person who lives in other people's skins.
- E.M. Doctorow

A novelist is, like all mortals, more fully at home on the surface of the present than in the ooze of the past.
- Vladimir Nabokov

I find in most novels no imagination at all. They seem to think the highest form of the novel is to write about marriage, because that's the most important thing there is for middle-class people.
- Gore Vidal

One should not be too severe on English novels; they are the only relaxation of the intellectually unemployed.
- Oscar Wilde

The novelist's—any writer's—object is to whittle down his meaning to the exactest and finest possible point. What, of course, is fatal is when he does not know what he does mean: he has no point to sharpen.
- Elizabeth Bowen

Writing a novel without being asked seems a bit like having a baby when you have nowhere to live.
- Lucy Ellman

Novels are to love as fairy tales to dreams.
- Samuel Taylor Coleridge

A novel…is a hiding place in which you can conceal two or three words which you hope your reader will find.
- Heinrich Böll

The monotony of staying in one place is the best thing for writing a novel. Having regular habits, a kind of security, but especially no big surprises, no shocks.
- Paul Theroux

Over time I've realized that the ideal novel that deeply stirs everyone will never be written. Even *Anna Karenina* grows tiresome for some readers.
- Scott Turow, *Writers [on Writing]*

It is important that a novel be approached with some urgency. Spend too long on it, or have great gaps between writing sessions and the unity of the work tends to be lost.
- Anthony Burgess

The object of the novelist is to keep the reader entirely oblivious of the fact that the author exists—even of the fact he is reading a book.
- Ford Maddox Ford

The main question to a novel is—did it amuse? Were you surprised at dinner coming so soon? Did you mistake eleven for ten? Were you too late to dress? And did you sit up beyond the usual hour? If a novel produces these effects, it is good; if it does not—story, language, love, scandal itself cannot save it. It is only meant to please; and it must do that or it does nothing.
- Sydney Smith

A novel is a spot where language, movement, feeling and thought gel for a moment, through the agency of, let's say, a particular volunteer, but it is not an object or a possession. It is an act of love.
- Jane Smiley, *Writers [on Writing]*

Basically, if you write novels, you sit alone in a room and fight the language.
- Alan Furst, *Writers [on Writing] Vol. II*

The whole process of writing a novel is having this great, beautiful idea and then spoiling it.
- Diane Johnson

First drafts are for learning what your novel or story is about.
- Bernard Malamud

If I were a writer, how I would enjoy being told the novel is dead. How liberating to work in the margins, outside a central perception. You are ghoul of literature. Lovely.
- Don Delillo

When stuff in life gets really tough, I would just die if I was not writing a novel. Once you think it up, it's like a whole other city with a little door and every time you sit down to write you just open the door and there you are—a wonderful vacation for two hours.
- Lee Smith

It was as if the novel was already written, floating in the air, on a network of electrons. I could hear it talking to itself. I sensed that if I would but sit and listen, it would come through, all ready.
- A.S. Byatt

The novel is the highest example of subtle interrelatedness that man has discovered.
- D.H. Lawrence

Writing a novel is not merely going on a shopping expedition across the border to an unreal land: it is hours and years spent in the factories, the streets, the cathedrals of the imagination.
- Janet Frame

Writing a novel proved to be the hardest, most self-analyzing task I had ever attempted, far worse than an autobiography: and its rewards were greater than I expected.
- Dick Francis, *The Sport of Queens*

If you caricature friends in your first novel they will be upset, but if you don't they will feel betrayed.
- Mordecai Richler

Before I start writing a novel I read *Candide* over again so that I may have in the back of my mind the touchstone of that lucidity, grace and wit.
- W. Somerset Maugham

Great fiction can change our lives; turn us around corners. No movie ever did that to me. I might walk and talk a bit differently for a few minutes after leaving an effective film but that's about it. Novels have heft; films are filmy.
- John Barth

My God, this novel makes me break out in a cold sweat! Do you know how much I've written in five months, since the end of August? Sixty-five pages!... It's a series of well-turned, ordered paragraphs which do not flow on from each other. I shall have to unscrew them, loosen the joints, as one does with the masts of a ship when one wants the sail to take more wind.
    - Gustave Flaubert

An old novel has a history of its own.
    - Alexander Smith

The suspense of a novel is not only in the reader, but in the novelist, who is intensely curious about what will happen to the hero.
    - Mary McCarthy

I'd rather have written Conrad's *Nostromo* than any other novel...chiefly because Nostromo, the man, intrigues me so much...I would rather have dragged his soul from behind his astounding and inarticulate presence than written any other novel in the world.
    - F. Scott Fitzgerald, *In His Own Time*

A first novel from an unknown author has everything to prove.
    - Christopher Evans, *Writing Science Fiction*

A novel is a work in which the greatest powers of the mind are displayed; in which the most thorough knowledge of human nature, the happiest delineation of its varieties, the liveliest effusions of wit or humor, are conveyed to the world in the best chosen language.
    - Jane Austen, *Northanger Abbey*

The novel is something that never was before and will not be again.
    - Eudora Welty

Oh, it's only a novel...in short, only some work in which the greatest powers of the mind are displayed.
    - Jane Austen

They can't yank a novelist like they can a pitcher. A novelist has to go the full nine, even if it kills him.
    - Ernest Hemingway

A good novel must be a vivid, continuous dream.
    - John Gardner

The unsuccessful novel reminds me of a top that has been spinning for a while. One can see the chapters begin to wander in loose, uneven circles…The successful novel, on the other hand, has a shape much like a bell…Every detail has purpose here…As soon as we have gained our bearings, we notice things beginning to open up, flaring outward the way a bell does.
  - Chitra Divakaruni, *Writers [on Writing] Vol. II*

I cringe when critics way I'm a master of the popular novel. What's an unpopular novel?
  - Irwin Shaw

I work continuously within the shadow of failure. For every novel that makes it to my publisher's desk, there are at least five or six that died on the way.
  - Gail Godwin

Popular novels in our age might serve the same function as stained-glass windows did in the Middle Ages.
  - Andrew Greeley

Novelists [fashion] nets to sustain and support the reader as he falls helplessly through the chaos of his own existence.
  - Fay Weldon

The world of the novel is one of empty rituals. Every act is bereft of substance and significance, and even death becomes a spectacle for which the good citizens buy tickets.
  - Azar Nafisi, *Reading Lolita in Tehran*

How do you write a novel? I think you have to answer that question one novel at a time. Do what works for this novel. For the next, you may have to invent the whole process all over again.
  - Bruce Holland Rogers, *Word Work*

A novel is never an answer; it's always a question.
  - Richard Peck

A novel is a mirror walking along the main road.
  - Stendhal (Marie Henri Beyle)

The traditional novel form continues to enlarge our experience in those very areas where the wide-angle lens and the Cinema screen tend to narrow it.
  - Daniel J. Boorstin

My test of a good novel is dreading to begin the last chapter.
- Thomas Helm

When I want to read a novel, I write one.
- Benjamin Disraeli, *Life of Benjamin Disraeli*

One becomes a writer, but one must be born a novelist. If a person has sensitivity, culture, and imagination, it is not difficult to become a writer. It is impossible to become a novelist, storyteller or fabler; either you have a natural gift for narrating, or you don't.
- Alberto Moravia

If you want to be a novelist you have to know people. You have to know the dimensions they have lived, or may live.
- Morris L. West.

I keep aiming toward that novel that is just that, a true novel, but a novel for our time, dealing with an essential theme and an essential message in a subterranean carefully hidden away, a message like a snake in the grass, as Trollope put it. There's to be no boy meets tractor, nor even a professor meets a sophomore.
- Hans Koning

Writing a novel is like building a wall brick by brick; only amateurs believe in inspiration.
- Frank Yerby

Novelists should never allow themselves to weary of the study of real life.
- Charlotte Brontë

A novelist must preserve a child-like belief in the importance of things which common sense considers of no great consequence.
- W. Somerset Maugham

The novelist is, after all, God's liar and if he does his job well, keeps his head down and his courage, he can sometimes find the truth that lives at the center of the lie.
- Stephen King, *Danse Macabre*

A writer without a sense of justice and of injustice would be better off editing the Year Book of a school for exceptional children than writing novels.
- Ernest Hemingway, *Writers at Work*

The novelist's job is to reveal and unfold, not simply portray. The novelist works with the things that pass unobserved by others, captures them in motion, brings them out into the open.
- Joao Guimaraes Rosa

Every author really wants to have letters printed in his papers. Unable to make the grade, he drops down a rung of the ladder and writes novels.
- P.G. Wodehouse, *Louder and Funnier*

I do not read anything but history and biography...I have no liking for novels or stories—none in the world...Are you saying, "You have written stories yourself?" Quite true: but the fact that an Indian likes to scalp people is no evidence that he likes to be scalped.
- Mark Twain, letter

The novelist talks as one individual to individuals—in a small personal voice.
- Doris Lessing

A novelist must be one of those on whom nothing is lost.
- Henry James

It takes a lot of energy and a lot of neurosis to write a novel...If you were really sensible, you'd do something else.
- Lawrence Durrell, *Washington Post*, 29 May '86

How does writing novels differ from writing short stories? I think a novel gathers its own impetus.
- Stephen King, *Secret Windows*

The business of the novelist is not to chronicle great events but to make small ones interesting.
- Arthur Schopenhauer

...the poem is primarily a dialogue with the self and the novel a dialogue with others...I suppose I have written novels to find out what *I thought* about something and poems to find out what I *felt* about something.
- May Sarton, *Journal of A Solitude*

Each sentence must have, at its heart, a little spark of fire, and this, whatever the risk, the novelist must pluck with his own hands from the blaze.
- Virginia Woolf

A novelist must preserve a childlike belief in the importance of things which common sense considers of no great consequence.
- W. Somerset Maugham, *A Writer's Notebook*

Essential characteristic of the really great novelist: a Christ-like, all embracing compassion.
- Arnold Bennett

In writing a novel, there is in the beginning what I would call a theme. It's not an idea but a feeling. Then this feeling goes on developing and unraveling itself, like a rope. This is why I say a novel writes itself. One writes a novel in order to know why one writes it. It is the same with life—you live not for some end, but in order to know why you live.
- Alberto Moravia

So, come on, really, how much is autobiographical? All of it. None.
- Sue Miller, *Writers [on Writing]*

8.

What makes for a good short story?

Alex Haley was down to two cans of sardines and 18 cents before he sold his first short story. Three years later he began his research which led to *Roots*.
- Don Freeman, *In a Flea's Navel*

I feel that it is in the short story that a writer distills the essence of his thought…Short-story writing—for me—is only looking closer than normal into the human heart.
- Mary Lavin

Find the key emotion; this may be all you need know to find your short story.
- F. Scott Fitzgerald

I think a surgeon is particularly suited by temperament to the short story form as opposed to the novel, because the short story is rather like a surgical operation. It has a beginning, middle and an end…You make an incision, you rummage around inside for a little while, then you stitch it up.
- Richard Selzer

I think one should work into a story the idea of not being sure of all things because that's the way reality is.
- Jorge Luis Borges

The best I do is tell you what a story is not. It is not a joke; it is not an anecdote; it is not a lyric rhapsody in prose; it is not case history; it is not a reported incident.
- Flanner O'Connor, *Esprit*

Some writers I know have stopped writing short stories because, as they say, "there is no market for them." Others like myself, the addicts, go on and I suspect would go on even if there really wasn't any home for them but a private drawer.
- Doris Lessing

A good short story is a work of art which daunts us in proportion to its brevity...
No inspiration is too noble for it; no amount of hard work is too severe for it.
      - Elizabeth Stuart Phelps

If you do not have an alert and curious interest in character and dramatic
situation, if you have no visual imagination and are unable to distinguish
between honest emotional reactions and sentimental approaches to life, you
will never write a competent short story.
      - Edward J. O'Brien

I asked Ring Lardner the other day how he writes his short stories, and he said
he wrote a few widely separated words or phrases on a piece of paper and then
went back and filled in the spaces.
      - Harold Ross

Every short story, at least for me, is a little act of discovery...A story that you
do not learn something from while you are writing it, that does not illuminate
something for you, is dead, finished before you started it.
      - Mary McCarthy, *Settling the Colonel's Hash*

It probably costs you nothing to write a short story but I find that it costs
me as many false starts—and therefore failures—as does a long one...I have
hardly ever started a story, long or short, on the right plan—the right plan
being the plan which will make it tell itself without my help—except after
three failures.
      - Mark Twain, letter

All the trash must be eliminated in the short story, whereas one can get away
with some of it in a novel.
      - William Faulkner

A short story reveals the truth in a way that the novel (even) with its wider
canvas cannot achieve.
      - Frank O'Connor

I hate writing short stories, as you know, and only do my six a year to have the
leisure to write my novels at leisure.
      - F. Scott Fitzgerald, *Letters*

The short-story writer must decide whose story it is going to be: the girl's, the
father's a hoodlum's, perhaps the mother's.
      - Isabelle Ziegler, *Creative Writing*

A collection of short stories is generally thought to be a horrendous clinker; an enforced courtesy for the elderly writer who wants to display the trophies of his youth, along with his trout flies.
- John Cheever

I think when one has finished writing a short story one should delete the beginning and the end.
- Anton Chekhov

Plays traditionally imitate actions; short stories frequently do not.
- Harold Bloom

Where does beauty come from in the short story? Beauty comes from form, from development of ideas, from after-effect…Sometimes spontaneity is the most sparkling kind of beauty.
- Eudora Welty, *The Reading and Writing of Short Stories*

In most English classes the short story has become a kind of literary specimen to be dissected. Every time a story of mine appears in a Freshman anthology, I have a vision of it, with its little organs laid open, like a frog in a bottle…A good story is literal in the same sense that a child's drawing is literal.
- Flannery O'Connor, *Mystery and Manners*

Fiction is art. Its purpose is not to instruct, but to please.
- W. Somerset Maugham

Fiction is art and art is the triumph over chaos…to celebrate a world that lies spread out around us like a bewildering and stupendous dream.
- John Cheever

There are no rules for real fiction, any more than there are rules for serious visual art or musical compositions.
- John Gardner

Fiction is about stuff that's screwed up.
- Nancy Kress

Story first.
- Sarah Harrison

The secret of successful fiction is a continual slight novelty.
- Edmund Gosse

I think fiction is about small ambition, small failed ambition.
  - Ethan Canin

Any fiction…is bound to be transposed autobiography.
  - Elizabeth Bowen

The secret of successful fiction is a continual slight novelty.
  - Edmund Gosse

A writer is congenitally unable to tell the truth and that is why we call what he writes fiction.
  - William Faulkner

If you write fiction you are, in a sense, corrupted. There's a tremendous corruptibility for the fiction writer because you're dealing mainly with sex and violence. These remain the basic themes, they're the basic themes of Shakespeare whether you like it or not.
  - Anthony Burgess

The fiction writer has to engage in a continual examination of conscience. He has to be aware of the freak in himself.
  - Flannery O'Connor

You can write anything you want to—a six-act blank verse, symbolic tragedy or a vulgar short story. Just so that you write it with honesty and gusto, and do not try to make somebody believe that you are smarter than you are. What's the use? You can never be smarter than you are.
  - Brenda Ueland

Facts and fictions are different truths.
  - Patricia MacLachlan, *The Facts and Fictions of Minna Pratt*

Fiction is not a competitive sport.
  - John Cheever

All fiction is for me a kind of magic and trickery—a confidence trick, trying to make people believe something is true that isn't.
  - Angus Wilson

Detail is the lifeblood of fiction.
  - John Gardner

It seems that the fiction writer has a revolting attachment to the poor, for even when he writes about the rich, he is more concerned with what they lack than with what they have.
- Flannery O'Connor

…if we can imagine the art of fiction come alive and standing in our midst, she would undoubtedly bid us to break her and bully her, as well as honour and love her, for so her youth is renewed and her sovereignty assured.
- Virginia Woolf, *The Common Reader*

The test of any good fiction is that you should care something for the characters; the good to succeed, the bad to fail. The trouble with most fiction is that you want them all to land in hell, together, as quickly as possible.
- Mark Twain

The good ended happily, and the bad unhappily. That is what Fiction means.
- Oscar Wilde

I've made up stuff that's turned out to be real, that's the spooky part.
- Tom Clancy

Whether it's done quickly or slowly, however splendid the results, the process of writing fiction is inherently, inevitably, indistinguishable from wasting time.
- Deborah Eisenberg

The reader expects to be transported into a fictional world and allowed to remain there until the story is complete. The writer's responsibility is to not interfere.
- Harvey Stanbrough, *Writing Realistic Dialogue & Flash Fiction*

Fiction may be said to be the caricature of history.
- Edward Bulwer-Lytton

Fiction reveals truths that reality obscures.
- Jessamyn West

Fiction is like a spider's web, attached ever so lightly perhaps, but still attached to life at all four corners. Often the attachment is scarcely perceptible.
- Virginia Woolf

Fiction is the truth inside the lie.
- Stephen King

The main concern of the fiction writer is with mystery as it is incarnated in human life.
- Flannery O'Connor

Writing fiction has developed in me an abiding respect for the unknown in a human lifetime and a sense of where to look for the threads, how to follow, how to connect, find in the thick of the tangle what clear line persists. The strands are all there: to the memory nothing is ever really lost.
- Eudora Welty, *One Writer's Beginning*

The beginning of knowledge is through the senses, and the fiction writer begins where the human perception begins. He appeals through the senses, and you cannot appeal through the senses with abstractions.
- Flannery O'Connor

The world that is in me is the only world I have by which to grasp the world outside and as I write fiction, it is the chart by which I must steer.
- Katherine Paterson

To serve the reader a fruitcake that you wouldn't eat yourself, to build the reader an uncomfortable house you wouldn't want to live in: this violates what seems to me the categorical imperative for any fiction writer. This is the ultimate breach of contract.
- Jonathan Franzen

Fiction never exceeds the reach of the author's courage.
- Dorothy Allison

The best fiction touches the deep layers in us.
- Jessica Page Morrell

Fiction writers are, by their very nature, middle children. They are searchers, doubters, malcontents. They believe themselves somehow abandoned, uncoddled, unloved. They deserve more, understand more, desire more. They are voyeurs, con artists, liars.
- John Gregory Brown, *Creating Fiction*

The difference between fiction and reality? Fiction has to make sense.
- Tom Clancy

Fiction is based on reality unless you're a fairytale artist.
- Hunter S. Thompson

Truth is stranger than fiction, but it is because fiction is obliged to stick to possibilities. Truth isn't.
- Mark Twain, *Following the Equator*

It is the tug of reality, its mystery and magnetism, that leads one into the writing of fiction—what then when one is not mystified, but stupefied? Not drawn but repelled.
- Philip Roth, *Writing American Fiction*

There is quite enough sorrow and shame and suffering and baseness in real life, and there is no need for meeting it unnecessarily in fiction.
- Theodore Roosevelt

I believe fiction can heal things, and I think we would all agree, now more than ever, that we can use some healing, and that we need it daily.
- Rick Bass

Fiction—if it aspires to be art—appeals to temperament. And in truth it must be, like painting, like music, like all art, the appeal of one temperament to all the other innumerable temperaments whose subtle and resistless power endows passing events with their true meaning, and creates the moral, the emotional atmosphere of the place and time.
- Joseph Conrad, Preface, *The Nigger of the "Narcissus"*

Writing fiction has become a priestly business in countries that have lost their faith.
- Gore Vidal

Fiction is an old word in the English language. It is derived from a verb meaning "to make," "to form," and sometimes "to feign."
- Isabelle Ziegler, *Creative Writing*

The good ended happily, and the bad unhappily. That is what fiction means.
- Oscar Wilde, *The Importance of Being Earnest*

Fiction without irony is like painting without perspective. Irony exposes the incongruities of everyday life—the half-truths, deceptions, and self-deceptions that help us all get through the day.
- David Bouchier, *Creating Fiction*

Fiction gives us a second chance that life denies us.
- Paul Theroux

Fiction is the art form of human yearning. A character may be besieged by problems, but that is not yearning. It is our yearning that defines us as human beings.
- Robert Olen Butler

One of the most succinct and perfect observations I have ever heard about the laws of fiction...was delivered by an early agent of mine..."Put your character in a situation and then get him out."
- George Abbe, *Stephen Vincent Benét on Writing*

In my first writing class, I was given the most valuable advice that a young writer could receive. The professor said, "Take a situation that intrigues you and ask yourself two questions: Suppose? And, What if? Then turn the situation into fiction.
- Mary Higgins Clark

Sometimes reality is too complex. Fiction gives it form.
- Jean-Luc Godard

To most readers the word "fiction" is an utter fraud. They are entirely convinced that each character has an exact counterpart in real life and that any small discrepancy with that counterpart is a simple error on the author's part. Consequently, they are totally at a loss if anything essential is altered. Make Abraham Lincoln a dentist, put the Gettysburgh Address on his tongue, and nobody will recognize it.
- Louis Auchincloss

In fiction, truth is the search for truth, nothing is pre-established and knowledge is only what both of us—reader and writer—can imagine.
- Carlos Fuentes

Fact and fiction: fiction and fact. Which stops where, and how much to put in of each? At what point does regurgitated autobiography graduate into memory shaped by art? How do you know when to stop telling it as it is, or was, and make it into what it ought to be—or what would make a better story?
- Gail Godwin, *The Writer on Her Work*

Reality is forced always to be extraordinary. Fiction is not allowed that freedom. Fiction has to be plausible; reality doesn't.
- Freeman Dyson

Writing fiction is...an endless and always defeated effort to capture some quality of life without killing it.
- Rose Wilder Lane

The good thing about writing fiction is that you can get back at people. I've gotten back at lawyers, prosecutors, judges, law professors and politicians. I just line 'em up and shoot 'em.
- John Grisham

Storytellers who dramatize their own era embrace its most resounding moments, moments when the spiritual compass by which we live (and write) has spun out of alignment. Realigning that compass, searching for a new magnetic north, is some of the best work fiction writers do.
- Julia Glass "In the Dust that Refuses to Settle: Writing Fiction After 9/11" *Publishers Weekly*, August 21, 2006

[My goal in writing fiction is] to cut up reality and make it more real... This is the intricate music of the art of fiction. It's the music I have always tried to play.
- John Steinbeck

I began to write fiction on the assumption that the true enemies of the novel were plot, character, setting and theme.
- John Hawkes

There is no excuse for anyone to write fiction for public consumption unless he has been called to do so by the presence of a gift. It is the nature of fiction not to be good for much unless it is good in itself. A gift of any kind is a considerable responsibility.
- Flannery O'Connor, *The Nature and Aim of Fiction*

Some people have the notion that you read the story and then climb out of it into the meaning, but for the fiction writer himself the whole story is the meaning, because it is an experience, not an abstraction.
- Flannery O'Connor, *On Writing*

Unless a reader is able to give something of himself, he cannot get from a novel the best it has to give. And if he isn't able to do that, he had better not read it at all. There is no obligation to read a work of fiction.
- W. Somerset Maugham

I write fiction because I need to organize the clutter of too many details into some meaning, because I enjoy turning something promising into something marvelous.
- Gail Godwin, "A Diarist on Diaries," Joyce Carol Oates, *First Person Singular*

For me, to love a work of fiction...it will tell me something remarkable, it will be beautifully executed, and it will be nested in truth.
   - Barbara Kingsolver, *Small Wonder*

In a battle of competing truths, fiction, if it is done right, will always win over what fondly passes for fact...Sources of fiction are myriad and complex—a character, a character in a situation, a phrase, a scene, a setting, a smell—anything at all but an idea attached to an intention.
   - Lynn Freed, *Reading, Writing and Leaving Home*

Fiction writers are...thoughtful interpreters of the world ...But instead of doing research or criticism—they doodle on the walls of the cave. They make art objects which must themselves be interpreted.
   - Annie Dillard, *Living by Fiction*

Everyone who works in the domain of fiction is a bit crazy. The problem is to render this craziness interesting.
   - Francois Truffaut

9.

How do you
handle criticism?

Writers have a little holy light within, like a pilot light, which fear is always blowing out. When a writer brings a manuscript fresh from the making, at the moment of greatest vulnerability, that's the moment for friends to help get the little holy light lit again.
- Cynthia Ozick

It's my experience that very few writers, young or old, are really seeking advice when they give out their work to be read. They want support; they want someone to say, "Good job."
- John Irving

Unfortunately many young writers are more concerned with fame than with their own work…It's much more important to write than to be written about.
- Gabriel Garcia Marquez

My relatives say that they are glad I'm rich, but that they simply cannot read me.
- Kurt Vonnegut

An artist who theorizes about his work is no longer artist but critic.
- H. G. Wells

The purpose of a writer is to be read, and the criticism which would destroy the power of pleasing must be blown aside.
- Samuel Johnson

Some old lady said that my book left a bad taste in her mouth. I wrote back to her and said, "You weren't supposed to eat it."
- Flannery O'Connor

Uninvited criticism is an insult.
- John L'Heureux

God knows people who are paid to have attitudes toward things, professional critics, make me sick; camp following eunuchs of literature. They won't even whore. They're all virtuous and sterile. And how well meaning and high minded. But they're all camp followers.
    - Ernest Hemingway

Always be nice to people younger than you, because they are the ones who will be writing about you.
    - Cyril Connolly

Honest criticism and sensible appreciation are directed not upon the poet but upon the poetry.
    - T.S. Eliot

For critics it's an easy task to point out that the author is always contradicting himself. The natural response would be: "Who else should I take the time to contradict?"
    - Jens Bjørneboe, Preface, *Aske, Vind og Jord*

A critic is a man who knows the way but can't drive the car.
    - Kenneth Tynan

Four hostile newspapers are more to be feared than a thousand bayonets.
    - Napoleon Bonaparte

Never pick a fight with people who buy ink by the barrel.
    - William Jefferson Clinton

We judge ourselves by what we feel capable of doing, but others judge us by what we have already done.
    - Leo Tolstoy

Only rocks can take hammering.
    - Anni Korpela

If you are attacked as regards your style, never reply; it is for your work alone to make answer.
    - Voltaire

No man has an appreciation so various that his judgment is good upon all varieties of literary work.
    - Mark Twain

A writer should have another lifetime to see if he's appreciated.
- Jorge Luis Borges

A good writer is not, per se, a good book critic. No more than a good drunk is automatically a good bartender.
- Jim Bishop

Keep away from people who belittle your ambitions. Small people always do that, but the really great make you feel that you, too, can become great.
- Mark Twain

I love criticism just so long as it's unqualified praise.
- Noel Coward

What you said hurt me very much. I cried all the way to the bank.
- Liberace

Critics are like horse-flies which hinder the horses in their ploughing of the soil.
- Anton Chekhov

The strength of criticism lies in the weakness of the thing criticized.
- Henry Wadsworth Longfellow

Remember: when people tell you something's wrong or doesn't work, they are almost always right. When they tell you exactly what's wrong and how to fix it, they are almost always wrong.
- Neil Gaiman

What I wish to do is to plead for passionate criticism for the sake of the passionate itself…To write passionately, the critic must invent, or, to use a more accurate word, he must create his criticism so that it reveals a work of art, through the critic's feelings.
- Barnett Newman, in Ken MacRorie, *Telling Writing*

To avoid criticism do nothing, say nothing, be nothing.
- Elbert Hubbard

Critics are like eunuchs in a harem; they know how it's done, they've seen it done every day, but they're unable to do it themselves.
- Brendan Behan

There is probably no hell for authors in the next world—they suffer so much from critics and publishers in this.
        - C.N. Bovee

Insects sting, not in malice, but because they want to live. It is the same with critics; they desire our blood, not our pain.
        - Friedrich Nietzsche

Some men are born mediocre, some men achieve mediocrity, and some men have mediocrity thrust upon them.
        - Joseph Heller

Mediocrity is more dangerous in a critic than in a writer.
        - Eugene Ionesco

The covers of this book are too far apart.
        - Ambrose Bierce, *The Devil's Dictionary*

Reading this book is like waiting for the first shoe to drop.
        - Robert Novak

Novels as dull as dishwater, with the grease of random sentiments floating on top.
        - Italo Calvino

On Robert Montgomery's Poems: His writing bears the same relation to poetry which a Turkey carpet bears to a picture. There are colours in the Turkey carpet out of which a picture might be made. There are words in Mr. Montgomery's writing which, when disposed in certain orders and combinations, have made, and will make again, good poetry. But, as they now stand, they seem to be put together on principle in such a manner as to give no image of anything in the heavens above, or in the earth beneath, or in the waters under the earth.
        - Macaulay Thomas Babington, *Literary Essays in the Edinburgh Review*

On Shakespeare: After all, all he did was string together a lot of old, well-known quotations.
        - H. L. Mencken

On Lillian Hellman: Every word she writes is a lie, including "and" and "the."
        - Mary McCarthy

On Henry James: [He] writes fiction as if it were a painful duty.
  - Oscar Wilde

On Henry James: He had a mind so fine that no idea could violate it.
  - T.E. Eliot

On Kipling: From the point of view of literature Mr. Kipling is a genius who drops his aspirates. From the point of view of life, he is a reporter who knows vulgarity better than any one has ever known it.
  - Oscar Wilde

On Gertrude Stein: She was a master at making nothing happen very slowly.
  - Clifton Fadiman

On William Faulkner and Ernest Hemingway: I have MORE to say than Hemingway, and God knows, I say it better than Faulkner.
  - Carson McCullers

On Virginia Woolf: Virginia Woolf's writing is no more than glamorous knitting. I believe she must have a pattern somewhere.
  - Edith Sitwell

On Ernest Hemingway: He has never been known to use a word that might send a reader to the dictionary.
  - William Faulkner

On William Faulkner: Poor Faulkner. Does he really think big emotions come from big words?
  - Ernest Hemingway

On George Bernard Shaw: He writes his plays for the ages—the ages between five and twelve.
  - George Nathan

On *Moby Dick*: Sad stuff. Mr. Melville's Quakers are wretched dolts and scrivellers and his mad captain is a monstrous bore.
  - *The Odessa Courier*

On Ezra Pound: To me Pound remains the exquisite showman without the show.
  - Ben Hecht

On Aldous Huxley: The stupid person's idea of a clever person.
  - Elizabeth Bowen

On *Tropic of Cancer* by Henry Miller: At last an unprintable book that is fit to read.
  - Ezra Pound

On Robert Browning: His verse is the beads without the string.
  - Gerard Manley Hopkins

On *Babbitt*: Babbitt as a book was planless; its end arrived apparently because its author had come to the end of the writing-pad, or rather, one might suspect from its length, to the end of all writing-pads then on the market.
  - Rebecca West

On Jack Kerouac and other Beat Generation writers: What they do isn't writing at all. It's typing.
  - Truman Capote

On Truman Capote: A great zircon in the diadem of American literature.
  - Gore Vidal

To me, Poe's prose is unreadable—like Jane Austen's. No, there is a difference. I could read his prose on a salary, but not Jane's.
  - Mark Twain

On *Leaves of Grass:* Here be all sorts of leaves except fig leaves.
  - Wendell Phillips

On E.M. Forster: E.M. Forster never gets any further than warming the teapot. He's a rare fine hand at that. Feel this teapot. Is it not beautifully warm? Yes, but there ain't going to be no tea.
  - Katherine Mansfield, *Diary*

On Harold Robbins: He is able to turn an unplotted, unworkable manuscript into an unplotted and unworkable manuscript with a lot of sex.
  - Tom Volpe

On Jane Austen: Every time I read *Pride and Prejudice* I want to dig her up and hit her over the skull with her own shinbone.
  - Mark Twain

On Andy Warhol: The only genius with an IQ of 60.
  - Gore Vidal

On John Dryden: His imagination resembles the wings of an ostrich.
  - Thomas Babington Macaulay

Just the omission of Jane Austen's books alone would make a fairly good library out of a library that hadn't a book in it.
  - Mark Twain

This paperback is very interesting, but I find it will never replace a hardcover book—it makes a very poor doorstop.
  - Alfred Hitchcock

Every time I read a Jane Austen novel, I feel like a bartender at the gates of heaven.
  - Mark Twain

He was such a bad writer, they revoked his poetic license.
  - Milton Berle

His style is chaos illumined by flashes of lightning. As a writer he has mastered everything except language.
  - Oscar Wilde

Be your own teacher and your own critic, develop that love and propensity for it that can bring such immeasurable returns.
  - Ruth Sawyer, *The Way of the Storyteller*

Don't be dismayed by the opinions of editors, or critics. They are only the traffic cops of the arts.
  - Gene Fowler

How people treat you is their karma; how you react is yours.
  - Wayne Dyer

Every writer wants at some time to be a critic.
  - William Zinsser, *On Writing Well*

Listening to critics is like letting Muhammad Ali decide which astronaut goes to the moon.
  - Robert Duvall

A young critic is like a boy with a gun; he fires at every living thing he sees. He thinks only of his own skill, not the pain he is causing.
- Henry Wadsworth Longfellow

It's ironic to discover that the critics who stop us in our tracks are within us... We don't need to push them away. On the contrary, we need to let them go.
- Hal Zina Bennett, *Write From the Heart*

Critics are like horse-flies which prevent the horse from ploughing.
- Anton Pavlovitch

[David Merrick] liked writers in the way that a snake likes live rabbits.
- John Osborne, *Almost a Gentleman*

I would rather be attacked than unnoticed. For the worst thing you can do to an author is to be silent as to his works.
- Samuel Johnson

Critics sometimes appear to be addressing themselves to works other than those I remember writing.
- Joyce Carol Oates

Asking a working writer what he thinks about critics is like asking a lamppost how it feels about dogs.
- Christopher Hampton

Everything that is written merely to please the author is worthless.
- Blaise Pascal

He shouldn't have written in such small print.
- William O. Douglas [on the difficulties of reading Sir Walter Scott's novels], *The Setons*

What distinguishes modern art from the art of other ages is criticism.
- Octavio Paz

Ah, Mailer is, as usual, lost for words.
- Gore Vidal

With nothing can one approach a work of art so little as with critical words: they always come down to more or less happy misunderstanding.
- Rainer Maria Rilke, *Letters to a Young Poet*

Oscar Wilde: I shall always regard you as the best critic of my plays.
Beerbohm Tree: But I have never criticized your plays.
Oscar Wilde: That's why.
> \- Hesketh Pearson, *Beerbohm Tree*

Critics are like brushers of noblemen's clothes.
> \- George Herbert

He's a writer for the ages—for the ages of four to eight.
This is not a novel to be tossed aside lightly. It should be thrown with great force.
> \- Dorothy Parker, *Wit's End*

A best-seller is the golden tomb of a mediocre talent.
> \- Logan Pearsall Smith, *Afterthoughts*

[Ring Lardner] never knew anything about composition, except as it concerned the shorter forms…it was his greatest fault—the fault of many men brought up in the school of journalism…It is a hell of a lot more difficult to build up a long groan than to develop a couple of short coughs!
> \- F. Scott Fitzgerald, *Letters* [to Max Perkins]

…She (Gertrude Stein) never could write dialogue. It was terrible. She learned how to do it from my stuff…and she was afraid people would notice it, where she'd learned it, so she had to attack me. It's a funny racket, really. But I swear she was damned nice before she got ambitious.
> \- Ernest Hemingway, *Green Hills of Africa*

The man who is asked by an author what he thinks of his work is put to the torture and is not obliged to speak the truth.
> \- Samuel Johnson

Did you ever know a writer to calmly take a just criticism and shut up?
> \- F. Scott Fitzgerald, *Letters*

Any fool can criticize, condemn, and complain—and most fools do.
> \- Dale Carnegie

The foulest Toadstool that has yet sprung from the reeking dunghill of present times.
> \- William Beckford, on *Frankenstein*

If another writer is in your estimation 98 percent bad and only 2 percent good, you must reckon with 2 percent. Not in justice to him, nor because you owe him at least that amount of fellowship. The reason is that you have to keep your eye in good training.
- David Greenhood, *The Writer on His Own*

How should you respond to feedback? Ideally with silence. Don't defend or explain yourself. If you are left with unresolved issues or are feeling uncomfortable because of something that was said, think of the experience as material for more writing.
- Linda Trichter Metcalf, Tobin Simon, *Writing the Mind Alive*

Writing is a process so when the critic attacks our souls, it delivers a early fatal blow...Self esteem is based on our ability to accept ourselves in our weaknesses as well as in our strengths.
- Janet Hagberg, *Wrestling With Your Angels*

In literary criticism the critic has no choice but to make over the victim of his attention into something the size and shape of himself.
- John Steinbeck, *Travels with Charlie*

Many thanks. I shall lose no time in reading it.
- Benjamin Disraeli [to an author who had presented him with an unwelcome book], *The Man Disraeli*

Scrutinize second; write first and freely.
- Julia Cameron, *The Right to Write*

It's ironic to discover that the critics who stop us in our tracks are within us...
- Hal Zina Bennett, *Write From the Heart*

You know who the critics are? The men who have failed in literature and art.
- Benjamin Disraeli, *Lothair*

[On a poor performance of *Hamlet*] There has long been a controversy over who wrote Shakespeare's plays—Shakespeare or Bacon. I propose to settle it today by opening their graves. Whoever turned over last night wrote *Hamlet*.
- Robert Hendrickson

Nothing touches a work of art so little as words of criticism; they always result in more or less fortunate misunderstandings.
- Rainer Maria Rilke, *Letter to a Young Poet*

Silencing the inner Judge when he goes too far does not mean that everything you write will be wonderful, or that someday you will not pick up something you wrote and discover that it really *was* trite and worthless after all...There is still another critic to deal with, one you are not equipped to face until you have come to some kind of terms with your internal enemy...Your audience: every soul out there who reads your work and feels compelled to comment on it.
- Victoria Nelson, *Writer's Block and How to Use It*

I will like and praise some things in a young writer which, yet, if he continues in, I cannot but justly hate him for.
- Samuel Johnson

I went for years without finishing anything. Because, of course, when you finish something you can be judged.
- Erica Jong

It is healthier, in any case, to write for the adults one's children will become than for the children one's "mature" critics often are.
- Alice Walker

The biggest critics of my books are people who have never read them.
- Jackie Collins

What a blessed thing it is, that Nature, when she invented, manufactured, and patented her authors, contrived to make critics out of the chips that were left!
- Oliver Wendell Holmes, Sr., *The Professor at the Breakfast Table*

Writing criticism is to writing fiction and poetry as hugging the shore is to sailing in the open sea.
- John Updike

The public is the only critic whose opinion is worth anything at all.
- Mark Twain

Virginia Woolf, I enjoyed talking to her, but thought *nothing* of her writing. I considered her "a beautiful little knitter."
- Edith Sitwell, letter to Geoffrey Singleton

Mr. Zola is determined to show that, if he has not got genius, he can at least be dull.
- Oscar Wilde

The cheerful clatter of Sir James Barrie's cans as he went round with the milk of human kindness.
    - Phillip Guedella, *Supers and Supermen*

To pass judgment on people or on characters in a book is to make silhouettes of them.
    - Cesare Pavese

Another reason I don't like critics (the one in myself as well as in other people) is that they try to teach something without *being* it.
    - Brenda Ueland, *If You Want to Write*

There is in the air about a man a kind of congealed jealousy. Only let him say he will do something and that whole mechanism goes to work to stop him.
    - John Steinbeck

The critic is interested in the novel; the novelist is interested in his neighbors.
    - Annie Dillard, *Living by Fiction*

Don't be too harsh to these poems until they're typed. I always think typescript lends some sort of certainty: at least, if the things are bad then, they appear to be bad with conviction.
    - Dylan Thomas, letter to Vernon Watkins

Poetry is an activity of the spirit; its roots lie deep in the subconscious nature, and it withers if that nature is denied, neglected, or negated."
    - Louise Bogan, *Journey Around My Room*

We must be careful what we say. No bird resumes its egg.
    - Emily Dickinson

The test of a good critic is whether he knows when and how to believe on insufficient evidence.
    - Samuel Butler

The play was consumed in wholesome fashion by large masses in places of public resort; the novel was self-administered in private.
    - Flann O'Brien, *At Swim-Two-Birds*

We writers all act and react on one another; and when I see a good thing in another man's book I react on it at once.
    - Stephen Leacock, *My Discovery of England*

From the moment I picked up your book [S. J. Perleman's *Dawn Ginsberg's Revenge*] until I laid it down, I was convulsed with laughter. Some day I intend reading it.
> - Groucho Marx

There are two ways of disliking poetry. One way is to dislike it, the other is to read "Pope."
> - Oscar Wilde

I have only ever read one book in my life, and that is *White Fang*. It's so frightfully good I've never bothered to read another.
> - [Uncle Matthew], Nancy Mitford, *Love in a Cold Climate*

Authors are judged by strange capricious rules. The great ones are thought mad, and the small ones fools.
> - Alexander Pope, *Three Hours after Marriage*

Pay no attention to what the critics say; there has never been set up a statue in honor of a critic.
> - Jean Sibelius

Don't labor for the admiration of the crowd, but be content with a few choice readers.
> - Horace

Praise nauseates you—but woe betide him who does not recognize your worth.
> - Dag Hammarskjöld, *Markings*

A lot of writers are killed off early. They just can't take the ridicule.
> - Norman Mailer

I don't care what is written about me, so long as it isn't true.
> - Dorothy Parker

When a man publishes a book, there are so many stupid things said that he declares he'll never do it again. The praise is almost always worse than the criticism.
> - Sherwood Anderson

The public will rail against a writer who holds up too bruising a mirror.
> - Lynn Freed, *Reading, Writing and Leaving Home*

Your manuscript is both good and original; but the part that is good is not original, and the part that is original is not good.
- Samuel Johnson

I never read a book before reviewing it; it prejudices a man so.
- Sydney Smith, *The Smith of Smiths*

A bad review may spoil your breakfast but you shouldn't allow it to spoil your lunch.
- Kingsley Amis, *Aren't We Due a Royalty?*

The reviewer always has hold of the wrong horror.
- Flannery O'Connor

It wasn't until the Nobel Prize that they really thawed out. They couldn't understand my books, but they could understand $30,000.
- William Faulkner

I am sitting in the smallest room of my house. I have your review before me. In a moment it will be behind me.
- Max Reger, *Lexicon of Musical Invective*

A person who publishes a book willfully appears before the populace with his pants down…If it is a good book nothing can hurt him. If it is a bad book, nothing can help him.
- Edna St. Vincent Millay

But by and large, with some exceptions, your good reviews are usually as stupid as your bad reviews.
- Fran Lebowitz

One of the earliest lessons I learned was not to read my reviews. Weigh them.
- Marion Zimmer Bradley

Any reviewer who expresses rage and loathing for a novel is preposterous. He or she is like a person who has put on full armor and attacked a hot fudge sundae.
- Kurt Vonnegut

I still feel bruised by that *Times* review. It did throw me off balance. It was like being tripped and thrown to the ground just as one has started a race to win.
- May Sarton, *Journal of a Solitude*

I have just read your lousy review. [Of his daughter Margaret's singing recital]. You sound like a frustrated old man who never made a success, an eight-ulcer man on a four-ulcer job...I have never met you but if I do, you'll need a new nose, a lot of beefsteak for black eyes, and a supporter below.
  - Harry S. Truman

It is safer to assume that every writer has read every word of every review, and will never forgive you.
  - John Leonard

They [Reviewers] are a poor lot, indeed, ill-paid, despised all around, and often wrong, but they have their pride.
  - Anthony Brandt, *Rotten Reviews*, Introduction

The artists who want to be writers, read the reviews; the artists who want to write, don't.
  - William Faulkner

I know there are authors who find it healthier for them, in their creative process, to just not look at any reviews, or bad reviews, or they have them filtered, because sometimes they are toxic for them. I don't agree with that kind of isolation. I'm very much interested in how African-American literature is perceived in this country, and written about, and viewed. It's been a long hard struggle, and there's a lot of work yet to be done. I'm especially interested in how women's fiction is reviewed and understood. And the best way to do that is to read my own reviews.
  - Toni Morrison, *Salon*, Feb 1998

Actors yearn for the perfect director, athletes for the perfect coach, priests for the perfect pope, presidents for the perfect historian. Writers hunger for the perfect reviewer.
  - Thomas Fleming, *NY Times* 6 Jan '85

Oh, great reviews are the worst. They mislead you more than the bad ones, because they only fuel your ego. Then you only want another one, like potato chips or something, and the best thing you get is fat and bloated. I'd rather just refuse, thanks.
  - Chazz Palminteri

A unanimous chorus of approval is not an assurance of survival; authors who please everyone at once are quickly exhausted.
  - André Gide

Book reviewers are little old ladies of both sexes.
    - John O'Hara

[on *Wuthering Heights* by Emily Brontë] Here all the faults of *Jane Eyre* (by Charlotte Brontë) are magnified a thousand fold, and the only consolation which we have in reflecting upon it is that it will never be generally read.
    - James Lorimer, *North British Review*

[on Emily Dickinson]
An eccentric, dreamy, half-educated recluse in an out-of-the-way New England village—or anywhere else—cannot with impunity set at defiance the laws of gravitation and grammar...Oblivion lingers in the immediate neighborhood.
    - Thomas Bailey Aldrich, *Atlantic Monthly*, 1892

[on M.M Kaye's *The Far Pavillions*] One of those big, fat paperbacks, intended to while away a monsoon or two, which, if thrown with a good over-arm action, will bring a water buffalo to its knees.
    - Nancy Banks-Smith, *Guardian*

The most insipid, ridiculous play that I ever saw in my life.
    - Samuel Pepys, *Diary* (on *A Midsummer Night's Dream*
    by Shakespeare)

I've been reading the reviews of my stories for twenty-five years, and can't remember a single point in any of them, or the slightest good advice. The only reviewer who ever made an impression on me was Skabichevsky, who prophesied that I would die drunk in the bottom of a ditch.
    - Anton Chekhov

This chamber music, this closet fiction, is executed behind too firmly closed windows...The book [*The Waves* by Virginia Woolf] is dull.
    - H.C. Harwood, *Saturday Review of Literature*

I no longer gave a sick dog's drop for the wisdom, the reliability and the authority of the public's literary mind, those creeps and old ladies of vested reviewing.
    - Norman Mailer

Some reviews give pain. That is regrettable, but no author has the right to whine. He was not obliged to be an author. He invited publicity, and he must take the publicity that comes along.
    - E.M Forster

Posterity will judge our works, and will judge our critics, too. If a critic savages you, the best response is to keep writing anyway. That'll show them.
- Bruce Holland Rogers, *Word Work*

The best compliment a writer can receive is, "I couldn't put it down."
- Brenda Hamilton

When you are a Bear of Very Little Brain and you Think of Things, you find sometimes that a Thing which seemed very Thingish inside you is quite different when it gets out into the open and has other people looking at it.
- A.A. Milne, *Winnie the Pooh*

10.

Writing is just telling a story - right?

God made man because he loves stories.
- Elie Wiesel

We're storytellers and what story could be more grand than the story of creation?
- Brian Greene, *The Fabric of the Cosmos*

It's all a question of story...The Old Story—the account of how the world came to be and how we fit into it—is not functioning properly, and we have not learned the New Story...we are between stories.
- Thomas Berry

Our personal stories can become the ground of new myths we need in order to create the world anew.
- Starhawk, *Truth or Dare*

Aslan, the Great Lion of God, tells you only your story.
- C.S Lewis

The stories we tell, whether human or divine, mythic or parabolic, order experience, construct meaning, and build community...We are our stories.
- Herbert Anderson and Edward Foley, *Mighty Stories, Dangerous Rituals*

...people live in stories that structure their worlds...Whoever can give his people better stories than the ones they live in like a priest in whose hands common bread and wine become capable of feeding the very soul...
- Hugh Kenner, *The Pound Era*

Stories sustain us—we need to share them with our friends. Even the act of telling them creates community and invites more stories.
- William G. Doty, *Mythography*

We tell ourselves stories in order to live…We look for the sermon in the suicide, for the social or moral lesson in the murder of five. We interpret what we see, select the most workable of the multiple choices.
- Joan Didion, *The White Album*

All stories are true stories, especially the artful lies we invent to satisfy the wishful thinker in us, for they present to us, in disguise often and at great distance, the way we are or would want to be.
- Lee K. Abbott, "The True Story of Why I Do What I Do"

Story is to human beings what the pearl is to the oyster.
- Joseph Gold

Life will go on as long as there is someone to sing, to dance, to tell stories and to listen.
- Oren Lyons

Without a story you have not got a nation, or a culture, or a civilization.
- Laurens Van der Post

The destiny of the world is determined less by the battles that are lost and won than by the stories it loves and believes in.
- Harold Goddard, *The Meaning of Shakespeare*

A story is a little knot or complex of that species of connectedness which we call relevance.
- Gregory Bateson, *Mind and Nature*

When one hears a story one takes pleasure in it for different reasons—for the euphony of its phrases, an aspect of the plot, or because one identifies with one of the characters. With certain stories certain individuals may experience a deeper, more profound sense of well-being…The listener who "takes the story to heart" will feel a pervasive sense of congruence within himself and also with the world.
- Barry Lopez, *Crossing Open Ground*

Stories exist to be exchanged. They are the currency of human growth.
- Jean Houston, *The Search for the Beloved*

Flood stories appear in 217 cultures.
- Bruce Feiler, *Walking the Bible*

My story is important not because it is mine...but because if I tell it anything like right, the chances are you will recognize that in many ways it is yours.

> - Frederick Buechner

We are all part of the old stories; whether we know the stories or not, the old stories know about us. From time immemorial, the old stories encompass all events, past and future.

> - Leslie Marmon Silko, *Yellow Woman and a Beauty of the Spirit*

We experience a frisson when we say the words story or soul because we know we are plunging into the liminal space that exists at the edge of the knowable and unknowable, the real and the wondrous.

> - Deena Metzger, *Nourishing the Soul*

Some stories leave a train of light behind them, meteor-like, so that much later than they strike our eyes we may see their meaning like an aftereffect.

> - Eudora Welty, *The Eye of the Story*

Sara Kendell once read somewhere that the tale of the world is like a tree...it encompassed the grand stories that caused some change in the world and were remembered in ensuing years as, if not histories, at least folktales and myths. By such reasoning, Winston Churchill could take his place in British folklore alongside the legendary Robin Hood; Merlin Ambrosilus had as much validity as Martin Luther. The scope of their influence might differ, but they were all of the same tale.

> - Charles de Lint, *Moonheart*

Story is very simple. A story is "something that happened and..."

> - Deena Metzger, *Nourishing the Soul*

A story should be something like the earth, a blazing fire at the core, but cool and green on the outside.

> - Madeleine L'Engle, *The Summer of the Great Grandmother*

All of us remembering what we have heard together—that creates the whole story, the long story of the people.

> - Leslie Marmon Silko, *Storyteller*

The universe is made of stories, not atoms.

> - Muriel Rukeyser

To tell a story you must travel inward…Story is the umbilical cord that connects us to the past, present and future…The Kalahari Bushmen have said, "A story is like the wind. It comes from a far-off place, and we feel it."
       - Terry Tempest Williams, *Pieces of White Shells*

No story sits by itself. Sometimes stories meet at corners and sometimes they cover one another completely, like stones beneath a river.
       - Mitch Albom, *The 5 People You Meet in Heaven*

Everywhere he looked, he saw a world made up of stories.
       - Leslie Marmon Silko

A story is like something you wind out of yourself. Like a spider, it is a web you weave, and you love your story like a child.
       - Katherine Anne Porter

A great hill marks the place where the Senecas first emerged from the Earth Mother…There too, it is said, the first stories ever heard were whispered from a crevice in the great, smooth rock…the Storytelling Stone.
       - Belden C. Lane, *Landscapes of the Sacred*

I hope you will go out and let stories happen to you, and that you will work with them, water them with your blood and tears and your laughter till they bloom, till you yourself burst into blossom…This is the work. The only work… Stories set the inner life into motion.
       - Clarissa Pinkola Estes, *Women Who Run with the Wolves*

There are many stories that live in the woods and around the sacred places of the world. Every once in a while they find someone that they like and they come to them.
       - Lynne V. Andrews, *Crystal Woman*

My story is important not because it is mine…but because if I tell it anything like right, the chances are you will recognize that in many ways it is yours.
       - Frederick Buechner

Change the name and the story is about you.
       - Horace

Borges said we go on writing the same story all our lives. The trouble is, it's usually a story that can never be told.
       - Robert Coover

A real story touches not only the mind but also the imagination and the unconscious depth in a person, and it may remain with him or her through many years, coming to the surface of consciousness now and then to yield new thoughts.
    - Helen M. Luke, *The Way of Woman*

It had been startling and disappointing to me to find out that story books had been written by *people*, that books were not natural wonders, coming up of themselves like grass.
    - Eudora Welty

There is a difference between taking a story literally and taking it seriously.
    - Robert S. McElvaine, *Eve's Seed*

The primary job that any writer faces is to tell you a story, a story out of human experience—I mean by that, universal mutual experience, the anguishes and troubles and griefs of the human heart, which is universal, without regard to race or time or condition.
    - William Faulkner, "Faulkner At West Point"

We are, each one of us, our own prisoner. We are locked up in our own story.
    - Maxine Kumin

It's all about letting the story take over.
    - Robert Stone

Stories are like fairy gold. The more you give away, the more you have.
    - Polly McGuire

There are no good stories. Only the singer really matters, seldom the song. What a writer brings to any story is an attitude, an attitude usually defined by the wound stripes of life.
    - John Gregory Dunne

I am always at a loss at how much to believe of my own stories.
    - Washington Irving

We construct a narrative for ourselves and that's the thread that we follow from one day to the next. People who disintegrate as personalities are the ones who lose that thread.
    - Paul Auster

I don't judge in my books. I don't have to have the antagonist get shot or the protagonist win. It's just how it comes out. I'm just telling a story.
- Elmore Leonard

In the tale, in the telling, we are all one blood. Take the tale in your teeth, then, and bite till the blood runs, hoping it's not poison; and we will all come to the end together, and even to the beginning: living, as we do, in the middle.
- Ursula K. Le Guin

"To begin at the beginning" was the old story-telling formula, and it was a very sound one, if "the beginning" could only be definitely ascertained!
- Jessie L. Weston, *From Ritual to Romance*

Stories exist to be exchanged. They are the currency of human growth. Stories conjugate. Alone you are stuck. In the exchange, both you and the story change.
- Jean Houston, *The Search for the Beloved*

We need myths to get by. We need story; otherwise the tremendous randomness of experience overwhelms us. Story is what penetrates.
- Robert Coover

Telling the proper stories is as if you were approaching the throne of Heaven in a fiery chariot.
- Baal Shem Tov

God made man because he loves stories.
- Nachman of Bratzlev

A good story cannot be devised; it has to be distilled.
- Raymond Chandler

Stories are living and dynamic. Stories exist to be exchanged. They are the currency of Human Growth.
- Jean Houston

Language is for telling, not for naming. All knowledge is made up of stories we can tell. Where we can tell no story, can have no knowledge.
- Richard Mitchell, *Less Than Words Can Say*

If a story is in you, it's got to come out.
- William Faulkner

It is the responsibility of writers to listen to gossip and pass it on. It is the way all storytellers learn about life.
　　- Grace Paley

Something from inside me takes lodging inside you.
　　- Native American storyteller

What do stories do when they are not being told? Do they live in villages?... Do they tell each other to each other?
　　- Howard Norman, *The Wishing Bone Cycle*

There are stories the man recites quietly into the room which slip from level to level like a hawk.
　　- Michael Ondaatje, *The English Patient*

Jesus employed his right brain...Storytellers work out of the right brain and speak to the right brain of others with messages of intellectual depth that strongly challenge left brains.
　　- Matthew Fox, *The Coming of the Cosmic Christ*

Storytellers always retell.
　　- Robert Bly and Marion Woodman, *The Maiden King*

A good story knows more than its teller.
　　- John O'Donohue, *Beauty*

Story telling is the oldest form of education...Story is the umbilical cord that connects us to the past, present and future.
　　- Terry Tempest Williams, *Pieces of White Shells*

Storytelling is bringing up, hauling up; it is not an idle practice...There must be a little spilled blood on every story if it is to carry the medicine.
　　- Clarissa Pinkola Estes, *Women Who Run with the Wolves*

A storyteller in Cree is literally "Someone-Who-Lies-Without-Hurting-Anyone."
　　- Kenneth Lincoln, *Native American Renaissance*

I like a good story well told. That is the reason I am sometimes forced to tell them myself.
　　- Mark Twain, speech

If the story is beautiful, its beauty belongs to us all. If the story is not, the fault is mine alone who told it.
- Swahili storyteller

Australian Aborigines say that the *big* stories—the stories worth telling and retelling, the ones in which you may find the meaning of your life—are forever stalking the right teller, sniffing and tracking like predators hunting their prey in the bush.
- Robert Moss, *Dreamgates*

That's what we all are—just stories. We only exist by how people remember us, by the stories we make of our lives. Without the stories, we'd just fade away.
- Charles de Lint

Tell a good story. And let it bring your characters to a different place (in soul and/or body) than where they started out.
- Catherine Breslin

There is no agony like bearing an untold story inside you.
- Z.N. Hurston

The reason for evil in the world is that people are not able to tell their stories.
- Carl Gustav Jung

Madame, all stories, if continued far enough, end in death, and he is no true storyteller who would keep that from you.
- Ernest Hemingway

Storytelling reveals meaning without committing the error of defining it.
- Hannah Arendt

Not only is your story worth telling, but it can be told in words so painstakingly eloquent that it becomes a song.
- Gloria Naylor

Man is essentially a storyteller. His search for a purpose, a cause, an ideal, a mission and the like is largely a search for a plot and a pattern in the development of his life story—a story that is basically without meaning or pattern.
- Eric Hoffer

No one ever told a story well standing up, or fasting.
- Honoré de Balzac

We are storied folk. Stories are what we are; telling and listening to stories is what we do.
- Arthur Kleinman

True stories carry and nurture us by helping us to see things as they are as well as what they can become.
- William R. White, *Stories for Telling*

If you tell me, it's an essay. If you show me, it's a story.
- Barbara Greene

Some stories must wait to be told. Any writer worth his salt knows this. Sometimes you wait for events to percolate in your subconscious until a deeper truth emerges; other times you're simply waiting for the principals to die. Sometimes it's both.
- Greg Iles, *Turning Angel*

By great story, I mean story that enables us to see patterns of connections, as well as symbols and metaphors to help us contain and understand our existence.
- Jean Houston

Once you're into a story everything seems to apply—what you overhear on a city bus is exactly what your character would say on the page you're writing. Wherever you go, you meet part of your story. I guess you're tuned in for it, and the right things are sort of magnetized.
- Eudora Welty

Who then…tells a finer tale than any of us? Silence does.
- Isak Dinesen, *Last Tales*

Language is for telling, not for naming. All knowledge is made up of stories we can tell. Where we tell no story, we can have no knowledge.
- Richard Mitchell, *Less Than Words Can Say*

The story is not in the plot but in the telling.
- Ursula K. Le Guin

It takes time, trust, and courage for the pattern of a story to emerge in perfect (or imperfect) symmetry. Trust is the most important because a writer must let it happen and believe that, in time, it will.
- Pamela Jane

To write a story is an act of Naming.
　　- Madeleine L'Engle, *Walking on Water*

There are three necessary elements in a story—exposition, development and drama. Exposition we may illustrate as "John Fortescue was a solicitor in the little town of X"; development as "One day Mrs. Fortescue told him she was about to leave him for another man"; and drama as "You will do nothing of the kind," he said.
　　- Frank O'Connor

If you write one story, it may be bad; if you write a hundred, you have the odds in your favor.
　　- Edgar Rice Burroughs

The story is a drill that keeps digging.
　　- Geoffrey O'Brien, *The Browser's Ecstasy*

"Talking story" is the breath of life.
　　- Maxine Hong Kingston

Writing and telling are almost the same, the way I do it.
　　- Daniel Pinkwater

The first law of storytelling: every man is bound to leave a story better than he found it.
　　- Mrs. Humphrey Ward

Our stories are simultaneously the same *and* different.
　　- Gabriele Lusser Rico

Some stories are true that never happened.
　　- Elie Weisel

There are only two or three human stories, and they go on repeating themselves as fiercely as if they had never happened.
　　- Willa Cather

We are lonesome animals. We spend all our life trying to be less lonesome. One of our ancient methods is to tell a story begging the listener to say—and to feel—Yes, that's way it is, or at least that's the way I feel it. You're not as alone as you thought.
　　- John Steinbeck

The flow of stories is medicine—similar medicine to listening to the ocean or gazing at sunrises.
- Clarissa Pinkola Estes

If there's anything worth calling theology, it is listening to people's stories, listening to them and cherishing them.
- Mary Pellauer

Inside the world of story, our minds run free—to do what children do when they are drawing—to color beyond the lines, all over the pages.
- Jimmy Neil Smith

Stories say: everything is near and close, everything is alive right here, a mystery is right here in everything. "It's all medicine"…Songs and stories bring the life of things in, make it so you can see and hear and touch it, give it a face and a voice, take care of it, bring it home like this. They can make a home out of the world. This is their power.
- Nick Johnson, *Arts Canada: Stones, Bones and Skin*

The Native American Lakota people tell the story of a white buffalo-calf woman who brought them their sacred pipe. When asked by a reporter if the story was true, one of the Lakota elders replied, "Well, I don't know whether it actually happened or not, but you can see for yourself that it's true.
- Ernie Carwile, *The Story Teller*

Some sacred stories carry a "need-to-be-told urgency" renewed in the tellings that feed the spirits that keep the world going.
- Kenneth Lincoln, *Native American Renaissance*

The extreme expression of his (Kalahari Bushman) spirit was in his story. He was a wonderful storyteller. The story was his most sacred possession. These people know what we do not: that without a story of your own to live you haven't got a life of your own.
- Laurens Van der Post

We're all storytellers. We all live in a network of stories. There isn't a stronger connection between people than storytelling.
- Jimmy Neil Smith

A defeated nation is always explaining itself. That's why the best storytellers are always from vanquished nations.
- Mark Richard

Stories that don't acknowledge the mystery at the center of things, don't challenge the version of reality most consenting adults rely upon day by day, are stories that disappear quickly into the ever-present buzz of entertainment.
- John Edgar Wideman

The best storyteller is one who lets you live if the weather is bad and you are hungry.
- [William Smith Smith] Kenneth Lincoln, *Native American Renaissance*

No one knows the whole fable; only parts of it.
- Edwin Muir

One doesn't write stories about people who are comfortable in their skins. You have to have trouble to write a story. If you don't have trouble, you don't have a story.
- Tobias Wolff

"Tell me a story" still comprise four of the most powerful words in English.
- Pat Conroy

Stories are like the wind.
- An African Bushman

Stories are relics that lie deep underground like fossils. Use your toolbox to dig them out. Sometimes you get a tiny shell; sometimes Tyrannosaurus Rex!
- Stephen King, *On Writing: A Memoir of the Craft*

Trust the tale, not the teller.
- D. H. Lawrence

There is no greater agony than bearing an untold story inside you.
- Maya Angelou

My stories run up and bite me in the leg—I respond by writing down everything that goes on during the bite. When I finish, the idea lets go and runs off.
- Ray Bradbury

A story really isn't any good unless it successfully resists paraphrase, unless it hangs on and expands in the mind.
- Flannery O'Connor, *On Writing*

Luck is a star; money is a plaything; time is a storyteller.
- Carl Sandburg

Stories told too long lose their audiences. Stories abbreviated too much have the sound of boredom. And boredom in the teller will kill any audience flat.
- Lynn Freed, *Reading, Writing and Leaving Home*

Storytelling is passing along gossip—it's *good* to talk. Talk is the exercise ground for writing.
- Natalie Goldberg, *Writing Down the Bones*

Story has the power to inspire and heal, to create archetypes of growth and to illumine the path before us…The metaphor of story is the language of the soul.
- Joan Borysenko

"And while we are sitting here waiting for the battle to begin," said one of the men to the king, "let me propose that we ask someone to tell a story—one which can pass the time without awakening heavy thoughts.
- Jens Bjørneboe, epigraph, *Winter in Bellapalma*

Stories set the inner life into motion.
- Clarissa Pinkola Estes, *Women Who Run with the Wolves*

The writer, like the shaman storyteller of ancient times, embraces his own life experiences, tells stories to the community…and in the process both storyteller and listeners are healed.
- Hal Zina Bennett, *Write From the Heart*

The greatest stories touch on the sacred, that moment when head and heart and soul combine.
- Jane Yolen, *Take Joy*

I hope you will go out and let stories happen to you, and that you will work with them, water them with your blood…till you yourself bloom.
- Clarissa Pinkola Estes, *Women Who Run with the Wolves*

Our responsibility, then, is to find and know the story that is our own.
- Gertrud Mueller Nelson, *Here All Dwell Free*

A story is a way to say something that can't be said any other way, and it takes every word in the story to say what the meaning is.
- Flannery O'Connor

Don't be afraid of writing bad, mawkish stories for that will show you many things about yourself, and your eye and taste and what you really feel and care about will become clearer to you.
- Brenda Ueland, *If You Want to Write*

I am also haunted by "the story I might not write." How I long to sneak into the future and snatch away the retrospect of one who could say: *"Oh yes, she wrote about this and this and this, while all the time, as close to her as her own skin, lay her real story, her true story, the whole story, the best story of all."*
- Gail Godwin, *The Writer on Her Work*

Stories take people on a journey, but they also escort them home again.
- Philip Martin

When we read a story, we inhabit it. The covers of the book are like a roof and four walls. What is to happen next will take place within the four walls of the story. And this is possible because the story's voice makes everything its own.
- John Berger

The test of a good story is in how much good stuff you can leave out.
- Ernest Hemingway

The secret is to start a story near the ending.
- Christ Offut

You want in all cases for the story to get through the writing.
- Alice Munro

I like stories with a strong action arc, solid dialogue and language that sings. I like stories that contain what Bernard Malamud called "the quality of afterthought."
- Grant Tracey, *North American Review*

We love stories mostly for two reasons: our readiness to comfort and entertain ourselves with fantasy, and our curiosity and desire for insight about reality. Though these seem like opposites, it is not always easy to separate them completely.
- Marjorie Boulton, *The Anatomy of the Novel*

Human beings are a story: they are living a story and anyone open to this story is living a part—perhaps all—of themselves.
- P.L. Travers

Good stories write themselves—bad ones have to be written…
- F. Scott Fitzgerald, *As Ever, Scotty-Fitz*

There is one story and one story only.
- Robert Graves

Stories do not tell themselves; whoever is telling a story has to be somewhere in relation to the story, in order to tell it.
- Marjorie Boulton, *The Anatomy of the Novel*

Once when my phone was out of order I went out very late at night to make a call from a public phone at a supermarket plaza. At something like two in the morning all the stores were closed but the plaza was not empty. There were three women there, one of them with a baby in a stroller. What were they doing there? It was several years before I figured out a possible answer, and that answer was a story.
- Janet Burroway

The best stories don't come from "good vs. bad" but from "good vs. good."
- Leo Tolstoy

If a nation loses its storytellers, it loses its childhood.
- William Hazlitt, Peter Handke

I had half a million words, but it wasn't a story.
- Jean Auel

My father told stories all the time when I was growing up. My mother used to call them "lies." I didn't know that "lies" was the name for stories in the black vernacular; I just thought it was her own word that she had made up. I was inspired by those "lies" though, and knew that I wanted to tell some too one day.
- Henry Louis Gates Jr., *Swing Low: Black Men Writing*

A good story has the same effect on me that I suppose a good drink of whiskey has on an old toper—it puts new life in me.
- Abraham Lincoln

Your life is full of stories; my life is full of stories. They are very occupying, but they are not really interesting. What is interesting is the way everyone tells their stories.
- Gertrude Stein

Tell the readers a story! Because without a story, you are merely using words to prove that you can string them together in logical sentences.
  - Anne McCaffrey

Sharing our stories can also be a means of healing. Grief and loss may isolate us, and anger may alienate us. Shared with others, these emotions can be powerfully uniting, as we see that we are not alone, and realized that others weep with us.
  - Susan Wittig Albert

Stories knit together the realities of past and future, of dreamed and intended moments. They teach us how we perceive and why we wonder.
  - Joan Halifax

There are stories in everything. I've got some of my best yarns from park benches, lampposts, and newspaper stands.
  - O. Henry

A human life is a story told by God and in the best of stories told by humans, we come closer to God.
  - Hans Christian Andersen

We live for and die for our stories.
  - George Gerbner

If stories come to you, care for them. And learn to give them away where they are needed. Sometimes a person needs a story more than food to stay alive.
  - Barry Lopez, *Crow and Weasel*

There have been great societies that did not use the wheel, but there have been no societies that did not tell stories.
  - Ursula K. Le Guin

…When their authors are now determined to die, stories often write themselves, and go where they want to go.
  - Umberto Eco, *The Island of the Day Before*

To be a person is to have a story to tell.
  - Isak Dinesen

The tale is often wiser than the teller.
  - Susan Fletcher, *Shadow Spinner*

A man is always a teller of tales, he lives surrounded by his stories and the stories of others, he sees everything that happens to him through them, and he tries to live his own life as if he were telling a story.

    - Jean-Paul Sartre

A lost coin is found by means of a penny candle; the deepest truth is found by means of a simple story.

    - Anthony de Mello

Every story you tell is your own story.

    - Joseph Campbell

In a constant process of creation and recreation, one transforms the other; stories make soul and soul speaks in story.

    - Deena Metzger

The one who tells the stories rules the world.

    - Hopi proverb

The job of an apple tree is to bear apples. The job of a storyteller is to tell stories, and I have concentrated on that obligation.

    - James A. Michener

Those who do not have power over the story that dominates their lives, power to retell it, rethink it, deconstruct it, joke about it, and change it as times change, truly are powerless, because they cannot think new thoughts.

    - Salman Rushdie

All sorrows can be borne if you put them into a story or tell a story about them.

    - Isak Dinesen

People live in stories that structure their worlds…Whoever can give his people better stories than the ones they live in is like the priest in whose hands common bread and wine become capable of feeding the very soul, and he may think of forging in some invisible smithy the uncreated conscience of his race.

    - Hugh Kenner, *The Pound Era*

When I write stories, I am like someone who is in her own country, walking along streets that she has known since she was a child, between walls and trees that are hers.

    - Natalia Ginzburg

All of us remembering what we have heard together—that creates the whole story, the long story of the people.
- Leslie Marmon Silko, *Storyteller*

Something from inside me takes lodging inside you.
- Native American Storyteller

If the story is beautiful, its beauty belongs to us all. If the story is not, the fault is mine alone who told it.
- Swahili Storyteller

A story isn't about a moment in time; a story is about *the* moment in time.
- W.D. Wetherell

The Swampy Cree say stories live in the world and may choose to inhabit people who then have the option of telling them back out into the world again.
- Lynn V. Andrews, *Flight of the 7th Moon*

Nothing is allowed to die in a society of storytelling people.
- Harry Crews

Jesus' stories don't illustrate a point: they are the point.
- William R. White, *Stories for the Gathering*

Stories are "love gifts."
- Lewis Carroll

The Catholic sacramental view of life is one that maintains and supports at every turn the vision that the storyteller must have if he is going to write fiction of any depth.
- Flannery O'Connor

A story is like something you wind out of yourself. Like a spider, it is a web you weave, and you love your story like a child.
- Katherine Anne Porter

So when the storyteller by the hearth starts out: "Once upon a time, a long way from here, lived a king who had three sons," that story will be telling us that things change; that events have consequences; that choices are to be made; that the kind does not live forever. Narrative is a stratagem of mortality.
- Ursula K. LeGuin, *Dancing at the Edge of the World*

What really happens is that the story-maker proves a successful "sub-creator." He makes a Secondary World which your mind can enter. Inside it, what he relates is "true," it accords with the laws of that world. You therefore believe it, while you are, as it were, inside.
- J.R.R. Tolkien

...stories are a history—of a sort...This does not mean that stories lie but rather than they look at humanity's history obliquely, through slotted eyes. Emily Dickinson once wrote something to that effect: "Tell all the Truth but tell it slant."
- Jane Yolen

What we want is a story that starts with an earthquake and builds to a climax.
- Samuel Goldwyn

Not to have any story to live out is to experience nothingness; the primal formlessness of human life below the threshold of narrative structuring. Why become anything at all? Does anything make any difference? Why not simply die?
- Michael Novak, *Ascent of the Mountain, Flight of the Dove*

I'm not a bright novelist, no Graham Greene or Paul Bowles...I'm a storyteller, my virtues are honesty, good intent, and the ability to entertain people of my own level of intellect.
- Stephen King, "How *It* Happened."

Know something, Sugar? Stories only happen to people who can tell them.
- Allan Gurganus

Storytelling is fundamental to the human search for meaning.
- Mary Catherine Bateson, *Composing a Life*

A good writer is basically a storyteller, not a scholar or a redeemer of mankind.
- Isaac Bashevis Singer

Storytelling is a bringing up, hauling up; it is not an idle practice.
- Clarissa Pinkola Estes, *Women Who Run with the Wolves*

I navigate life using stories where I find them, and I hold tight to the ones that tell me new kinds of truths.
- Barbara Kingsolver, *Small Wonder: Essays*

Stories are for those late hours in the night when you can't remember how you got from where you were to where you are.
- Tim O'Brien

Even the pre-literary tradition of oral culture had complex tapestries of story that left the most subtle openings into the resonance fields of myth and mystery.
- John O'Donohue, *Beauty: The Invisible Embrace*

Life will go on as long as there is someone to sing, to dance, to tell stories.
- Oren Lyons

No matter what form the dragon may take, it is the mysterious passage past him, or into his jaws, that stories of any depth will be concerned to tell.
- Flannery O'Connor, *Mystery and Manners*

Story Types: "Ha-Ha!" (stories that are funny); "Aha!" (stories that surprise or delight the mind); "Ahhh…." (stories that touch deep emotions; "Amen" (stories that move the spirit.)
- Elizabeth Ellis, [Jack Maguire,] *The Power of Personal Storytelling*

As our ancestors knew very well, storytelling adds a layer of richness to everyday life. Stories become real for us, and simple objects—trees or candles or rocks— take on special meanings because we have encountered them in our stories.
- Robin Moore

Draw your chair up close to the edge of the precipice and I'll tell you a story.
- F. Scott Fitzgerald

If the stories come to you, care for them. And learn to give them away where they are needed.
- Barry Lopez

Many people think of storytelling as something that is done at bedtime, that it is something done for small children. But when I use the term storytelling, I'm talking about something much bigger than that. I'm talking about something that comes out of an experience and an understanding of that original view of creation—that we are all part of a whole; we do not differentiate or fragment stories and experiences.
- Leslie Marmon Silko, "Language and Literature from a Pueblo Indian Perspective"

Some people think we're made of flesh and blood and bones. Scientists say we're made of atoms. But I think we're made of stories. When we die, that's what people remember, the stories of our lives and the stories that we told.
- Ruth Stotter

We create stories and stories create us. It is a rondo.
- Chinua Achebe

Time is a good storyteller.
- Irish Saying

Death of the Father would deprive literature of many of its pleasures. If there is no longer a Father, why tell stories? Doesn't every narrative lead back to Oedipus? Isn't storytelling always a way of searching for one's origin, speaking one's conflicts with the Law, entering into the dialectic of tenderness and hatred?
- Roland Barthes

The stories have grown the storytellers, grown them into who they are.
- Clarissa Pinkola Estes

We ride stories like rafts, or lay them out on the table like maps. They always, eventually, fail and have to be reinvented. The world is too complex for our forms ever to encompass for long.
- William Kittredge, *The Nature of Generosity*

"Who are you?" someone asks. "I am the story of my self," comes the answer.
- N. Scott Momaday

There are just three essentials to a good story: humanity, a point, and the storyteller.
- J. Frank Dobie

Stories are greater than we are, their capacious narratives give us wiggle room to dream It is why children's eyes light up and gaze far off when we read them tales of elves, kings and Ents. Our families and communities connect us to the old and new stories, and guide us to "lean into the light."
- Paul Hawken, *Blessed Unrest*

There is only one story of time and space and it is constantly retold: someone far away tries to come home.

    - Michael Joyce, *Twilight, A Symphony*

If we had time and no money, living by our wits, what story would you tell?

    - Adrienne Rich

Is rewriting as difficult as it sounds?

Only the hand that erases can write the true things.
- Meister Eckhart

You must often make erasures if you mean to write what is worthy of being read a second time.
- Horace

Review. Reread. Rewrite.
- George Mair, *How to Write Better in One Hour*

Murder your darlings.
- Arthur Quiller-Couch

Let your darlings out, but murder them.
- Joseph Campbell

The first draft is the down draft. You just get it down. The second draft is the up draft—you fix it up. The third draft is the dental draft, where you check every tooth, to see if it's loose or cramped or decayed, or…healthy.
- Anne Lamott, *Bird by Bird*

What I have crossed out I didn't like. What I haven't crossed out I'm dissatisfied with.
- Cecil B. De Mille

Muddiness is not merely a disturber of prose, it is also a destroyer of life, of hope.
- Berel Lang, *Soundings*

Clarity. Clarity. Clarity. When you become hopelessly mired in a sentence, it is best to start fresh.
- William Strunk, Jr. and E.B. White

In the interests of clarity, it seemed necessary to constantly remind myself to pay not the slightest attention to the elegance of the presentation; I adhered conscientiously to the rule of the brilliant theoretician, Ludwig Boltzmann, to leave elegance to tailors and shoemakers.
        - Albert Einstein

To write simply is as difficult as to be good.
        - W. Somerset Maugham

The shorter and the plainer the better.
        - Beatrix Potter

Anything is better than not to write clearly. There is nothing to be said against lucidity, and against simplicity only the possibility of dryness. This is a risk well worth taking when you reflect how much better it is to be bald than to wear a curly wig.
        - W. Somerset Maugham

Making the simple complicated is commonplace; making the complicated simple, awesomely simple, that's creativity.
        - Charles Mingus

Vigorous writing is concise. A sentence should contain no unnecessary words, a paragraph no unnecessary sentence, for the same reason that a drawing should have no unnecessary lines and a machine no unnecessary parts.
        - William Strunk Jr. and E.B. White, *The Elements of Style*

If writing isn't clear, it's nothing. If readers have to guess at your meaning, only some will guess right. Leave nothing to chance, writer. In your control of the language lies your authority.
        - Bill Roorbach, *Writing Life Stories*

Never express yourself more clearly than you are able to think.
        - Niels Bohr

It is a safe rule to apply that, when a mathematical or philosophical author writes with a misty profundity, he is talking nonsense.
        - *An Introduction to Mathematics*, 1948

There is nothing in the world that should not be expressed in such a way that an affectionate seven year old boy can see and understand it.
        - Leo Tolstoy

Put it before them briefly so they will read it, clearly so they will appreciate it, picturesquely so they will remember it and, above all, accurately so they will be guided by its light.
- Joseph Pulitzer

Put the argument into a concrete shape, into an image, some hard phrase, round and solid as a ball, which they can see and handle and carry home with them, and the cause is half won.
- Ralph Waldo Emerson

The greatest thing a soul ever does…is to *see* something and tell what it *saw* in a plain way."
- John Ruskin

When all things are equal, translucence in writing is more effective than transparency, just as glow is more revealing than glare.
- James Thurber

Confident writers have the courage to speak plainly; to let their thoughts shine rather than their vocabulary.
- Ralph Keyes

There is something about plain writing which smacks of moral goodness. Interestingly, some writers turn to it more and more as they get older. There is a modesty to it.
- Annie Dillard, *Living by Fiction*

Everything should be made as simple as possible, but not simpler.
- Albert Einstein

Use dense words. A dense word is a word that crowds a lot of meaning into a small space. The fewer words you use to express an idea, the more impact that idea will have.
- Gary Provost, *100 Ways to Improve your Writing (Mentor)*

Say all you have to say in the fewest possible words, or your reader will be sure to skip them; and in the plainest possible words or he will certainly misunderstand them.
- John Ruskin

Simplicity, coupled with clarity, equals elegance.
- Jon Franklin, *Writing for Story*

Be simple and clear—Be not occult...Clearness, simplicity, not twistified or foggy sentences at all...
- Walt Whitman, early notebooks

Never be so brief as to be obscure.
- Tryon Edwards

Good writing is essentially clear thinking made visible.
- Ambrose Bierce

Clutter is the disease of American writing...the secret of good writing is to strip every sentence to its cleanest components.
- William Zinsser, *On Writing Well*

To get the right word in the right place is a rare achievement. To condense the diffused light of a page of thought into the luminous flash of a single sentence, is worthy to rank as a prize composition just by itself...Anybody can have ideas—the difficulty is to express them without squandering a quire of paper on an idea that ought to be reduced to one glittering paragraph.
- Mark Twain

The great enemy of clear language is insincerity. When there is a gap between one's real and one's declared aims, one turns, as it were instinctively, to long words and exhausted idioms, like a cuttlefish squirting out ink.
- George Orwell

And how is clarity to be achieved? Mainly by taking trouble; and by writing to serve people rather than to impress them.
- F. L. Lucas

In all pointed sentences, some degree of accuracy must be sacrificed to conciseness.
- Samuel Johnson

Good prose is like a windowpane.
- George Orwell

The three chief qualities of style are clearness, force and ease...the rule of clearness is not to write, so that the reader can understand, but so that he cannot possibly misunderstand.
- Christopher Morley

To be clear is the first duty of a writer; to charm and to please are graces to be acquired later.
- Brander Matthews

Those who write clearly have readers, those who write obscurely have commentators.
- Albert Camus

If you can describe clearly without a diagram the proper way of making this or that knot, then you are a master of the English language.
- Hilaire Belloc

Clarity is the perception of wisdom...being able to perceive and understand the illusion, and to let it play. It is being able to see beyond the activities of the personality to the force of the immortal soul.
- Gary Zukav

If a man writes clearly, anyone can see if he fakes.
- Ernest Hemingway

Every life contains within it a potential for clarification.
- Peter Hoeg

Take care of the sense and the sounds will take care of themselves.
- Lewis Carroll

Nothing conduces to brevity like a caving in of the knees.
- Oliver Wendell Holmes Jr., *Yankee from Olympus*

Simplify. Then complicate all over again.
- Paul West

Good writers are those who keep their language efficient. That is to say, keep it accurate, keep it clear.
- Ezra Pound

Producing writing is not so much like filling a basin or pool once, but rather getting water to keep flowing through till finally it runs clear.
- Peter Elbow, *Writing Without Teachers*

Vigorous writing is concise.
- William Strunk, Jr., "The Elements of Style"

By clarity I mean that there is the same lovely limpid quality in a good story that you find in a well-kept fish pond.,...when the fish rises and swims across the pool, it is somehow illuminated by the water, made bigger, clearer, sweeter, more important.

- Jane Yolen, *Take Joy*

As with all other aspects of the narrative art, you will improve with practice, but practice will never make you perfect. Why should it? What fun would that be?

- Stephen King

I see but one rule: to be clear.

- Stendhal (Marie-Henri Beyle)

It is my ambition to say in ten sentences what others say in a whole book.

- Friedrich Nietzsche

Calvin: I used to hate writing assignments, but now I enjoy them I realized that the purpose of writing is to inflate weak ideas, obscure poor reasoning, and inhibit clarity. With a little practice, writing can be an intimidating and impenetrable fog! Want to see my book report?
Hobbs: (reading the title) *The Dynamics of Interbeing and Monological Imperatives in Dick and Jane: A Study in Psychic Transrelational Gender Modes.*
Calvin: Academia, here I come!

- Calvin and Hobbs

Talent is ordinary. Disciplined talent is rare.

- James Michener

In Tibetan, the term for discipline is *tsul trim. Tsul* means "appropriate or just," and *trim* means "rule" or "way." So discipline is to do what is appropriate or just; that is, in an excessively complicated age, to simplify our lives.

- Sogyal Rinpoche, *The Tibetan Book of Living and Dying*

Discipline is a dedication to your truth. Discipline makes something come from nothing.

- Nancy Slonim Aronie, *Writing From the Heart*

Doing something does not require discipline. It creates its own discipline— with a little help from caffeine.

- Annie Dillard

Surely the writer is to address a world of laborers, and such therefore must be his own discipline.
- Henry David Thoreau, *A Week on the Concord and Merrimack Rivers*

The discipline of the written word punishes both stupidity and dishonesty.
- John Steinbeck

Be accurate with the facts. You will be repeated. When you write a book, you are *committing history.*
- Dan Poynter, *The Self-Publishing Manual*

It has been said that if you don't have discipline, it is like trying to walk without legs.
- Chogyam Trungpa

As I see discipline it means that power of the will to work long enough at any one effort until the habit be established. It means the aptitude for obeying a higher command.
- Ruth Sawyer, *The Way of the Storyteller*

Discipline is the basic set of tools we require to solve life's problems. Without discipline we can solve nothing.
- M. Scott Peck

Discipline is a dedication to your truth. Discipline makes something come from something.
- Nancy Slonim Aronie, *Writing From the Heart*

The discipline of the writer is to learn to be still and listen to what his subject has to tell him.
- Rachel Carson

The qualities that make a true artist [are] nearly the same qualities that make a true athlete.
- John Gardner

You learn from music, from watching great athletes at work—how disciplined they are, how they move. You learn these things by watching a shortstop at work, how he concentrates on one thing at a time. You learn from classic music, from the blues and jazz, from bluegrass. From all this, you learn how to sustain a great line without bringing in unnecessary words.
- Ernest Gaines

A discipline is a learning, and a disciple in a learner, one who follows a teaching…it requires an unflinching attention and a faithful care.
    - Mary Caroline (M.C.) Richards, *Centering*

Some people regard discipline as a chore. For me, it is a kind of order that sets me free to fly.
    - Julie Andrews

Without discipline, there is no life at all.
    - Katharine Hepburn

Discipline is the refining fire by which talent becomes ability.
    - Roy L. Smith

Every author's fairy godmother should provide him not only with a pen but also with a blue pencil.
    - F.L. Lucas, *Style*

One cannot collect all the beautiful shells on the beach. One can collect only a few, and they are more beautiful if they are few.
    - Anne Morrow Lindbergh

Rewriting ripens what you've written.
    - Duane Alan Hahn

Anton Chekov gave some advice about revising a story: first, he said, throw out the first three pages…It depends on the length of the story, naturally; if it's very short, you can only throw out the first three paragraphs. But there are few first drafts to which Chekhov's Razor doesn't apply.
    - Ursula Le Guin

Half my life is an act of revision.
    - John Irving

…only what fits is allowed.
    - Norman Podhoretz, *Making It*

Clutter is the disease of American writing. We are a society strangling in unnecessary words, circular constructions, pompous frills and meaningless jargon.
    - William Zinsser

I started all over again on page 1, circling the 262 pages like a vulture looking for live flesh to scavenge.
- John Gregory Dunne

Revision, once well done, becomes a sort of automatic itch which you scratch in the next work without thinking about it.
- Romulus Linney

Rereading reveals rubbish and redundancy.
- Duane Alan Hahn

Remember the waterfront shack with the sign FRESH FISH SOLD HERE. Of course it's fresh, we're on the ocean. Of course it's for sale, we're not giving it away. Of course it's here, otherwise the sign would be someplace else. The final sign: FISH.
- Peggy Noonan

There is but one art, to omit.
- Robert Louis Stevenson

In baseball you only get three swings and you're out. In rewriting, you get almost as many swings as you want, and you know, sooner or later, you'll hit the ball.
- Neil Simon

The beautiful part of writing is that you don't have to get it right the first time, unlike, say, a brain surgeon.
- Robert Cormier

Writing is rewriting. A writer must learn to deepen characters, trim writing, intensify scenes. To fall in love with the first draft to the point where one cannot change it is to greatly enhance the prospects of never publishing.
- Richard North Patterson

Writing and rewriting are a constant search for what it is one is saying.
- John Updike

Rewriting is like scrubbing the basement floor with a toothbrush.
- Pete Murphy

Never be afraid to write for the wastebasket.
- Phyllis A. Whitney, *Writing Juvenile Stories and Novels*

What I had to face, the very bitter lesson that everyone who wants to write has got to learn, was that a thing may in itself be the finest piece of writing one has ever done, and yet have absolutely no place in the manuscript one hopes to publish.
    - Thomas Wolfe

The wastebasket is a writer's best friend.
    - Isaac Bashevis Singer

The most valuable of talents is never using two words when one will do.
    - Thomas Jefferson

Sometimes I think I write to throw away; it's a process of distillation.
    - Donald Bartheleme

I love revision. Where else can spilled milk be turned into cream?
    - Katherine Paterson

Substitute "damn" every time you're inclined to write "very;" your editor will delete it and the writing will be just as it should be.
    - Mark Twain

Revision is one of the exquisite pleasures of writing.
    - Bernard Malamud

Of every four words I write, I strike out three.
    - Nicolas Boileau

Writing is not like painting where you add. It is not what you put on the canvas that the reader sees. Writing is more like sculpture where you remove, you eliminate in order to make the work visible. Even those pages you remove somehow remain.
    - Elie Wiesel

The time to begin writing an article is when you have finished it to your satisfaction. By that time you begin to clearly and logically perceive what it is you really want to say.
    - Mark Twain

I am one of those people who write short. A great deal of my revisions is spent fleshing out and very little writing.
    - Katherine Paterson

There's got to be white space around the word, silence around the voice. Listing is not describing. Only the relevant belongs. Some say God is in the details; some say the Devil is in the details. Both are correct...Tactically speaking, I'd say go ahead and crowd in the first draft—put everything in. Then in revising decide what counts, what tells; and cut and recombine till what's left is what counts. Leap boldly.
     - Ursula LeGuin

Generally, I write everything many times over. All my thoughts are second thoughts.
     - Aldous Huxley, *Writers at Work*

What I have crossed out I didn't like. What I haven't crossed out I'm dissatisfied with.
     - Cecil B. de Mille

I'm not a good writer, but I'm a good re-writer.
     - James Michener

Nothing you write, if you hope to be any good, will ever come out as you first hoped.
     - Lillian Hellman

The purpose of revision is not to correct, but to discover.
     - Lucy McCormick Calkins

...there are days when the result is so bad that no fewer than five revisions are required. In contrast, when I'm greatly inspired, only four revisions are needed.
     - John Kenneth Galbraith

Every new revision brings a writer back to square one. We are beginners in our art every time.
     - Jane Yolen, *Take Joy*

Often I think writing is a sheer paring away of oneself leaving always something thinner, barer, more meager.
     - F. Scott Fitzgerald, *Letters*

Read and revise, reread and revise, keeping reading and revising until your text seems adequate to your thought.
     - Jacques Barzun, *Simple and Direct*

The manuscript you submit [should not] contain any flaws that you can identify. It is up to the writer to do the work, rather than counting on some stranger in Manhattan...
- Richard North Patterson

It would take him [F. Scott Fitzgerald] five starts and seventeen versions before he could resolve it into his brutally personal work *Tender Is the Night.*
- Scott Berg, *Max Perkins Editor of Genius*

Writing is about hypnotizing yourself into believing in yourself, getting some work done, then unhypnotizing yourself and going over the material coldly.
- Anne Lamott, *Bird by Bird*

In composing, as a general rule, run your pen though every other word you have written and you have no idea what vigor it will give your style.
- Sydney Smith

Cut down on your "Lard Factor." Half the words you're using aren't necessary.
- Richard Lanhamin, *Revising Prose*

If it sounds like writing, I rewrite it.
- Elmore Leonard

I feel like a lot of time my writing is like having about twenty boxes of Christmas decorations. But no tree. You're going, where do I put this? Then they go, Okay, you can have a tree, but we'll blindfold you and you gotta cut it down with a spoon.
- Carolyn Chute

Let alone re-write, he doesn't even re-read.
- Clive James, *The Dreaming Swimmer*

I try to leave out he parts that people skip.
- Elmore Leonard

I have performed the necessary butchery. Here is the bleeding corpse.
- Henry James [when asked to cut three lines from a 5,000 word article]

...there are days when the result is so bad that no fewer than five revisions are required. In contrast, when I'm greatly inspired, only four revisions are needed.
- Kenneth Galbraith

I quit writing if I feel inspired, because I know I'm going to have to throw it away.
- Frank Yerby

I once tried doing thirty-three, [revisions] but something was lacking, a certain—how shall I say—*je ne sais quoi*. On another occasion I tried forty-two versions, but the final effect was too lapidary.
- S. J. Perelman. Interview, *Writers at Work*

I can't write five words but that I change seven.
- Dorothy Parker

Blot out, correct, insert, refine
Enlarge, diminish, interline.
- Jonathan Swift, *On Poetry*

Don't tear up the page and start over when you write a bad line…
- Garrison Keillor

You become a good writer as you become a good joiner: by planing down your sentences.
- Anatole France

Erskine Caldwell once admitted to having rewritten a manuscript as many as sixteen times. Hemingway rewrote the ending of *A Farewell to Arms* thirty-nine times in manuscript form and worked it over thirty times in proof form.
- William Gentz and Elaine Wright Colvin,
  The Religious Writer's Marketplace

I find that revising in this case [*Tender Is the Night*] is pulling up the weaker section of the book and then the next weakest, etc.
- F. Scott Fitzgerald [To Max Perkins] *Letters*

Some of the best writing comes when you rehash…I compare it to preparing a lens for a telescope. For months, all you're doing is grinding it into the generalized shape of what a lens should be. Once the rough-cut bowl is formed, it's not going to reflect an image. In writing you can have your skeleton, your structure, but it doesn't reflect. The reflection comes in the polish. What a person will see, what a person will feel, comes in the polish…it forms the image you're trying to create.
- Donald Perry

There may be two or three more drafts after the third to polish up. But the third is the one where it all comes together for me.
- Phyllis Reynolds Naylor

Less is more.
- Robert Browning

But those books were not meant to become anything more than a lesson to me on what it takes to write fiction: persistence imposed by a limited focus…The focus required of a priest, a nun, a convict serving a life's sentence.
- Amy Tan, explaining why she threw away a thousand pages of manuscript that could have become several books, [Donald McQuade, Robert Atwan, *The Writer's Presence*]

Read over your compositions and, when you meet a passage which you think is particularly fine, strike it out.
- Samuel Johnson

I'm a rewriter. That's the part I like the best…once I have a pile of paper to work with, it's like having the pieces of a puzzle. I just have to put the pieces together to make a picture.
- Judy Blume

When you write…some things that come very late in the creation change what you were conceiving back when you started. Therefore, you have to go back and revise.
- William Kennedy

I have often rewritten—often several times—every word I have ever published. My pencils outlast their erasers.
- Vladimir Nabokov

When rewriting, move quickly. It's a little like cutting your own hair.
- Robert Stone

I rewrite a great deal. I'm always fiddling, always changing something. I'll write a few words—then I'll change them. I add. I subtract. I work and fiddle and keep working and fiddling, and I only stop at the deadline.
- Ellen Goodman

You let the story cool off and then, instead of rewriting, you relive it.
- Ray Bradbury

I liked the piece enough to rewrite it. I took out a couple of paragraphs…This is the kind of absurdity you fall into when you write about anything, let alone about yourself. You're so pleased and grateful to be writing at all, especially at the beginning, that you babble. It doesn't hurt much to babble in a first draft, so long as you have the sense to cut out the irrelevancies later.
    - Annie Dillard, "How I Wrote the Moth Essay—and Why"

The writer must learn that writing is re-writing. He must be able to cut away at his script without quivering, to carve up his child without flinching.
    - Isabelle Ziegler, *Creative Writing*

He [E. B. White] rewrote pieces twenty times or more, and sometimes pleaded with the postmaster of North Brooklyn, Maine, to return a just-mailed manuscript so he could punch up its ending or rewrite the lead.
    - Ralph Keyes, *The Courage to Write*

I turn sentences around. That's my life. I write a sentence and then I turn it around. Then I look at it and I turn it around again. Then I have lunch.
    - Philip Roth, *Ghost Writer*

The first draft of anything is shit.
    - Ernest Hemingway

It's perfectly okay to write garbage—as long as you edit brilliantly.
    - C. J. Cherryh

You need not expect to get your book right the first time. Go to work and revamp or rewrite it. God only exhibits his thunder and lightning at intervals, and so they always command attention. These are God's adjectives. You thunder and lightning too much, the reader ceases to get under the bed, by and by.
    - Mark Twain

Rewriting is largely a question of seeing the wood for the trees.
    - Christopher Evans, *Writing Science Fiction*

Each of the large ones (essays) took nine months to a year. I've had thousands of pages for a 30-page essay—30 or 40 drafts of every page.
    - Susan Sontag

In six pages I can't even say hello.
    - James Michener

Perhaps in order to write a really great book, you must be rather unaware of the fact. You can slave away at it and change every adjective to some other adjective, but perhaps you can write better if you leave the mistakes.

    - Jorge Luis Borges, interview, *Writers at Work*

Doing work which has to be done over and over again helps us recognize the natural cycles of growth and decay, of birth and death, and thus become aware of the dynamic order of the universe.

    - Fritjof Capra

I have heard that an eagle misses seventy percent of its strikes. Why should I expect to do better?

    - Sophy Burnham, *For Writers Only*

It is dangerous to leave written that which is badly written. A chance word, upon paper, may destroy the world. Watch carefully and erase, while the power is still yours, I say to myself, for all that is put down, once it escapes, may rot its way into a thousand minds, the corn become a black smut, and all libraries, of necessity, be burned to the ground as a consequence. Only one answer: write carelessly so that nothing that is not green will survive.

    - William Carlos Williams

Any fool can write. It takes a visionary to erase.

    - Rebbe Isreal

12.

What do I need to know about research?

Basic research is what I am doing when I don't know what I am doing.
- Wernher von Braun

What is research, but a blind date with knowledge.
- William Henry

Research is the process of going up alleys to see if they are blind.
- Marston Bates

Research serves to make building stones out of stumbling blocks.
- Arthur D. Little

I didn't want to have reams of data that would give me no place to invent. It was important to me, therefore, that whatever I invented call up the research, rather than the research dictate what I was going to write.
- Toni Morrison [Referring to *Beloved* and her research on slavery in an interview with Sigmund Koch]

Allow the material you've gathered to have its own influence on plot and character, as well as on description and local or historical detail.
- David Poyer

[on writing from tape recordings] Too many books in my field smell of tape. When you record, there are just too many words and there is a temptation to use them all.
- John McPhee, *People Books, Book People* [David W. McCullough]

Bees are sometimes drowned in the honey which they collect—so are some writers lost in their collected learning.
- Nathanial Hawthorne, *Journals*

If we knew what we were doing it wouldn't be research.
  - Albert Einstein

Research is usually a policeman stopping a novel from progressing.
  - Brian Moore

You can overdo research if you allow it to become an excuse for putting off that confrontation with the blank page or screen. You can always read another book or interview another source. But do you need to?
  - Marshall Cook, *Freeing Your Creativity*

The trick in doing a historical novel…is to digest the research…You learn how hard it is to separate what belongs only to your time from the era you are trying to re-create.
  - Norman Mailer, *The Spooky Art*

The greatest part of a writer's time is spent in reading, in order to write; a man will turn over half a library to make one book.
  - Samuel Johnson

Let's get one thing straight: Research is a creative process. And just like the other creative processes, research gets hampered when we close down its possibilities, narrow too much our definitions.
  - Bill Roorbach, *Writing Life Stories*

The digging is never done because the shovel scrapes at life itself. It is not possible to get it all, or even very much of it, but I gather what I can of the rough, tumbling crowd, the lone walkers and the voluble talkers, the high lonesome singers, the messages people write and leave for me to read.
  - Annie Proulx, *Writers [on Writing]*

Research can be a big clunker. It's difficult to know how you can make the historical light.
  - Michael Ondaatje

For fiction, poetry, or nonfiction, the more research you do, the more materials you will have to play with. You are writing for readers—a very educated bunch in this country. It's hard and interesting to tell them something they don't know. The more you read, the better you will know what they know.
  - Annie Dillard, *"Notes for Young Writers"*

When I was sitting writing *The Shadow of the Glen* I got more aid than any learning would have given me from a chink in the floor of the old Wicklow house where I was staying, that let me hear what was being said by the servant girls in the kitchen.

    - J. M. Synge

It took seven years for Tom Clancy to research his first novel. It took less than a week for him to research his fifth one.

    - Oscar Collier, *How To Write & Sell Your First Novel*

There is no need for the writer to eat a whole sheep to be able to tell what mutton tastes like. It is enough if he eats a cutlet.

    - W. Somerset Maugham

Facts tell us everything and nothing.

    - Nancy Willard

When a writer omits things he does not know, they show like holes in his writing.

    - Ernest Hemingway, *Writers at Work*

Don't worry about blind alleys. Most lead somewhere.

    - Julia Cameron, *The Right to Write*

Frederick Forsyth, author of *The Day of the Jackal* and other books, claims to hate writing and to do it only because he loves research.

    - Sophy Burnham, *For Writer's Only*

Dictionaries are like watches; the worst is better than none, and the best cannot be expected to go quite true.

    - Samuel Johnson

A definition is the enclosing a wilderness of ideas within a wall of words.

    - Samuel Butler

Lexicographer: A writer of dictionaries, a harmless drudge.

    - Samuel Johnson

At painful times, when composition is impossible and reading is not enough, grammars and dictionaries are excellent for distraction.

    - Elizabeth Barrett Browning

Any word you have to hunt for in a thesaurus is the wrong word. There are no exceptions to this rule.
> - Stephen King, "Everything You Need to Know About
> Writing Successfully—in Ten Minutes"

The first dictionary which could be read with pleasure.
> - Lord Macaulay on Samuel Johnson's *Dictionary of the*
> *English Language*

The greatest masterpiece in literature is only a dictionary out of order.
> - Jean Cocteau

Actually if a writer needs a dictionary he should not write. He should have read the dictionary at least three times from beginning to end and then have loaned it to someone who needs it.
> - Ernest Hemingway

I suppose that so long as there are people in the world, they will publish dictionaries defining what is unknown in terms of something equally unknown.
> - Flann O'Brien, *Myles Away from Dublin*

I've been in *Who's Who* and I know what's what, but it'll be the first time I ever made the dictionary.
> - Mae West, letter [upon learning an inflatable life jacket was
> named after her]

What's another word for Thesaurus?
> - Steven Wright

13.

How do I go about writing films and plays?

Playwriting is simply showing how words influence actions and vice versa.
- David Mamet [Donald McQuade, Robert Atwan, *The Writer's Presence*]

You write a hit play the same way you write a flop.
- William Saroyan

If you would shut your door against the children for an hour a day and say: "Mother is working on her five-act tragedy in blank verse!" you would be surprised how they would respect you. They would probably all become playwrights.
- Brenda Ueland, *If You Want to Write*

In a good play, everyone is in the right.
- Fredrich Hebbel

Drama is life with the dull bits cut out.
- Alfred Hitchcock

A play should give you something to think about. When I see a play and understand it the first time, then I know it can't be much good.
- T.S. Eliot

The great dramatist has something better to do than to amuse either himself or his audience. He has to interpret life.
- George Bernard Shaw

I have always been able to attach my demons to my chariot.
- Ingmar Bergman

Playwriting gets into your blood and you can't stop it. At least not until the producers or the public tell you to.
- T.S. Eliot

On a purely theatrical plane Strindberg has become an inspiration, whereas Ibsen has become a burden, an immovable gravestone which preserves that form of theater which Ibsen mastered and therefore wished to keep unchanged. In dramatic world literature Strindberg has many descendants, Ibsen none.
   - Jens Bjørneboe, "Strindberg the Fertile"

The potential playwright…is in love with the theater and woos it relentlessly. He doesn't' read plays; he sees them…the writer has much to accomplish in his first act if he is going to get his audience back for the second one.
   - Isabelle Ziegler, *Creative Writing*

Remember the fable about the elusive bluebird? A man searched all over the world for the blue bird of happiness, and when he returned home he found it had been there all the time. It is unnecessary to torture your brain, to weary yourself by searching for a premise, when there are so many ready to hand. Anyone who has a few strong convictions is a mine of premises.
   - Lajos Egri, *Art of Dramatic Writing*

…here I was twenty-nine years old and I wasn't a very good poet and I wasn't a very good novelist, I thought I would try writing a play, which seems to have worked out a little better.
   - Edward Albee, interview, *Writers at Work*

Everyone judges plays as if they were very easy to write. They don't know that it is hard to write a good play, and twice as hard and tortuous to write a bad one.
   - Anton Chekhov

Most playwrights go wrong on the fifth word. When you start a play and you type "Act one, scene one" your writing is every bit as good as Arthur Miller or Eugene O'Neil or anyone. It's that fifth word where amateurs start to go wrong.
   - Meredith Wilson

A playwright knows that what is most private in her heart of hearts is also the most astonishing.
   - Tina Howe

It's hard enough to write a good drama, it's much harder to write a good comedy, and it's hardest of all to write a drama with comedy. Which is what life is.
   - Jack Lemmon

If there is a gun hanging on the wall in the first act, it must fire in the last.
- Anton Chekhov

Drama is a gun that doesn't go off.
- Jonis Agee

The theatre is a communal event, like church. The playwright constructs a mass to be performed for a lot of people. She writes a prayer, which is just the longings of one heart.
- Marsha Norman

When I am writing I must be alone; if I have eight characters of a drama to do with I have society enough; they keep my busy; I must learn to know them.
- Henrik Ibsen

I write fiction because it's a way of making statements I can disown, and I write plays because dialogue is the most respectable way of contradicting myself.
- Tom Stoppard

When a play enters my consciousness, it is already a fairly developed fetus. I don't put down a word until the play seems ready to be written.
- Edward Albee

We rely upon the poets, the philosophers, and the playwrights to articulate what most of us can only feel in joy or sorrow. They illuminate the thoughts for which we can only grope; they give us the strength and balm we cannot find in ourselves. Whenever I feel my courage wavering I rush to them. They give me the wisdom of acceptance, and the will and resilience to push on.
- Helen Hayes

There is more of yourself in a book than in a play. That's why we know all about Dickens and not much about Shakespeare. Ben Jonson murdered people; Marlowe was a spy; Shakespeare just sat in the corner and took notes.
- John Mortimer

No art passes our conscience in the way film does, and goes directly to our feelings, deep down into the dark rooms of our souls.
- Ingmar Bergman

Literature and painting both exist as art from the very start; the cinema doesn't.
- Jean-Luc Godard

It struck me that movies had spent more than half a century saying, "They lived happily ever after," and the following quarter-century warning that "they'll be lucky to make it through the weekend. " Possibly now we are entering a third era in which the movies will be sounding a note of cautious optimism: "You know it just might work."
      - Nora Ephron

For me, the cinema is not a slice of life, but a piece of cake.
      - Alfred Hitchcock

MGM bores me when I see them, but I don't see them much. They have been a help in getting me introductions to morticians, who are the only people worth knowing.
      - Evelyn Waugh

The cinema, like the detective story, makes it possible to experience without danger all the excitement, passion and desirousness which must be repressed in a humanitarian ordering of life.
      - Carl Jung

My belief is that no movie, nothing in life, leaves people neutral. You either leave them up or you leave them down.
      - David Puttnam

In good films, there is always a directness that entirely frees us from the itch to interpret.
      - Susan Sontag

Don't worry about a commercial script. *Million Dollar Baby* and *Crash* could not have been any less commercial, but they worked. My best advice is don't listen to studios, or your agent, or anyone else telling you what they want. Never ask what the studios are looking for, or what producers need. Let it come from your gut.
      - Paul Haggi

You sell a screenplay like you sell a car. If somebody drives it off a cliff, that's it.
      - Rita Mae Brown

People sometimes say that the way things happen in the movies is unreal, but actually it's the way things happen to you in life that's unreal.
      - Andy Warhol

They have followed their usual procedure and handed my treatment over to several other people to make a screenplay out of it. By the time they are ready to shoot it may have been through 20 pairs of hands. What will be left? One shudders to think. Meanwhile, they have paid me a lot of money...
    - Aldous Huxley

Television has raised writing to a new low.
    - Samuel Goldwyn

Writing for television is a special kamikaze mission.
    - Don Freeman, *In a Flea's Navel*

There are days when any electrical appliance in the house, including the vacuum cleaner, seems to offer more entertainment than the TV set.
    - Harriet van Horne

I'm always amazed that people will actually choose to sit in front of the television and just be savaged by stuff that belittles their intelligence.
    - Alice Walker

The business of scriptwriting is really about rewriting. I think begin creative is about being destructive...When you finish a draft and you send it off, you think "OK, now that is it." But it never is.
    - Peter Berry, *The Writer*, April 2005

A "treatment" helps you write your script; the log line and synopsis help you sell it. You need to know how to do all three.
    - Michael Thunder

You have all the scenes. Just go home and word it in.
    - Samuel Goldwyn

Never judge a book by its movie.
    - J. W. Eagan

Reading a novelization of your own screenplay is like watching someone else kiss your girlfriend.
    - Don Marquis

I can't think of any one film that improved on a good novel, but I can think of many good films that came from very bad novels.
    - Gabriel Garcia Marquez

Turning one's novel into a movie script is rather like making a series of sketches for a painting that has long ago been finished and framed.
- Vladimir Nabokov

Don't listen to the cautious producer inside of you, but listen to the roaring side of you.
- Peter Berry

I write scripts to serve as skeletons awaiting the flesh and sinew of images.
- Ingmar Bergman

Being a writer in Hollywood is like going into Hitler's Eagle's Nest with a great idea for a Bar Mitzvah.
- David Mamet

Some years ago, not long after I moved to Los Angeles from New York, I attended a television industry party. When a man asked my profession, I told him that I was a writer. He sipped his drink. "Half-hour or hour?" he inquired. There was a long silence. "Lifelong," I replied.
- Carol Muske Dukes

Here I am paying big money to you writers and what for? All you do is change the words.
- Samuel Goldwyn

Strip away the phony tinsel of Hollywood and you'll find the real tinsel underneath.
- Oscar Levant

I'm a Hollywood writer, so I put on a sports jacket and take off my brain.
- Ben Hecht

You can take all the sincerity in Hollywood, place it in the navel of a fruit fly and still have room enough for three caraway seeds and a producer's heart.
- Fred Allen

Having your book turned into a movie is like seeing your oxen become bouillon cubes.
- John LeCarre

14.

Can I write poetry?

Poetry: the best words in the best order.
- Samuel Taylor Coleridge

Poetry is nothing but healthy speech.
- Henry David Thoreau

Poetry is truth in its Sunday clothes.
- Joseph Roux

Poetry is an echo, asking a shadow to dance.
- Carl Sandburg

Poetry is the art of substantiating shadows.
- Edmund Burke

A poem is a momentary stay against confusion…Like a piece of ice on a hot stove the poem must ride on its own melting…Poetry is a way of taking life by the throat.
- Robert Frost

A poem is like a deed in that it is to be judged as a manifestation of the personality of its maker.
- Dag Hammarskjöld, *Markings*

Poetry is the language of a state of crisis.
- Stephane Mallarmé

Poetry is ordinary language raised to the Nth power. Poetry is boned with ideas, nerved and blooded with emotions, all held together by the delicate, tough skin of words.
- Paul Engle, NY *Times* 17 Feb '57

A poem is never finished, only abandoned.
> - Paul Valery

A good poem is almost always good housekeeping.
> - Don Welch

A poem is true if it hangs together. Information points to something else. A poem points to nothing but itself.
> - E.M. Forster, *Two Cheers for Democracy*

The poem is the point at which our strength gave out.
> - Richard Rosen

Poetry is not always words.
> - Audrey Foris

Poetry is devil's wine.
> - St. Augustine

Poetry lies its way to the truth.
> - John Ciardi, *Saturday Review* 28 Apr '62

You will find poetry nowhere unless you bring some of it with you.
> - Joseph Joubert

Poetry began, I think, as a mnemonic device to enable an illiterate populace to remember prayers, to recite the order of worship, or, in a more secular use, to recount the inventories of warehouses in ancient Babylon. That's why we wrote in rhyme and meter, so that we could remember…
> - Peter Davison, *Breathing Room*

Poetry is a rich, full-bodied whistle, cracked ice crunching in pails, the night that numbs the leaf, the duel of two nightingales, the sweet pea that has run wild.
> - Boris Pasternak, *Life* 13 Jun '60

Poetry is not a turning loose of emotion, but an escape from emotion; it is not the expression of personality but an escape from personality.
> - T.S. Eliot

Poetry is thoughts that breathe, and words that burn.
> - Thomas Gray

Poetry is when an emotion has found its thought and the thought has found words.
- Robert Frost

Poetry takes something that we know already and turns it into something new.
- T.S. Eliot

Poetry is life distilled.
- Gwendolyn Brooks

A poem is a serious joke, a truth that has learned jujitsu.
- William Stafford

Poetry, like the moon, does not advertise anything...The success of the poem is determined, not by how much the poet felt in writing it, but by how much the reader feels in reading it.
- John Ciardi

What is a Professor of Poetry? How can poetry be professed?
- W.H. Auden

Poetry is like a plant. It wants to grow toward the sun of spirit and vision.
- Barron Wormser, *The Road Washes Out in Spring*

Poetry is to be read and reread till it reveals its secrets. It is better to read one poem ten times than to read ten poems once.
- Leo Stein

We don't read and write poetry because it's cute. We read and write poetry because we are members of the human race. And the human race is filled with passion. And medicine, law, business, engineering, these are noble pursuits and necessary to sustain life. But poetry, beauty, romance, love, these are what we stay alive for.
- *Dead Poet's Society*

Poetry ennobles the heart and the eyes, and unveils the meaning of all things upon which the heart and eyes dwell.
- Edith Sitwell

If you have a poem within you today, I can guarantee you a tomorrow.
- T. Guillemets

The impact of poetry is so hard and direct that for the moment there is no other sensation except that of the poem itself.
    - Virginia Woolf

There's a current in poetry that is electric—not metaphorical electricity but a real, static charge, the hoodoo of the rhythmic words.
    - Baron Wormser, *The Road Washes Out in Spring*

There is something about poetry beyond prose logic, there is mystery in it, not to be explained but admired.
    - Edward Young

If you are going deeply into poetry, give your whole self to it—go the whole hog. Too many take it carefully, and fail. If it is to be your life, make everything else subordinate to it.
    - Robert Frost to Daniel Smythe, Jay Parini, *Robert Frost: A Life*

Poetry is the only art people haven't yet learnt to consume like soup.
    - W.H. Auden

Three days without bread, yes. One day without poetry, never!
    - Baudelaire

"I can repeat poetry as well as other folk it if comes to that—" "Oh, it needn't come to that!" Alice hastily said.
    - Lewis Carroll, *Through the Looking-Glass*

Poetry is the language of a state of crisis.
    - Stéphane Mallarmé

Poetry is I say essentially a vocabulary just as prose is essentially not…So that is poetry really loving the name of anything and that is not prose.
    - Gertrude Stein, *Lectures in America*

The compulsion to make rhymes was born in me. For those sated readers of my work who wish ardently that I would stop, the future looks dark indeed.
    - Noël Coward, foreword to *The Lyrics of Noel Coward*

A memorable poem, like memorable weather, depends upon contrast for its effect.
    - Edgar H. Knapp, *Introduction to Poetry*

All bad poetry springs from genuine feeling.
> - Oscar Wilde

Breathe-in experience,
Breathe-out poetry.
> - Muriel Rukeyser

The best craftsmanship always leaves holes and gaps...so that something that is *not* in the poem can creep, crawl, flash or thunder in.
> - Dylan Thomas

Each memorable verse of a true poet has two or three times the written content.
> - Alfred de Musset, *L Poète déchu*

Writing is like this—you dredge for the poem's meaning the way police dredge for a body. They think it is down there under the black water, they work the grappling hooks back and forth.
> - Paul Engle, *Life* 28 May '56

I gave up on new poetry myself thirty years ago, when most of it began to read like coded messages passing between lonely aliens on a hostile world.
> - Russell Baker

Poetry often enters through the window of irrelevance.
> - M.C. Richards

I don't create poetry, I create myself; for me my poems are a way to me.
> - Edith Södergran

In writing poetry we keep approaching what we know we cannot know, but we keep on because we feel an inexplicable assurance that it is worth knowing.
> - David Greenhood, *The Writer on His Own*

Everyone has one good poem in his hidden head.
> - Don Welch

The mind wraps itself around a poem. It is almost sensual, particularly if you work on a computer. You can turn a poem round and about and upside down, dancing with it a kind of bolero of two snakes twisting and coiling, until the poem has found its right and proper shape.
> - Marge Piercy

If I knew how to write a poem, I wouldn't.
 - James Galvin, *Sonora Review*

You can't write poetry on the computer.
 - Quentin Tarantino

I feel that poetry is the completely personal expression of someone about his feelings and reactions to the world. I think it is only interesting in proportion to how interesting the person who writes it is.
 - Diane Wakoski

I've done as many as eighty drafts of one poem…I've found students shocked to learn that it can take me three years to finish a poem.
 - Carolyn Forche, *The Writing Business*

The mind that finds its way to wild places is the poet's; but the mind that never finds its way back is the lunatic's.
 - G.K.Chesterton

I am two fools, I know: for loving, and for saying so in whining poetry.
 - John Donne

Genuine poetry can communicate before it is understood.
 - T.S. Eliot, *Dante*

In order that human beings bring about the most radiant conditions for themselves to inhabit, it is essential that the vision of reality which poetry offers be transformative, more than just a printout of the given circumstances of its time and place.
 - Seamus Heaney, "Joy or Night"

Perhaps no person can be a poet, or can even enjoy poetry, without a certain unsoundness of mind.
 - Thomas Babbington Macaulay

No poems can please for long or live that are written by water-drinkers.
 - Horace (Quintus Horatius Flaccus), *Satires*

It is the job of poetry to clean up our word-clogged reality by creating silences around things.
 - Stephen Mallarmé

I come here to speak poetry. It will always be in the grass. It will also be necessary to bend down to hear it. It will always be too simple to be discussed in assemblies.

- Boris Pasternak, speech

The words in a poem, after all, are on furlough from daily life.
- Baron Wormser, *The Road Washes Out in Spring*

The beginner hugs his infant poem to him and does not want it to grow up. But you may have to break your poem to remake it.
- May Sarton

When power leads man toward arrogance, poetry reminds him of his limitations. When power narrows the areas of man's concern, poetry reminds him of the richness and diversity of his existence. When power corrupts, poetry cleanse, for art establishes the basic human truths which must serve as the touchstone of our judgment.
- John F. Kennedy, Address, Amherst College, Oct. 6, 1963

The poem…is a light by which we may see—and what we see is life.
- Robert Penn Warren, *Saturday Review*, 22 Mar '58

Science is for those who learn; poetry, for those who know.
- Joseph Roux, *Meditations of a Parish Priest*

Most people read [poetry] listening for echoes because the echoes are familiar to them. They wade through it the way a boy wades through water, feeling with his toes for the bottom: The echoes are the bottom.
- Wallace Stevens, *Secretaries of the Moon*

Poetry should surprise by a fine excess and not by singularity—it should strike the Reader as a working of his own highest thoughts, and appear almost a Remembrance.
- John Keats

A poem must not mean, but be.
- Archibald MacLeish

Poetry is certainly something more than good sense, but it must be good sense…just as a palace is more than a house, but it must be a house.
- Samuel Coleridge

My poems are hymns of praise to the glory of life.
> \- Edith Sitwell

May Ireland hurt you into poetry.
> \- W.H. Auden

Poetry is a mixture of common sense, which not all have, with an uncommon sense, which very few have.
> \- John Masefield

Our of the quarrel with others we make rhetoric; out of the quarrel with ourselves we make poetry.
> \- William Butler Yeats

If you know what you are going to write when you're writing a poem, it's going to be average.
> \- Derek Walcott

Poetry is written vision. You have to show new ways of seeing things to be a real poet.
> \- Jane Reichhold, *Another Attempt to Define Haiku*

...creation and appreciation of haiku demand: Selflessness, Loneliness, Grateful Acceptance, Worldlessness, Non-intellectuality, Contradictoriness, Humor, Freedom, Non-morality, Simplicity, Materiality, Love and Courage.
> \- R. H. Blyth, *Haiku*

The primary purpose of reading and writing haiku is sharing moments of our lives that have moved us, pieces of experience and perception that we offer or receive as gifts. At the deepest level, this is the one great purpose of all art, and especially of literature.
> \- William R. Higginson, *The Haiku Handbook*

To haiku's finest artists its brevity was seen less as a barrier than challenge to the imagination, demanding that however broad in implication the poem would have to be of single impact.
> \- Lucien Stryk, *The Dumpling Field*

The only problem
With Haiku is that you just
Get started and then
> \- Roger McGough

Haiku sees into the heart of things and is supremely alive here and now.
- Frederick Franck, *The Awakened Eye*

A poem is solitary and on its way.
- Paul Celan

The moon glows, flowers bloom, insects cry, water flows…this is the essence of haiku…separate yourself from historical limitations—there you'll find the essence of true art, religion and science.
- Santoka Taneda

Poetry is plucking at the heartstrings, and making music with them.
- Dennis Gabor

I want to…read poems filled with terror and music that changes laws and lives.
- Leonard Cohen

Poetry is the impish attempt to paint the color of the wind.
- Maxwell Bodenheim

A sliver of the moon lost in the belly of a golden frog.
- Carl Sandburg, NY *Times*, 13 Feb '59

Poetry is a packsack of invisible keepsakes.
- Carl Sandburg

The really terrifying thing is that writing poetry is not something people necessarily get better at. There is no guarantee that they will exceed their early promise.
- Jacob Polley

Poetry is as exact a science as geometry.
- Gustave Flaubert

Poetry is the journal of a sea animal living on land, wanting to fly in the air… Poetry is a search for syllables to shoot at the barriers of the unknown and the unknowable. Poetry is a phantom script telling how rainbows are made and why they go away.
- Carl Sandburg, *Poetry Considered*

Poetry is a mirror which makes beautiful that which is distorted.
- Percy Shelley, *A Defence of Poetry*

Above all, a haiku must be very simple and free of all poetic trickery and make a little picture and yet be as airy and graceful as a Vivaldi Pastorella.
- Jack Kerouac

Poems of great energy are usually distillations of words and sentiments outside themselves. Poems are by nature a compression.
- Peter J. Kreeft, *Heaven, the Heart's Deepest Longing*

Arranging a bowl of flowers in the morning can give a sense of quiet in a crowded day—like writing a poem or saying a prayer.
- Anne Morrow Lindbergh

Poetry should be great and unobtrusive, a thing which enters into one's soul, and does not startle or amaze it with itself, but with its subject.
- John Keats

Poetry is nearer to vital truth than history.
- Plato, *Ion*

Any fool can take a bad line out of a poem; it takes a real pro to throw out a good line.
- Theodore Roethke

Poetry is the art of creating imaginary gardens with real toads.
- Marianne Moore

Poetry does not feed, but men have died for want of it.
- Robert Kennedy

Poetry is the spontaneous overflow of powerful feelings…emotion recollected in tranquility.
- William Wordsworth

You can learn about the pine only from the pine, or about bamboo only from bamboo…The object and yourself must become one, and from that feeling of oneness issues your poetry.
- Matsuo Basho

If Galileo had said in verse that the world moved, the inquisition might have let him alone.
- Thomas Hardy

Poetry is what Milton saw when he went blind.
- Don Marquis

Poetry is the breath and finer spirit of all knowledge.
- William Wordsworth

Poetry takes something that we know already and turns it into something new.
- T.S. Eliot

Anything can be poetry that is felt as poetry.
- Mary Caroline (M.C.) Richards, *Centering*

You always run up against poetry in England.
- Virginia Woolf, letter to Vita Sackville-West

There is poetry as soon as we realize that we possess nothing.
- John Cage

Poetry is the alchemy which teaches us to convert ordinary materials into gold.
- Anäis Nin, *The Novel of the Future*

Who can tell the dancer from the dance?
- W.B. Yeats

Poetry heals the wounds inflicted by reason.
- Novalis

If I were obliged, not to define poetry, but to name the class of things to which it belongs, I should call it a secretion...like turpentine in the fir...or like the pearl in the oyster.
- A.E. Housman

Poetry is not a turning loose of emotion, but an escape from emotion; it is not the expression of personality, but an escape from personality. But, of course, only those who have personality and emotions know what it means to want to escape from such things.
- T.W. Eliot

A good poem contains both meaning and music.
- Eve Merriam

Poetry is the revelation of a feeling that the poet believes to be interior and personal which the reader recognizes as his own.
- Salvatore Quasimodo

The sound of a word is at least as important as the meaning.
- Jack Prelutsky

Poetry and mysticism both derive from a common source, the ground or depth of the soul where the Mystery of Being is experienced. But the poet is always driven to "symbolize" his experience, to express it in words or in paint or in music. The mystic sees the experience in itself, beyond words or sounds or images.
- Bede Griffiths, *Return to the Center*

Poetry…is the opening and closing of a door, leaving those who look through to guess about what was seen during a moment.
- Carl Sandburg

If I feel physically as if the top of my head were taken off, I know that is poetry.
- Emily Dickinson

Poetry is a river, many voices travel in it. Poem after poem moves along in the exciting crests and falls of the river waves. None is timeless; each arrives in an historical context; almost everything in the end, passes.
- Mary Oliver, *A Poetry Handbook*

The outer world (of nature) is needed to activate the inner world, the world of poetry, imagination and spirituality.
- Thomas Berry, at the Parliament of World Religions

Poetry is the language in which man explores his own amazement.
- Christopher Fry

I am overwhelmed by the beautiful disorder of poetry, the eternal virginity of words.
- Theodore Roethke

The one man who should never attempt an explanation of a poem is its author. If the poem can be improved by its author's explanation, it never should have been published.
- Archibald MacLeish

For women, then, poetry…is a vital necessity of our existence. It forms the quality of light within which we predicate our hopes and dreams toward survival and change, first made into language, then into idea, then into more tangible action. Poetry is the way we help give name to the nameless so it can be thought. The farthest horizons of our hopes and fears are cobbled by our poems carved from the rock experiences of our daily lives.
- Audre Lorde, *Sister/Outsider*

Poetic reverie is a reverie which poetry puts on the right track, the track of expanding consciousness follows. This reverie is written, or, at least promises to be written. It is already facing the great universe of the blank page. Then images begin to compose and fall into place.
- Gaston Bachelard, *The Poetics of Reverie*

Poetry is the insulation that lies between the inner walls of the mind.
- Robert M. Hensel

Poetry is a response to the daily necessity of getting the world right.
- Wallace Stevens, *Opus Posthumous*

For most people, poetry is a solitary affair, like meditation or prayer.
- Bill Moyers, *Fooling with Words*

Poetry does not move us to be just or unjust in itself. It moves us to thoughts in whose light justice and injustice are seen with a fearful sharpness of outline.
- J. Bronowski, *The Common Sense of Science*

There's an awful lot of fussing and fiddling; I feel that the writing of a poem is a very conscious act…very often poems begin, for me, with words. So that very often when I leap out of bed in the dark, the thing that I want to jot down is a set of words in a certain order, which will be the nucleus of whatever is going to come.
- Anthony Hecht, in Mihaly Csikszentmihalyi, *Creativity*

We are protected, mercifully on the whole, from the knowledge of the power of our thoughts. That is one reason why I never put my darkest thoughts into poetry.
- Katherine Raine [Robin Skelton, *The Poet's Calling*]

We live in a culture in which it is easier to publish a book about poetry than a book of poems.
- Theodore Roethke

Consider: I. That the whole world is material for poetry; II. That there is not a specifically poetic material.
- Wallace Stevens

Poetry is just the evidence of life. If your life is burning well, poetry is just the ash.
- Leonard Cohen

Eloquence is heard, poetry is overheard.
- John Stuart Mill. "Thoughts on Poetry and Its Varieties"

I don't look on poetry as closed works. I feel they're going on all the time in my head and I occasionally snip off a length.
- John Ashbery, London *Times*, 23 Aug '84

The success of the poem is determined, not by how much the poet felt in writing it, but by how much the reader feels in reading it.
- John Ciardi

Wanted: a needle swift enough to sew this poem into a blanket.
- Charles Simic

Stickiness, memorability, is one sign of a good poem. You hear it and a day later some of it is still there in the brainpan…What makes a poem memorable is its narrative line. A story is easier to remember than a puzzle.
- Garrison Keillor, *Good Poems*

Poetry should help, not only to refine the language of the time, but to prevent it from changing too rapidly.
- T.S. Eliot

You will find poetry nowhere unless you bring some of it with you.
- Joseph Joubert

A poem is never a put-up job, so to speak. It begins as a lump in the throat, a sense of wrong, a homesickness, a lovesickness. It is never a thought to begin with…A poem is best read in the light of all the other poems every written.
- Robert Frost, *Robert Frost On Writing*, Elaine Berry

If after I read a poem the world looks like that poem for 24 hours, or so, I'm sure it's a good one.
- Elizabeth Bishop

Poems of great energy are usually distillations of words and sentiments outside themselves. Poems are by nature a compression.
> - Guy Davenport, *The Geography of the Imagination*

Poetry is as necessary to comprehension as science. It is as impossible to live without reverence as it is without joy.
> - Henry Beston, *The Outermost House*

A poem is a pheasant disappearing into the brush.
> - Wallace Stevens

Poetry is a deal of joy and pain and wonder, with a dash of the dictionary.
> - Kahlil Gibran

In writing poetry, all of one's attention is focused on some inner voice.
> - Li Young Lee

The poem is a thousand times closer to the concerto or the painting than it is to the sermon, speech, article, editorial, or discussion.
> - Rod Jellema

Poetry should surprise by a fine excess, and not be singularity...if poetry comes not as naturally as leaves to a tree it had better not come at all.
> - John Keats, letter

Poetry is the art of overhearing ourselves say things from which it is impossible to retreat. A true line acts like a lightning rod in a storm...The difficult part about writing poetry is that you must go your own way to write the poem. But having done that, the poem must belong to everyone.
> - David Whyte, *The Heart Aroused*

A perfect poem is impossible. Once it had been written, the world would end.
> - Robert Graves

Herman has taken to writing poetry. You need not tell anyone, for you know how such things get around.
> - Elizabeth Melville, letter

Not gods, nor men, nor even booksellers have put up with poets' being second-rate.
> - Horace

I can understand your wanting to write poems, but I don't quite know what you mean by "being a poet"…
- T.S. Eliot, *World Within World*

Poets, like small children and magicians, cannot help believing that words may affect reality.
- Robin Skelton, *The Poet's Calling*

Yes, there is a Nirvana; it is in leading your sheep to a green pasture, and in putting your child to sleep, and in writing the last line of your poem.
- Kahilil Gibran

One of my latest sensations was going to Lady Airlie's to hear Browning read his own poems—with the comport of finding that, at least, if you don't understand them, he himself apparently understands them even less. He read them as if he hated them and would like to bite them to pieces.
- Henry James

I like the poem on the page and not at the podium. I like to address the poem in peace and quiet, not on the edge of a folding chair with a full bladder. I can't stand a poem I can't see.
- Ted Kooser

The poet presents his thoughts festively, on the carriage of rhythm: usually because they could not walk.
- Friedrich Wilhelm Nietzche

Poets are simply those who have made a profession and a lifestyle of being in touch with their bliss.
- Joseph Campbell

The true poet is all the time a visionary and whether with friends or not, as much alone as a man on his deathbed.
- W.B. Yeats.

A poet's work is to name the unnameable, to point at frauds, to take sides, start arguments, shape the world, and stop it going to sleep.
- Salman Rushdie

God is the perfect poet.
- Robert Browning

Poets are the athletes of language.
- Robert W. Boynton and Maynard Mack, *Introduction to the Poem*

A poet looks at the world the way a man looks at a woman.
- Wallace Stevens, *Opus Posthumous*

The poet is a good citizen turned inside out.
- W.B. Yeats

My opinion is that a poet should express the emotion of all the ages and thoughts of his own.
- Thomas Hardy

No poet or novelist wishes he were the only one who ever lived, but most of them wish they were the only one alive, and quite a number fondly believe their wish has been granted.
- W.H. Auden

A poet can't afford to be aloof. The tools of his trade are the people he bumps up against.
- Rod McKuen, *On Being a Writer*

I may as well tell you, here and now, that if you are going about the place thinking things are pretty, you will never make a modern poet. Be poignant, man, be poignant!
- P.G. Wodehouse, *The Small Bachelor*

Being a poet is one of the unhealthier jobs—no regular hours, so many temptations!
- Elizabeth Bishop

The poet may be used as a barometer, but let us not forget that he is also part of the weather.
- Lionel Trilling

Poets are almost always bald when they get to be about forty.
- John Masefield

As to experience—well, think how little some good poets have had, or how much some bad ones have.
- Elizabeth Bishop

Poets are the antennae of the race.
- Ezra Pound

A poet never takes notes. You never take notes in a love affair.
- Robert Frost, *Interviews with Robert Frost*

He would be a poet…who nailed words to their primitive senses, as farmers drive stakes in the spring, which the frost has heaved; who derived his words as often as he used them—transplanted them to his page with earth adhering to their roots.
- Henry David Thoreau, *Walking*

Poets are like baseball pitchers. Both have their moments. The intervals are the tough times.
- Robert Frost

Poets are like magicians, searching for the magical phrases to pull rabbits out of people's souls.
- Glade Byron Addams

The poet advises: "Read me. Read me again."
- René Char

Immature poets imitate; mature poets steal.
- T.S. Eliot, *The Sacred Wood*

All poets adore explosions, thunderstorms, tornadoes, conflagrations, ruins, scenes of spectacular carnage.
- W.H. Auden, *The Dyer's Hand*

It is a great fault, in descriptive poetry, to describe everything.
- Alexander Pope

The poet who writes "free" verse is like Robinson Crusoe on his desert island: he must do all his cooking, laundry and darning for himself.
- W.H. Auden, *The Dyer's Hand*

What a mystery Auden is! He has made a new kind of poetry, far more original even than Eliot, I think, a kind of poetry based on the antithesis of the "poetic" as we used to know it, never inflated, ironic, anti-romantic, witty.
- May Sarton, *Journal of a Solitude*

There are four orders of poets: 1) Those who see clearly, but feel too little; 2) Those who feel strongly, but think less and see untruly; 3) Those who feel greatly, think deeply, see lucidly; 4) The one who synthesizes all these perceptions, yet the vision takes him over and he speaks beyond himself.
- John Ruskin

A poet dares be just so clear and no clearer...He unzips the veil from beauty, but does not remove it. A poet utterly clear is a trifle glaring.
- E.B. White

Writing a poem is...a kind of possible love affair between something like the heart and the learned skills of the conscious mind. They make appointments with each other and keep them and something begins to happen.
- Mary Oliver, *A Poetry Handbook*

I write very personal poems but I hope that they will become the central theme to someone else's private life.
- Anne Sexton

If your everyday life seems poor to you, do not accuse it; accuse yourself, tell yourself you are not poet enough to summon up its riches; since for the creator there is no poverty and no poor or unimportant place.
- Rainer Maria Rilke

I try to keep a clear line between say...journal jottings and poems—and again, the real line is in the music and the density—although, to be fair, not all my poems are that dense in terms of content analysis, but have maybe a musical density sometimes.
- Gary Snyder, *The Real Work*

I have not written in sonnet form for a long time, but at every major crisis in my life when I reach a point of clarification, where pain is transcended by the quality of the experience itself, sonnets come. Whole lines run through my head and I cannot stop writing until whatever it is gets said.
- May Sarton, *Journal of A Solitude*

The poet doesn't invent. He listens.
- Jean Cocteau

Poets are mysterious, but a poet when all is said and done is not much more mysterious than a banker.
- Allen Tate

A good poet is someone who manages, in a lifetime of standing out in thunderstorms, to be struck by lightning five or six times; a dozen or two dozen times and he is great.
- Randall Jarrell, *Poetry and the Age*

The poet only asks to get his head into the heavens. It is the logician who seeks to get the heavens into his head. And it is his head that splits.
- G. K. Chesterton

When asked why he decided to become a poet at the age of seven, Gyögy Faludy answered, "Because I was afraid to die."
- Mihaly Csikszentmihalyi, *Creativity*

One of the ridiculous aspects of being a poet is the huge gulf between how seriously we take ourselves and how generally we are ignored by everybody else.
- Billy Collins

Poets stick to nothing deliberately, but let what will stick to them, like burrs when they walk in the fields.
- Robert Frost, *The Poet's Calling*, Robin Skelton

To be a poet is a condition, not a profession.
- Robert Frost

Poets will never be the highest-paid writers in the world. Instead, poetry will go on cutting a hand-made path through the mass-market insanity. For me, anyway, that path is the one that leads to the Chapel of the Grail.
- Jeanette Winterson

Poets, like small children and magicians, cannot help believing that words may affect reality...Poets are absolutely unable to "put away childish things."
- Robin Skelton, *The Poet's Calling*

A poet must leave traces of his passage, not proof.
- René Char

Poetry is the synthesis of hyacinths and biscuits.
- Carl Sandburg

The words for "poet," "singer," and "magician" go back to the same linguistic root not only in Latin but in many other languages.
- Joachim Berendt, *Nada Brahma: The World is Sound*

I'd as soon write free verse as play tennis with the net down.
   - Robert Frost, *Interviews with Robert Frost*

People who can write poems, or who want to write poems, are people who don't have walls…Without walls you feel physically, through the cells, something beyond the immediate physical reality…Poets don't have the protection and the blindness that the walls offer.
   - Jeni Couzyn, *The Poet's Calling*, Robin Skelton

God robbed poets of their minds that they might be made expressions of his own.
   - Theodore Roethke, from his notebooks

Poems flew at him…until just words beat at his head like many wings.
   - Mary von Schrader Randall Jarrell's second wife

Most people think of poets as 1/3 lazy, 1/3 phony, and 1/3 organically eccentric.
   - Hart Crane

The poet is a liar who always speaks the truth.
   - Jean Cocteau

In Russia all tyrants believe poets to be their worst enemies.
   - Yevgeny Yevtushenko, *A Precocious Autobiography*

No honest poet can ever feel quite sure of the permanence of what he has written; he may have wasted his time and messed up his life for nothing.
   - T.S. Eliot

Remind yourself once more of the absolute holiness of your task.
   - Theodore Roethke

A true poet does not bother to be poetical. Nor does a nursery gardener scent his roses.
   - Jean Cocteau

The poet knows himself only on the condition that things resound in him, and that in him, at a single awakening, they and he come forth together out of sleep.
   - Jacques Maritain

A poet can't afford to be aloof. The tools of his trade are the people he bumps up against.
- Rod McKuen, *On Being a Writer*

Children and lunatics cut the Gordian knot which the poet spend his life patiently trying to untie.
- Jean Cocteau

Everything in creation has its appointed painter or poet and remains in bondage like the princess in the fairy tale 'til its appropriate liberator comes to set it free.
- Ralph Waldo Emerson

Only the poet who writes, speaks his message across the millennia to other hearts.
- Loren Eiseley, *The America Scholar*

Nothing whips my blood like verse.
- William Carlos Williams, *The Selected Letters of William Carlos Williams*

"Therefore" is a word the poet must not know.
- André Gide

Poets are the only people to whom love is not only a crucial, but an indispensable experience, which entitles them to mistake it for a universal one.
- Hannah Arendt

Poets are soldiers that liberate words from the steadfast possession of definition.
- Eli Khamarov, *The Shadow Zone*

Hölderlin says: "What endures/the poets create." The creation of such permanence is the result of following longing to the outposts, beyond every cozy or settled shelter, until some echo of the eternal belonging is sounded.
- John O'Donohue, *Eternal Echoes*

Poets are the unacknowledged legislators of the world.
- Percy Bysshe Shelley

A poet's autobiography is his poetry. Anything else can be only a footnote.
- Yevgeny Yevtushenko, *The Sole Survivor*

A poet is, before anything else, a person who is passionately in love with language.
- W.H. Auden, NY *Times* 9 Oct.'60

A poet is an unhappy being whose heart is torn by secret sufferings, but whose lips are so strangely formed that when the sighs and the cries that escape them, they sound like beautiful music.
- Søren Kierkegaard

A poet is a penguin—his wings are to swim with.
- e.e.cummings, *1: Six Non-Lectures*

A poet can survive almost anything but a misprint.
- Oscar Wilde

Poets are the mortals who, singing earnestly of the wine-god, sense the trace of the fugitive gods, stay on the gods' tracks, and so trace for their kindred mortals the way toward the turning.
- Martin Heidegger, *Poetry, Language, Thought*

Everyone starts out as a poet, then realizes it's too hard.
- James Joyce

Every poet knows the pun is...a matching and shifting of vowels and consonants, an adroit assonance sometimes derided as jackassonance.
- Louis Untermeyer, *Bygones*

If everyone became a poet, the world would be so much better. We would all read to each other.
- Nikki Giovanni

15.

How do I go about writing comedy and satire?

Humor is wonderful food for the soul. Too much seriousness violates the laws of nature. Living a humorless life, turning a blind eye to the paradoxes around and within us, or never laughing at ourselves shrinks the soul.
- Mathew Fox, *Handbook for the Soul*

Even the gods love jokes.
- Plato

You grow up the day you have the first real laugh at yourself.
- Ethel Barrymore

A laugh is the shortest distance between two people.
- Victor Borge

At the height of laughter the universe is flung into a kaleidoscope of new possibilities.
- Jean Houston

Laughter is cosmic joy juice…we pretend we are separate from one another. But the contagion of laughter reminds us we are one.
- Annette Goodheart, *New Realities*

Mirth cleanses the mind of its crazy cobweb designs, leaving space for nurturing to take place.
- Peter Balin, *The Flight of the Feathered Serpent*

Humor attends the embraces of incompatibles…Humor mischievously furnishes time out.
- Sidney Cox, *Indirections for Those Who Want to Write*

Humor is by far the most significant activity of the human brain.
- Edward De Bono

Comedy keeps the heart sweet.
- Mark Twain, "About Play-Acting"

My mother wanted us to understand that the tragedies of your life one day have the potential to be comic stories the next.
- Nora Ephron

Total absence of humor renders life impossible.
- Colette

Drama is like a plate of meat and potatoes; comedy is rather the dessert, a bit like meringue.
- Woody Allen

Humor is just another defense against the universe.
- Mel Brooks

Humor has a tremendous healing effect...[it] is the sudden seeing of the opposite of what we expect to see. As soon as we can say, "I see the other side," a tension is released and reconciliation can take place—that is what humor is all about.
- Herbert B. Puryear, *Edgar Cayce: Reflections of the Path*

The human race has one really effective weapon, and that is laughter.
- Mark Twain

Tension is wonderful for making people laugh.
- John Cleese

The secret of humor is surprise.
- Aristotle

Freud relished anecdotes and jokes, particularly Jewish jokes, because they were so pregnant with unconscious meanings. Like metaphors, jokes suggest rather than announce their meaning.
- Bruno Bettelheim, *Freud and Man's Soul*

Comedy is slightly cruel, slightly crass and if you want to make it palatable, it has to be slightly civilized...To write comedy, you need an above-average gift for self-expression, for writing, but the important thing, is, to go with above-average talent, you should have average tastes.
- Carl Reiner

Comedy is not so much what you do as what you don't do.
- Groucho Marx

Comedy is tragedy that happens to other people.
- Angela Carter

Comedy, if it's about anything at all, is about something gone wrong.
- Steve Allen

Comedy is an escape, not from truth but from despair; a narrow escape into faith.
- Christopher Fry

All I need to make a comedy is a part, a policeman and a pretty girl.
- Charlie Chaplin

I was doing stand-up at a restaurant and there was a chalkboard on the street out front. It said, Soup of the Day: Cream of Asparagus Ellen DeGeneres.
- Ellen De Generes

Humor is comedy in slow motion.
- Garrison Keillor

Humorists can never start to take themselves seriously. It's literary suicide.
- Erma Bombeck

Comedy naturally wears itself out—destroys the very food on which it lives…
- William Hazlitt

It's much easier to write a solemn book than a funny book. It's harder to make people laugh than it is to make them cry. People are always on the verge of tears.
- Fran Lebowitz

The only rules comedy can tolerate are those of taste, and the only limitations are those of libel.
- James Thurber

I always loved comedy, but I never knew it was something you could learn to do. I always thought that some people are born comedians—just like some people are born dentists.
- Paul Reiser

It's hard enough to write a good drama, it's much harder to write a good comedy, and it's hardest of all to write a drama with comedy. Which is what life is.
- Jack Lemmon

Comedy comes from conflict, from hatred.
- Warren Mitchell

The comic spirit is given to us in order that we may analyze, weigh, and clarify things in us which nettle us, or which we are outgrowing, or trying to reshape.
- Thornton Wilder

The humorous story may be spun out to great length, and may wander around as much as it pleases, and arrive nowhere in particular; but the comic and witty stories must be brief and end with a point. The humorous story bubbles gently along, the others burst.
- Mark Twain, "How to Tell a Story"

A man's got to take a lot of punishment to write a really funny book.
- Ernest Hemingway

I have a fine sense of the ridiculous, but no sense of humor.
- Edward Albee

Among those whom I like or admire, I can find no common denominator, but among those whom I love, I can: all of them make me laugh.
- W.H. Auden

Analyzing humor is like dissecting a frog. Few people are interested and the frog dies of it.
- E.B. White

Our "humor" is our general elasticity of mood, our resiliency, our give-and-take, our play, our flow.
- Jack Maguire, *The Power of Personal Storytelling*

The strongest should come first in comedy because once a character is really established as funny everything he does becomes funny. At least that's the way in life…
- F. Scott Fitzgerald, *The Pat Hobley Stories*

Comedy is tragedy plus time.
- Carol Burnett

If you're not allowed to laugh in heaven, I don't want to go there.
  - Martin Luther

Humor is the most engaging cowardice.
  - Robert Frost, *Selected Letters of Robert Frost*

Comedy is simply a funny way of being serious.
  - Peter Ustinov

The wit makes fun of other persons; the satirist makes fun of the world; the humorist makes fun of himself.
  - James Thurber

I don't analyze something and then do a cartoon about it…Funny words, or at least words I think are funny, often get me going in the direction of a gag…The source should never show. The newspapers I give a real going over are small-town newspapers written by amateurs…I agree with E. B. White when he says that analyzing humor is like dissecting a frog. You can spread the pieces all over the table, but in the process you lose something. The important thing for me is to see the little things that everyone sees, the things they see and ignore, things that are so familiar you don't notice them, and laugh at them until they are drawn on paper.
  - George Booth, *People Books, Book People* [David W. McCullough]

Defining and analyzing humor is a pastime of humorless people.
  - Robert Benchley

In merciless and rollicking comedy life is caught in the act.
  - George Santayana

There are things of deadly earnest that can only be mentioned under the cover of a joke.
  - J. J. Procter

If I want to tell a joke, I tell the truth: There's nothing funnier.
  - George Bernard Shaw

Humor is, I think, the subtlest and chanciest of literary forms. It is surely not accidental that there are a thousand novelists, essayists, poets or journalists for each humorist. It is a long, long time between James Thurbers.
  - Leo Rosten

Nine-tenths of the value of a sense of humor in writing is not in the things it makes one write but in the things it keeps one from writing. It is especially valuable in this respect in serious writing, and no one without a sense of humor should ever write seriously. For without knowing what is funny one is constantly in danger of being funny without knowing it.
> - Robert Benchley

The humorous story is told gravely; the teller does his best to conceal the fact that he even dimly suspects that there is anything funny about it.
> - Mark Twain, "How to Tell a Story"

Humor is also a way of saying something serious.
> - T.S. Eliot

Humor is emotional chaos remembered in tranquility.
> - James Thurber

Wherever you find humor, you find pathos close beside it.
> - Edwin P. Whipple

You can only be funny if you have matters of great importance on your mind.
> - Kurt Vonnegut

If you can find humor in it, you can survive it.
> - Bill Cosby

I regard the writing of humor as a supreme artistic challenge.
> - Herman Wouk, *Book-of-the-Month Club News*

The humour of Dostoievsky is the humour of a bar-loafer who ties a kettle to a dog's tail.
> - W. Somerset Maugham

Humor is mankind's biggest blessing.
> - Mark Twain

Common sense and a sense of humor are the same thing, moving at different speeds. A sense of humor is just common sense, dancing.
> - William James

Comedy is simply a funny way of being serious.
> - Peter Ustinov

Vulgarity is a necessary part of a complete author's equipment; and the clown is sometimes the best part of the circus.
- George Bernard Shaw

A humorist's funny bone is like an athlete's muscles or a singer's vocal cords. They work best when they're warmed up first.
- Melvin Helitzer, *Comedy Writing Secrets*

My one rule is to be true rather than funny.
- Bill Cosby

Humor is a rubber sword—it allows you to make a point without drawing blood.
- Mary Hirsch

It's very much easier to be tragic than it is to be comic.
- Robertson Davies in Mihaly Csikszentmihalyi, *Creativity*

I think it's the duty of the comedian to find out where the line is drawn and cross it deliberately.
- George Carlin

Comedy has to be based on truth. You take the truth and you put a little curlicue at the end.
- Sid Caesar

…humor is written backwards. That means you find the cliché you want to work on, then build a story around it. The trick is not to telegraph it…On the West Coast they say that not waiting until the last word to divulge the surprise is going past the "post office window." On the East Coast, more racetrack oriented, they call it going past the "pay off window."
- Melvin Helitzer, *Comedy Writing Secrets*

Many a true word is spoken in jest.
- English Proverb

Humor is…despair refusing to take itself seriously.
- Arland Ussher

A joke is total knowledge in a nanosecond.
- Steve Martin

Humor is reason gone mad.
> - Groucho Marx

"Black humor" is a sophomoric attempt to disguise self-hatred.
> - Paul Horgan, *Approaches to Writing*

Tragedy is a close-up; comedy, a long shot.
> - Buster Keaton

After God created the world, He made man and woman. Then, to keep the whole thing from collapsing, He invented humor.
> - Bill Kelly

Laughter is carbonated holiness.
> - Anne Lamott

A caricature is putting the face of a joke on the body of a truth.
> - Joseph Conrad

Humor is merely tragedy standing on its head with its pants torn.
> - Irvin Cobb

An emotional man may possess no humor, but a humorous man usually has deep pockets of emotion, sometimes tucked away or forgotten.
> - Constance Rourke

Chaos in the midst of chaos isn't funny, but chaos in the midst of order is.
> - Steve Martin

The opposite of gravity is levity.
> - Nancy Margulies

Wit is a weapon. Jokes are a masculine way of inflicting superiority. But humor is the pursuit of a gentle grin, usually in solitude.
> - Frank Muir

I have a "call" to literature of a low order—i.e. humorous. It is nothing to be proud of, but it is my strongest suit...seriously scribbling to excite the laughter of God's creatures.
> - Mark Twain

The person who knows how to laugh at himself will never cease to be amused.
- Shirley MacLaine

Jokes of the proper kind, properly told, can do more to enlighten questions of politics, philosophy, and literature than any number of dull arguments.
- Isaac Asimov

Humor results when society says you can't scratch certain things in public, but they itch in public.
- Tom Walsh

There must be courage; there must be no awe. There must be criticism, for humor, to my mind, is encapsulated in criticism. There must be a disciplined eye and a wild mind.
- Dorothy Parker

A brilliant epigram is a solemn platitude gone to a masquerade ball.
- Lionel Strachey

The absolute truth is the thing that makes people laugh.
- Carl Reiner

Everything is funny as long as it is happening to somebody else.
- Will Rogers

A poor joke must invent its own laughter.
- Latin Proverb

A satirist is a man whose flesh creeps so at the ugly and the savage and the incongruous aspects of society that he has to express them as brutally and nakedly as possible in order to get relief.
- John Dos Passos, *Occasions and Protests*

The satirist shoots to kill while the humorist brings his prey back alive and eventually releases him again for another chance.
- Peter De Vries

Satires which the censor can understand are justly forbidden.
- Karl Kraus

In the end, everything is a gag.
- Charlie Chaplin

You can't blunt the edge of wit or the point of satire with obscurity. Try to imagine a famous witty saying that is not immediately clear.
        - James Thurber

16.

What should I know about editors and publishers?

Editor: The author's first real reader.
  - William Sloane, *The Craft of Writing*

They are conceited and troublesome, and don't pay enough...I hate editors, for they make me abandon a lot of perfectly good English words.
  - Mark Twain

I love deadlines. I like the whooshing sound they make as they fly by.
  - Douglas Adams

One should fight like the devil the temptation to think well of editors. They are all, without exception—at least some of the time, incompetent or crazy.
  - John Gardner

[An editor is someone who] Rides in the whirlwind and directs the storm.
  - Joseph Addison

The unconscious creates, the ego edits.
  - Stanley Kunitz

Aspiring authors rarely meet editors, and so they imagine a race of deities in the misty heights of the publishing empyrean. Wrathful and capricious, these higher beings decree which writerlings shall be raised from obscurity and which consigned to the hell of the unpublished.
  - Arthur Plotnik, *The Elements of Authorship*

And let me say this about editors in general: Not having a good one is like doing brain surgery with a butter knife—you can do it, but you're always paranoid the other surgeons are rolling their eyes when you're not looking. What a relief to have someone standing next to you hand you a sharp scalpel and just say, "Cut that thing, Gary! Right there! Cut it, damn you!"
  - Gary Larson, *The Complete Far Side*

There are two kinds of editors, those who correct your copy and those who say it's wonderful.
        - Theodore H. White

Editors drive us nuts. We go from near-worshipful groveling when we submit to bitter cursing when they reject us.
        - Ken Rand

The road to ignorance is paved with good editors.
        - George Bernard Shaw

An editor selects manuscripts; a publisher selects editors.
        - M. Lincoln Schuster

An editor is someone who separates the wheat from the chaff and then prints the chaff.
        - Adlai Stevenson

How often we recall, with regret, that Napoleon once shot at a magazine editor and missed him and killed a publisher. But we remember with charity, that his intentions were good.
        - Mark Twain

An editor ought to have a pimp for a brother, so he'd have somebody to look up to.
        - Gene Fowler

You don't want to depend on an editor. If you want to regret something for the rest of your life, you want to make sure you're responsible for it.
        - Robert Stone

Editing tends to make best-sellers read more like each other.
        - Norman Mailer, *The Spooky Art*

A gifted editor once told me that what she most looked for in a new writer was "the glint of obsession."
        - Sarah Harrison

The writer who can't do his job looks to his editor to do it for him, though he won't dream of sharing his royalties with that editor.
        - Alfred Knopf

Editing is the same as quarreling with writers.
- Harold Ross

The better a book is, the slower I go.
- Max Perkins, A Scott Berg, *Max Perkins: Editor of Genius*

To editors dullness, not dishonesty, is the unforgivable sin.
- Donna Woolfolk Cross, *Word Abuse*

It's best for writers to determine where they stand with an editor before asking for more money.
- Steven Biller

Re-vision is re-seeing the topic so the writer can discover meaning. Editing is making the meaning clear so a reader can understand the meaning.
- Donald Murray

You write to communicate to the hearts and minds of others what's burning inside you. And we edit to let the fire show through the smoke.
- Arthur Polotnik

If navigating the editor-writer relationship is like dating, then an editor's long-term commitment to you must be a marriage made in heaven.
- Gretchen Roberts

The job of editor in a publishing house is the dullest, hardest, most exciting, exasperating and rewarding of perhaps any job in the world.
- John Hall Wheelock

Some editors are failed writers, but so are most writers.
- T. S. Eliot

The successful editor is one who is constantly finding new writers, nurturing their talents, and publishing them with critical and financial success.
- A. Scott Berg

I am thoroughly convinced that editors don't help authors.
- Henry Louis Mencken

An editor should tell the author his writing is better than it is. Not a lot better, a little better.
- T. S. Eliot

Don't forget, both you and the editor are putting on an unceasing act for the public, and between you there should be the same relation that exists between the magician and his assistant, offstage.
- Jack Woodford

Don't ever get to feeling important about yourself…an editor can only get as much out of an author as the author has in him.
- Maxwell Perkins

The only way I can write a decent story is to imagine no one's going to accept it and who cares. Self-consciousness about editors is ruinous to me. They can make their criticisms afterwards…
- F. Scott Fitzgerald, *Letters*

Great editors do not discover nor produce great authors; great authors create and produce great publishers.
- John Farrar

Remember that the editor is only a lens for the reader, a front for the market.
- Sherwood Eliot Wirt, *The Making of a Writer*

In an art form like film-making, we know that editing and revising cannot be dismissed as superfluous, for they are an integral part of the whole process. In fact, what we eventually see on the screen is not what was filmed, but what was edited.
- William Irmscher, *Teaching Expository Writing*

Editors are extremely fallible people, all of them. Don't put too much trust in them.
- Max Perkins

There is a difference between a book of two hundred pages from the very beginning, and as book of two hundred pages which is the result of an original eight hundred pages. The six hundred are there. Only you don't see them.
- Elie Wiesel

No passion in the world is equal to the passion to alter someone else's draft.
- H.G. Wells

An editor has been defined as someone who tells a writer when to stop writing.
- Kenneth Atchity, *A Writer's Time*

An editor likes what an editor likes, and often an editor cannot tell you what the editor likes until a neatly typed, polished manuscript is on the desk.
- Charles Austin, *The Complete Guide to Writing Nonfiction*, ed. by Glen Evans

If that first and most important paragraph does not slap and sparkle like the sun in water, then we editors can't bother unduly with the rest.
- Brian Vachon

No need to change title. Easier to change publishers.
- Graham Greene, telegram to publisher, *Aren't We Due a Royalty Statement?*

The editor is an intermediary between creativity and its markets.
- Kenneth Atchity, *A Writer's Time*

The poem will please if it is lively—if it is stupid it will fail—but I will have none of your damned cutting and slashing.
- Lord Byron, letter to publisher

An editor must engage himself to that most difficult of human problems—making up his mind.
- Fredson Bowers

An editor does not add to a book. At best, he serves as a handmaiden to an author. Don't ever get to feeling important about yourself, because an editor at most releases energy. He creates nothing.
- Max Perkins [A. Scott Berg, *Max Perkins—Editor of Genius*]

Your best defense to protect yourself in dealing with agents and editors is to be like a toasted marshmallow, crisp and tough on the outside, while maintaining your warmth and softness on the inside—the softness that gave you the sensitivity to understand your material.
- Frances Spatz Leighton

It [*Auntie Mame*] circulated for five years, through the halls of fifteen publishers, and finally ended up with Vanguard Press, which, as you can see, is rather deep into the alphabet.
- Patrick Dennis

[about her first editor at Houghton Mifflin] You hear all these terrible stories about how nobody wants to read a [first novel]; my experience hasn't been that way. There are a lot of schleppy editors; there are a lot of schleppy anything, but there are a lot of good editors and good houses who are just waiting and who are willing to take the risk. I had 100 pages and no more, and I had never written a novel before.
>   - Alice McDermott, *A Voice of One's Own*, Mickey Pearlman and
>   Katherine Usher Henderson

No passion in the world is equal to the passion to alter someone else's draft.
>   - H. G. Wells

Never throw up on an editor.
>   - Ellen Datlow

There are basically three kinds of rejection letters. The printed form, the modified printed form and the personal. They all hurt.
>   - Jane Yolen, *Take Joy*

Rejection is painful and constant.
>   - Bill Roorbach, *Writing Life Stories*

Rejection feels awful…Acceptance feels wonderful.
>   - Bruce Holland Rogers, *Word Work*

You have to know how to accept rejection and reject acceptance.
>   - Ray Bradbury

If a publisher declines your manuscript, remember it is merely the decision of one fallible human being, and try another.
>   - Stanley Unwin

…a rejection…may well reflect more unfavorably on the editor's ability than yours.
>   - Judith Appelbaum

The writer must learn to live with his rejection slips, use them for scrap paper, not label them "End of the World."
>   - Isabelle Ziegler, *Creative Writing*

For every person who will say yes, there are twenty who will say no. For a positive response you must find the twenty-first person.
>   - Chuck Reaves, *The Theory of 21*

The great American novel has not only already been written; it has already been rejected.
>   - Frank Dane

Rejection slip quotations:

It is impossible to sell animal stories in the U.S.A.
>   - George Orwell's *Animal Farm*

The girl doesn't, it seems to me, have a special perception or feeling which would lift that book above the "curiosity" level.
>   - Anne Frank, *Diary of Anne Frank*

Burn it, son, burn it. Fire is a great refiner.
>   - Harry Crews' short stories

This manuscript of yours that has just come back from another editor is a precious package. Don't consider it rejected. Consider that you've addressed it "to the editor who can appreciate my work" and it has simply come back stamped "not at this address." Just keep looking for the right address.
>   - Barbara Kingsolver

I discovered that rejections are not altogether a bad thing. They teach a writer to rely on his own judgment and to say in his heart of hearts, "To hell with you."
>   - Saul Bellow

There are few things more frustrating than having a story turned down because it doesn't fit publishing policies; this still leaves unanswered the question of whether the story is any good in its own right.
>   - Christopher Evans, *Writing Science Fiction*

When the English writer Barbara Pym's eighth novel was arbitrarily turned down by the publisher of her first seven, she was unable to write a line for the next sixteen years.
>   - Victoria Nelson, *Writer's Block and How to Use It*

No matter how good you are, nobody is going to come knocking at your door. You have to take the risk of rejection, and get that material out there… Understand, too, that things get rejected for a lot of reasons. Your writing may be wonderful—it may be your timing, your subject, or an editor's quirks that get between you and a sale. Try to find your richest joy and satisfaction in the writing itself. Let the rest be gravy. Good gravy, but gravy.
- Elizabeth Berg, *Escaping Into the Open*

Tony Hillerman was instructed to "get rid of all that Indian stuff" if he wanted to revise and have the editor reconsider that first novel.
- Bruce Holland Rogers, *Word Work*

A writer needs the sensitivity of a butterfly in touching the outside world—and the skin of a rhino to withstand its disregard.
- Sophy Burnham, *For Writers Only*

Your manuscript is both good and original; but the part that is good is not original, and the part that is original is not good.
- Commonly misattributed to Samuel Johnson

"We have read your manuscript with boundless delight. If we were to publish your book it would be impossible for us to publish any work of lower standard. And as it is unthinkable that in the next thousand years we shall see its equal, we are, to our regret, compelled to return your divine composition, and to beg you a thousand times to overlook our short sight and timidity."
- from a Chinese Publisher

No author is a man of genius to his publisher.
- Heinrich Heine

What the public wants, no one knows. Not even the publishers.
- Henry Miller

I'm not saying all publishers have to be literary, but *some* interest in books would help.
- A.N. Wilson

The big houses…basically give a book a six-week look; then they move on.
- Ken Blanchard, *Fast Company*, Nov. 2005

A lot of publishers treat authors like nuisances. We treat them like partners.
- Steve Piersanti, Berrett Koehler Catalogue

Writers are always a great nuisance to the publishers. If they could do without them, they would.
- Fay Weldon

The publisher is a middleman, he calls the tune to which the whole rest of the trade dances; and he does so because he pays the piper.
- Geoffrey Faber

Publishing skills are far more important than publishing technology. It would be better to have 500 words of the right content handwritten on scrap paper, delivered by snail mail, than to have 5,000 words of waffle sent by high-speed wireless to your mobile phone.
- Gerry McGovern and Rob Norton, *Content Critical*

Lightning does occasionally strike and occasionally the result isn't a corpse.
- Tillie Olsen

Great editors do not discover nor produce great authors; great authors create and produce great publishers.
- John Farrar

Publication is a self-invasion of privacy.
- Marshall McLuhan

Publication is not a gauge of excellence. This is harder to learn than anything about publishing, and very important.
- Annie Dillard, "Notes for Young Writers"

The fact is, fiction hasn't a chance to breathe under the weight of publishing anxieties…It should ride them out, not carry them on its back.
- Lynn Freed, *Reading, Writing and Leaving Home*

A certain editor and publisher said that you can't publish more than one book a year because you are then automatically considered a hack. I pointed out that Charles Dickens wrote every week, and that they were wrong. Totally.
- Robert Ludlum, in Richard Joseph, *Bestsellers: Top Writers Tell How*

As repressed sadists are supposed to become policemen or butchers so those with irrational fear of life become publishers.
- Cyril Connolly

Most writers can write books faster than publishers can write checks.
- Richard Curtis

A publisher is a man who is blamed if a book fails and ignored if it proves a success.
- John Fox, Jr.

If book publishers can't see the writing on the wall, it is because the writing is not on the wall. It is on the computer screen.
- Dan Poynter, *The Self-Publishing Manual*

Publishers are all cohorts of the devil; there must be a special hell for them somewhere.
- Johann Wolfgang von Goethe

Writers take their words seriously—perhaps the last professional class that does—and they struggle to steer their own through the crosswinds of meddling editors and careless typesetters and obtuse and malevolent reviewers into the lap of the ideal reader.
- John Updike

A young musician plays scales in his room and only bores his family. A beginning writer, on the other hand, sometimes has the misfortune of getting into print.
- Marguerite Yourcenar

All publishers are Columbuses. The successful author is their America.
- Mark Twain, *Autobiography of Mark Twain*

The walls are the publishers of the poor.
- Eduardo Galeano

Bringing out our little books was hard work. The great puzzle lay in the difficulty of getting answers of any kind from the publishers to whom we applied.
- Charlotte Bronte

A new firm of publishers has written to me proposing to publish "the successor" of *A Shropshire Lad*. But as they don't also offer to write it, I have had to put them off.
- A.E. Housman, letter

Being published by Oxford University Press is rather like being married to a duchess: the honour is almost greater than the pleasure.
- G.M Young, letter

Publishing is the only industry I can think of where most of the employees spend most of their time stating with great self-assurance that they don't know how to do their jobs. "I don't know how to sell this," they explain, frowning, as though it's your fault. "I don't know how to package this. I don't know what the market is for this book. I don't know how we're going to draw attention to this." In most occupations, people try to hide their incompetence; only in publishing is it flaunted as though it were the chief qualification for the job.
- Donald Westlake

A publisher who writes is like a cow in a milk bar.
- Arthur Koestler

A publisher is simply a useful middle-man.
- Oscar Wilde

There are men that will make you books, and turn them loose into the world, with as much dispatch as they would do a dish of fritters.
- Miguel de Cervantes

Manuscript: something submitted in haste and returned at leisure.
- Oliver Herford

A lot of manuscripts that come in, you wonder by what outrageous fantasy the author believes that this should be pressed into print.
- Lawrence Ferlinghetti

Typos are very important to all written form. It gives the reader something to look for so they aren't distracted by the total lack of content in your writing.
- Randy K. Milholland, *Something Positive Comic*

Publishing a volume of verse is like dropping a rose-petal down the Grand Canyon and waiting for the echo.
- Don Marquis

Publication—is the auction of the Mind of Man.
- Emily Dickinson

Publication is to thinking as childbirth is to the first kiss.
  - Friedrich Von Schlegel

The publishing industry is desperate for original thinkers with an elegant writing style. If you're genuinely good, you will get published eventually.
  - Peter Rubie

Writing is not the lottery. New writers have to be realistic about what it takes to get published. But there is one similarity to the lottery: You have to play to win.
  - Lori Perkins

Let your literary compositions be kept from the public eye for nine years at least.
  - Horace

You've got to write X number of words before you can write anything that can be published, but nobody is able to tell you how many words that is. You will know when you get there, but you don't know how long it will take.
  - Larry Brown

…hardly anybody treats getting published as if it were a rational, manageable activity—like practicing law or laying bricks—in which knowledge coupled with skill and application would suffice to ensure success.
  - Judith Applebaum and Nancy Evans, *How to Get Happily Published*

In a profession where simple accounting is preferable to a degree in English, illiteracy is not considered to be a great drawback.
  - Dominic Behan, *The Public World of Parable Jones*

Proof-reader, n. A malefactor who atones for making your writing nonsense by permitting the compositor to make it unintelligible.
  - Ambrose Bierce, *The Devil's Dictionary*

It has been calculated that each copy of the Guttenberg Bible…required the skins of 300 sheep.
  - From an article on printing

The printing press is either the greatest blessing or the greatest curse of modern times, one sometimes forgets which.
  - James Matthew Barrie

Printing was the reformation; Gutenberg made Luther possible.
- Will Durant, *The Story of Civilization, Vol. 6*

...the Protestants probably could not have pulled off their Reformation without the newfangled printing press, which Luther himself called "God's highest act of grace."...Even in 1455 Johannes Gutenberg already recognized the evangelical power of his invention: "Let us break the seal which seals up the holy things and give wings to Truth in order that she may win every soul that comes into the world by her word, no longer written at great expense by hands easily palsied, but multiplied like the wind of an untiring machine."
- Erik Davis, *TechGnosis*

I was in a Printing-house in Hell, and saw the method in which knowledge is transmitted from generation to generation.
- William Blake, *The Marriage of Heaven and Hell*

Our English word *text* comes from the German *textura*, meaning "tapestry." Early medieval manuscripts bear a closer resemblance to a medieval tapestry than to a modern page of writing.
- Leonard Schlain, *The Alphabet Versus the Goddess*

Publishing is as much about what you don't publish as what you do.
- Gerry McGovern and Rob Norton, *Content Critical*

And it does no harm to repeat, as often as you can, "Without me the literary industry would not exist: the publishers, the agents, the sub-agents, the sub-sub-agents, the accountants, the libel lawyers, the departments of literature, the professors, the theses, the books of criticism, the reviewers, the book pages—all this vast and proliferating edifice is because of this small, patronized, put-down and underpaid person.
- Doris Lessing

In a world dominated by information, publishing skills are no longer something that's nice to have. They are a must-have.
- Gerry McGovern and Rob Norton, *Content Critical*

Yesterday Mr. Hall wrote that the printer's proof-reader was improving my punctuation for me and I telegraphed orders to have him shot without giving him time to pray.
- Mark Twain

Self-publishing is a perfect example of the American dream. It is stimulating, demanding, and rewarding. For many it has proved to be the do-it-yourself way to fame and fortune.
- Tom Ross and Marilyn Ross

Beatrix Potter's Peter Rabbit books were turned down so often that she finally published them herself.
- Sophy Burnham, *For Writers Only*

The self-publisher really has control of his or her destiny to a much larger degree than does a writer merely submitting a manuscript [to a publisher]... It does not matter whether you sell out to a large New York book publisher or publish yourself, the author must do the promotion.
- Dan Poynter, *The Self-Publishing Manual*

Initially a "royalty" was a license to print fee paid to the crown.
- Dale Spender, *Nattering on the Net: Women, Power, and Cyberspace*

He received—nothing. But for that he paid more than others for their treasures.
- Dag Hammarskjöld, *Markings*

Write without pay until someone offers pay. If nobody offers pay within three years, the candidate may look upon this circumstance as a sign...that sawing wood is what he was intended for.
- Mark Twain

What a writer likes to write most is his signature on the back of a check.
- Brendan Francis

Literature doesn't matter! The only thing that matters is money and getting your teeth fixed.
- Delmore Schwartz

Writing for a penny a word is ridiculous. If a man wants to make a million dollars, the best way would be to start his own religion.
- L. Ron Hubbard

Let authors write for glory and reward. The truth is well paid when she is sung and heard.
- James J. Corbett

Frankly, I have no taste for either poverty or honest labor, so writing is the only recourse left for me.
- Hunter S. Thompson

There are hardly a half a dozen writers in England today who have not sold out to the enemy. Even when their good work has been a success, Mammon grips them and whispers: More money for more work.
- Aleister Crowley

Write a novel if you must, but think of money as an unlikely accident. Get your reward out of writing it, and try to be content with that.
- Pearl Buck

I'd like to have money. And I'd like to be a good writer. These two can come together, and I hope they will, but if that's too adorable, I'd rather have money.
- Dorothy Parker

Writing is turning one's worst moments into money.
- J.P. Donleavy

It is not the being paid money in advance that jars the sensitive artist: it is the having to work.
- P.G. Wodehouse

Be careful of doing great business and making great profits. It will spoil you.
- Leonard Bishop, *Dare to be a Great Writer*

I loathe writing. On the other hand I'm a great believer in money.
- S.J. Perelman

The best work never was and never will be done for money.
- John Ruskin

I have always believed that writing advertisements is the second most profitable form of writing. The first, of course, is ransom notes.
- Philip Dusenberry

Someday I hope to write a book where the royalties will pay for the copies I give away.
- Clarence Darrow

Writing is the only profession where no one considers you ridiculous if you earn no money.
    - Jules Renard

A person is a fool to become a writer. His only compensation is absolute freedom.
    - Roald Dahl

Almost anyone can be an author; the business is to collect money and fame from this state of being.
    - A.A. Milne

The only two kinds of books [that] could earn an American writer a living are cookbooks and detective novels.
    - Rex Stout

I never had any doubts about my abilities. I knew I could write. I just had to figure out how to eat while doing this.
    - Cormac McCarthy

The two most beautiful words in the English language are: "Check enclosed."
    - Dorothy Parker

Whatever money or praise comes from writing seems totally unreal to me. The money always seems like play money or found money, totally unrelated to the writing that brought it. The praise or criticism always seems like it's being said not about me but about someone I don't know, a stranger.
    - Harry Crews

If you want to get rich from writing, write the sort of thing that's read by persons who move their lips when reading.
    - Don Marquis

Nothing written for pay is worth printing. Only what has been written against the market.
    - Ezra Pound

O Time, Strength, Cash, Patience!
    - Herman Melville as he wrote *Moby Dick*

Writers don't need love. All they require is money.
    - John Osborne

Write without pay until somebody offers to pay.
- Mark Twain

There's no money in poetry, but there's no poetry in money, either.
- Robert Graves

A woman must have money and a room of her own if she is to write fiction.
- Virginia Woolf

Thinking to get at once all the gold that the goose could give, he killed it, and opened it only to find—nothing.
- Aesop

Writing is the hardest way of earning a living, with the possible exception of wrestling alligators.
- Olin Miller

17

What can you tell me about writing in different genres?

Romance writing isn't different from any other sort of popular fiction in that—plot, narrative setting, dialogue—everything has to be there. You have to have good, interesting, strong characters.
 - Nora Roberts

A historical romance is the only kind of book where chastity really counts.
 - Barbara Cartland

As long as the plots keep arriving from outer space, I'll go on with my virgins.
 - Barbara Cartland, *New Yorker* 9 Aug '76
 (on publication of her 217th book)

Science fiction properly conceived, like all serious fiction…is a way of trying to describe what is in fact going on, what people actually do and feel, how people relate to everything else in this vast sack, this belly of the universe, this womb of things to be and tomb of things that were, this unending story.
 - Ursula K. LeGuin, *Dancing at the Edge of the World*

No one suggests that writing about science will turn the entire world into a model of judgment and creative thought. It will be enough if they spread the knowledge as widely as possible.
 - Isaac Asimov

To write good SF today…you must push further and harder, reach deeper into your own mind until you break through into the strange and terrible country wherein live your own dreams.
 - Gardner Dozois

Science fiction…contains stories dealing with: other times, other worlds, other beings, other states of mind.
 - Christopher Evans, *Writing Science Fiction*

I don't try to write it. I don't sit down and say to myself, now I'm going to think up a science fiction idea…What happens is, something or other catches my attention and a few words or images join together in a provocative manner. Or sometimes a whole scene leaps into my head…And what it usually turns out to be is another science fiction story.
- Robert Sheckley, "The Search for the Marvellous,"
Science Fiction At Large, ed. Peter Nicholls

It has been said that every writer has one obsessive theme to which he constantly returns. This is even more true inside science fiction that out of it.
- Peter Nicholls, *Science Fiction at Large*

There is nothing fantastic or ultra-dimensional about crab grass…unless you are a SF writer, in which case pretty soon you are viewing crab grass with suspicion…One day the crab grass suit will fall off and their true identity will be revealed. By then the Pentagon will be full of crab grass and it'll be too late. The crab grass, or what we took to be crab grass, will dictate terms.
- Philip K. Dick

Science fiction writers foresee the inevitable and although problems and catastrophes may be inevitable, solutions are not.
- Isaac Asimov

The great game in science fiction is titled What If, and it is perhaps one of the things that topples a mainstream novel over into the SF category.
- Harry Harrison, "Worlds Beside Worlds,"
Science Fiction At Large, ed. Peter Nicholls

The fancy that extraterrestrial life is by definition of a higher order than our own is one that soothes all children, and many writers.
- Joan Didion

If science fiction is…a true metaphor to our strange times, then surely it is rather stupid and reactionary to try to enclose it in the old limits of an old art—like trying to turn a nuclear reactor into a steam-engine.
- Ursula K. Le Guin, "Science Fiction and Mrs. Brown"
Science Fiction At Large, ed. Peter Nicholls

SF is the literature of the theoretically possible and F is the literature of the impossible.
- Piers Anthony

SF is in part a fiction of ideas, so I took that aspect of the genre for my blend.
- Dean Koontz

Science fiction writers, I am sorry to say, really do not know anything. We can't talk about science, because our knowledge of it is limited and unofficial, and usually our fiction is dreadful.
- Philip K. Dick

Isaac Asimov once said that science fiction was born when it became evident that our world was changing within our lifetimes and therefore thinking about the future became a matter of individual survival.
- Kevin Kelly

I'm sure we would not have had men on the Moon if it had not been for Wells and Verne and the people who write about this and made people think about it. I'm rather proud of the fact that I know several astronauts who became astronauts through reading my books.
- Arthur C. Clarke

I suspect one of the reasons that fantasy and science fiction appeal so much to younger readers is that, when the space and time have been altered to allow characters to travel easily anywhere through the continuum and thus escape physical dangers and timepiece inevitabilities, mortality is so seldom an issue.
- Thomas Pynchon

Science fiction balances you on a cliff. Fantasy shoves you off.
- Ray Bradbury, Introduction, *The Circus of Dr. Lao*

A good science fiction story is a scenario in depth—a whole possible future.
- Stewart Brand, *The Clock of the Long Now*

I remember writing a science fiction novel which went nowhere because it was about the problems of heat-death on re-entry in the space program. I had worked out a very ingenious way to surmount that, and then the very moment it was finished and mailed off to my agent, they orbited a dog in the space capsule, and they found that the heat and re-entry problem just did not exist.
- Marion Zimmer Bradley

SF bears the same relation to fiction that Scientology bears to science. It works for some, but it won't bear looking at.
- Thomas M Disch, "The Embarrassments of Science Fiction," *Science Fiction At Large*, ed. Peter Nicholls

In sci-fi convention, life-forms that hadn't developed space travel were mere prehistory—horse-shoe crabs of the cosmic scene—and something of the humiliation of being stuck on a provincial planet in a galactic backwater has stayed with me every since.
- Barbara Ehrenreich

A good science fiction story is a story with a human problem, and a human solution, which would not have happened without its science content.
- Theodore Sturgeon

Space or science fiction has become a dialect for our time.
- Doris Lessing

Every now and then someone comes up to a science fiction writer, smiles a crazy secret in-the-know smile and smirks, "I know what you're writing is true and it's in code. All you SF writers are receivers for Them." Naturally I ask who "Them" is. The answer is always the same; "You know. Up there. The space people. They're already here, and they're using your writing. You know it too."…In truth, we may be influenced, especially during dream states, by a noösphere…This might not be the Creator, but it would be as close to Infinite Mind as we might get, and close enough.
- Philip K. Dirk, "Man, Android and Machine,"
Science Fiction At Large, ed. Peter Nicholls

[to science writers] You're the only ones with guts enough to *really* care about the future, who really notice what machines do to us, what wars do to us… [and] whether the space voyage for the next billion years or so is going to be Heaven or Hell.
- Kurt Vonnegut, *God Bless You Mr. Rosewater*

If science fiction is the mythology of modern technology, then its myth is tragic.
- Ursula K. Le Guin

I will reveal a secret to you. I like to build universes that *do* fall apart. I like to see them come unglued, and I like to see how the characters in the novels cope with the problems.
- Philip Dick, "How to Build a Universe That Doesn't
Fall Apart Two days Later"

To see clearly is poetry, prophesy and religion, all in one.
- John Ruskin

Science fiction does not remain fiction for long. And certainly not on the Internet.
- Vinton Cerf

Ultimately, our responsibility as spiritual-book writers is to remind our readers of their own courage and their capacities for knowing, and then get out of the way for them to do the rest.
- Hal Zina Bennett, *Writing Spiritual Books*

The Book of Kells was the work of an angel, not of man.
- Geraldus Cambrensis

The abstract labels for what we call "spiritual" are all too narrow—they can't catch it, they're diminishing terms.
- Jane Hirschfield

Writing is like praying, because you stop all other activities, descend into silence, and listen patiently to the depths of your soul, waiting for the true words to come. When they do, you thank God because you know the words are a gift, and you write them down as honestly and as cleanly as you can.
- Helen Prejean, *Death of Innocents*

All human beings have an innate need to hear and tell stories and to have a story to live by…religion, whatever else it has done, has provided one of the main ways of meeting this abiding need.
- Harvey Cox, *The Seduction of the Spirit*

…one of the meanings of religion is to bind back to the origin. At this point in God's being, we are all bound together at the same source. Stories begin in silence waiting for a word. In stories we rely on remembering, and remembering implies celebrating the word you have heard that you must now speak, that is the visitation of the Spirit in your life.
- Charles and Anne Simpkinson, *Sacred Stories*

Today's editors prefer their theology in small doses and wrapped in human terms—something the guy next door can relate to.
- Steve Lawhead

If you're a person of faith and believe you have been called to a sacred profession, that alone should move you. With a single phrase you can heal a wound or tear it open.
- Jerry B. Jenkins

The key to non-anxious sermon-writing is that it's not about me. It's about the congregation. I honor the fact that the listeners bring more to the sermons than I do. I remind myself of the hundreds of times someone says, "I loved how you said…" and then tell me things that they heard that were nowhere in my text and that I never said. But they heard what they needed to hear.
    - Sean Parker Dennison, *Ministrare*

The religious press today is looking for information, not piety; for reality, not Pollyanna; for inspiration, not poetic ramblings.
    - Antoinette Bosco in *The Complete Guide to Writing Nonfiction*, ed. by Glen Evans

In the entire vocabulary of philosophy, of theology, or of sociology the easiest word for us to define is "evil." Evil is the enemy of love. Simply that. But "love" is not definable. Likewise "truth" and "beauty"…evil is ever at pains to define each of these unfenceable ideas…And evil is always the aggressor…Love spreads without aggression, and contracts without diminution…Evil may in the end prevail in the story but not in the universe…evil cannot put love out of existence.
    - David Greenhood, *The Writer on His Own*

Write what you know and believe in its worth.
    - George Devine

The novelist with Christian concerns will find in modern life distortions which are repugnant to him, and his problem will be to make these appear as distortions to an audience which is used to seeing them as natural; and he may well be forced to take ever more violent means to get his vision across to this hostile audience.
    - Flannery O'Connor, *The Fiction Writer and His Country*

All the sweetness of religion is conveyed to children by the hands of storytellers and image-makers. Without their fictions the truths of religion would for the multitude be neither intelligible nor even apprehensible; and the prophets would prophesy and the philosophers celebrate in vain. And nothing stands between the people and the fictions except the silly falsehood that the fictions are literal truths, and that there is nothing in religion but fiction.
    - George Bernard Shaw

The problem with writing about religion is that you run the risk of offending sincerely religious people, and then they come after you with machetes.
    - Dave Barry

The difficulty in being human is that one can never be merely human. Whether we like it or not, each one of us has kinship with the divine. This kinship can remain dormant for a long time or it can find other forms of expression. Sooner or later it will assert itself in a form that is no longer possible to ignore…The source of our creative longing and passion is the Divine Imagination.

- John O'Donohue, *Beauty: The Invisible Embrace*

The universe will reward you for taking risks on its behalf.

- Shakti Gawain

To serve a work of art is almost identical with adoring the Master of the Universe in contemplative prayer. In contemplative prayer the saint (who knows himself to be sinner, for none of us is whole, healed and holy twenty-four hours a day) turns inward in what is called "the prayer of the heart," not to find self, but to lose self in order to be found.

- Madeleine L'Engle, *Walking on Water*

Good writing is always religious. Joyce was religious. He may have been profane, but he was always religious. Becket is religious. Dostoevsky. Tolstoy. That's really the only kind of writing I'm interested in.

- Edna O'Brien

18.

Do you have a writing method?

There is no method except to be very intelligent.
- T.S. Eliot

There is no method except yourself.
- Harold Bloom

Ring the bells that can still ring. Forget your perfect offering. There is a crack in everything.
- Leonard Cohen

A writer is not so much someone who has something to say as he is someone who has found a process that will bring about new things he would not have thought of if he had not started to say them.
- William Stafford

The writer should never be afraid of staring. There is nothing that doesn't require his attention.
- Flannery O'Connor, *On Writing*

Be direct. Indirectness ruins good writing…A writer must preserve a balance between sensitivity and vitality. High brow writers are sensitive but not vital. Commercial writers are vital but not sensitive. Trying to keep the balance is always hard. It is the whole job of living.
- Margaret Craven, *Again Calls the Owl*

Commit yourself to the process, NOT the project. Don't be afraid to write badly, everyone does. Invest yourself in the lifestyle…NOT in the particular piece of work.
- Frank Conroy

I always start writing with a clean piece of paper and a dirty mind.
- Patrick Dennis

I put a piece of paper under my pillow, and when I could not sleep, I wrote in the dark.
- Henry David Thoreau

I meditate and put on a rubber tire with three bottles of beer. Most of the time I just sit picking my nose and thinking.
- James Gould Cozzens

For me the discipline of writing and the discipline of prayer are identical, in that I have to let myself be got out of the way because that's not a do-it-yourself activity, and listen…When you write, don't think, write…When I'm truly praying, I'm not thinking. I'm not speaking. I'm shutting up, so perhaps if God has something to say I can hear it. So writing too is an act of listening, listening to what has to be said.
- Madeleine L'Engle

If my doctor told me I had only six minutes to live, I wouldn't brood; I'd type a little faster.
- Isaac Asimov

If you are a genius, you'll make your own rules, but if not—and the odds are against it—go to your desk, no matter what your mood, face the icy challenge of the paper—write.
- J.B. Priestly

The skill of writing is to create a context in which other people can think.
- Edwin Schlossberg

Four basic premises of writing: clarity, brevity, simplicity and humanity.
- William Zinsser

The way you define yourself as a writer is that you write every time you have a free minute. If you didn't behave that way you would never do anything.
- John Irving

Don't think. Write. We think before we write a story, and afterward, but during the writing, we listen.
- Madeleine L'Engle

It's always done one word at a time.
- Stephen King, *On Writing: A Memoir of the Craft*

You write by sitting down and writing. There's no particular time or place—you suit yourself, your nature. How one works, assuming he's disciplined, doesn't matter. If he or she is not disciplined, no sympathetic magic will help.

- Bernard Malamud

All good things…come by grace and grace comes by art and art does not come easy.

- Norman Maclean, *A River Runs Through It*

I don't wait for moods. You accomplish nothing if you do that. Your mind must know it has got to get down to work.

- Pearl S. Buck

It is wise…to have not simply a set time for writing—it need not be daily and yet be regular—but also a set "stint" for the day, based on a true, not vainglorious estimate of your powers. Then, when you come to a natural stop somewhere near the set amount, you can knock off with a clear conscience.

- Jacques Barzun

Writing is easy; all you do is sit staring at a blank sheet of paper until the drops of blood form on your forehead.

- Gene Fowler

Good writing is clear thinking made visible.

- Bill Wheeler

Good writers are those who keep the language efficient. That is to say, keep it accurate, keep it clear.

- Ezra Pound

New writers are often told, "Write what you know." I would broaden that by saying, "Write what you know emotionally."

- Marjorie Franco

Write *from* what you know *into* what you don't know.

- Grace Paley

Their language is exquisite, their scenes divine, but what have these writers done lately? Not a damn thing. Think about it…Past masters are done. Their achievements are finite, known, measurable. Present writers, on the other hand, live in possibility. Your masterpiece could be just around the corner.

- Allegra Goodman

Write while the heat is in you. The writer who postpones the recording of his thoughts uses an iron which has cooled to burn a hole with. He cannot inflame the minds of his audience.
          - Henry David Thoreau

Good writing is always entertaining or useful or both. It is not a puzzle, or a sermon, or executed by a superior person for inferiors.
          - William Sloane, *The Craft of Writing*

Easy writing makes hard reading.
          - Ernest Hemingway

Of all that is written, I love only what a person has written with his own blood.
          - Friedrich Nietzsche

The strokes of the pen need deliberation as much as the sword needs swiftness.
          - Julia Ward Howe

Never go off on tangents, which are lines that intersect a curve at only one point and were discovered by Euclid, who lived in the 3rd century B.C., which was the end of the middle Formative Period in Meso-America, where many principal sites of settlement in the area that we now know as Belize, a common destination for SCUBA-diving tourists.
          - Philip Greenspun, "Thoughts on Writing," Philip.greenspun.com

The creative power, which bubbles so pleasantly in beginning a new book, quiets down after a time, and one goes on more steadily. Doubts creep in. Then one becomes resigned. Determination not to give in, and the sense of an impending shape, keep one at it more than anything.
          - Virginia Woolf

I don't need time. What I need is a deadline.
          - Duke Ellington

Make 'em laugh; make 'em cry; make 'em wait.
          - Charles Reade

Write about it by day, and dream about it by night.
          - E. B. White

Every morning I jump out of bed and step on a land mine. That land mine is me.
- Ray Bradbury

For a while, I took the night boats between Boston and New York, the Fall River Line, the New Bedford Line, the Cape Line, all going to N.Y. at night. The rhythm of the water might have helped my sentence structure a little, at least I thought it did.
- Erskine Caldwell

At night, when the objective world has slunk back into its cavern and left dreamers to their own, there come inspirations and capabilities impossible at any less magical and quiet hour. No one knows whether or not he is a writer unless he has tried writing at night.
- H. P. Lovecraft

It doesn't matter which leg of your table you make first, so long as the table has four legs and will stand up solidly when you have finished it.
- Ezra Pound, *ABC of Reading*

Nighttime is really the best time to work. All the ideas are there to be yours because everyone else is asleep.
- Catherine O'Hara

The only way to write is to write today.
- Susan Shaughnessy, *Walking on Alligators*

Today is a dawdly day. They do seem to alternate. I do a whole of a day's work and then the next day, flushes with triumph, I dawdle…The crazy thing is that I get about the same number of words down either way.
- John Steinbeck

An old racetrack joke reminds you that your program contains all the winners' names. I stare at my typewriter keys with the same thought.
- Mignon McLaughlin, *The Neurotic's Notebook*

There is a belief perpetuated through the generations that a writer can be creative for only four hours a day. All but holy writ, the belief has gained widespread acceptance within the literary community. Of course, what it actually represents is the world's best excuse not to work a full day.
- Matt Braun, *How to Write Western Novels*

The act of writing requires a constant plunging back into the shadow of the past where time hovers ghostlike.
  - Ralph Ellison, *Writers at Work*

Write so that every word can be used against you!
  - Jens Bjørneboe, *Powderhouse*

I make an index of my notes and then get to the writing as soon as I can. I do a rough draft, and then I rewrite and rewrite.
  - Tracy Kidder

I am a completely horizontal author. I can't think unless I'm lying down, either in bed or stretched on a couch and with a cigarette and coffee handy.
  - Truman Capote

It is widely rumored, and also true, that I wrote my first novel in a closet… Fish gotta swim, birds gotta fly, writers will go to stupefying lengths to get the infernal roar of words out of their skulls and onto paper.
  - Barbara Kingsolver, *Small Wonder*

On sunny, calm days I may even work in the bottom of my canoe, floating on the lake…a yellow pad works anywhere. No word processors for me! I want no machinery or electricity between my brain, hand, pen and paper.
  - Anne Labastille, *Woodswoman II: Beyond Black Bear Lake*

It seems to me that those songs that have been any good, I have nothing much to do with the writing of them. The words have just crawled down my sleeve and come out on the page.
  - Joan Baez

Just get it down on paper, and then we'll see what to do about it.
  - Maxwell Perkins

We cannot write well or truly but what we write with gusto.
  - Henry David Thoreau

Brian Aldiss, who writes a novel and several short stories each year, says he places completed pages face down and won't backtrack until the first draft is completed. This way he sustains the necessary "vision" and "creative glow." Later, "creative hope mixed with critical discontent" carries him through the rewrites.
  - Arthur Plotnik, *The Elements of Authorship*

I listen to the voices.
  - William Faulkner

If one waits for the right time to come before writing, the right time never comes.
  - James Russell Lowell

You have to have a routine and live up to it and then hope for the best.
  - Walker Percy

We have to be continually jumping off cliffs and developing wings on the way down.
  - Kurt Vonnegut

James Michener actually goes into physical training like a boxer before he begins a book, so the least you can do is take a few deep breaths, put your pulse rate into second gear, and deliver a supply of oxygen to the brain.
  - Gary Provost, *100 Ways to Improve your Writing (Mentor)*

Enthusiasm and inspiration, these unconscious forces, are inhibited and suppressed right up until you have reinvented your cosmos, chosen your world, and have yourself decided what rules you will make into laws and follow. You have become conscious in your work and only when the conception of your book is thought through and worked out, crystal clear as a theorem in geometry, can your unconscious get back to work...Your work has now become so concrete, so difficult and so arduous that it can only be compared to hewing stone.
  - Jens Bjørneboe, "Alone with the Paper"

A writer needs certain conditions in which to work and create. She needs a piece of time, a peace of mind; a quiet place; and a private life.
  - Margaret Walker

Many writers do little else but sit in small rooms recalling the real world.
  - Annie Dillard

Here, beside this great black surface that is my desk, I feel as though I am on a desert island.
  - Etty Hillesum

In the writing process, the more a thing cooks, the better.
  - Doris Lessing

I don't know exactly how it's done; I let it alone a good deal.
        - Saul Bellow

One of the few things I know about writing is this: Spend it all, shoot it, play it, lose it, all, right away, every time. Do not hoard what seems good for a later place in the book, or for another book, give it, give it all, give it now…Some more will arise for later, something better. These things fill from behind, from beneath, like well water. Similarly, the impulse to keep to yourself what you have learned is not only shameful, it is destructive. Anything you do not give freely and abundantly becomes lost to you. You open your safe and find ashes.
        - Annie Dillard, *The Writing Life*

If one wants to write, one simply has to organize one's life in a mass of little habits.
        - Graham Greene

I caution writers all the time to slow down and pay more attention to the work in front of them than to the end result. I don't think you write one book and get anywhere. I think you write five books and then maybe you are finally on the right path.
        - Sue Grafton

Sleep on your writing; take a walk over it; scrutinize it of a morning; review it of an afternoon; digest it after a meal; let it sleep in your drawer a twelvemonth; never venture a whisper about it to your friend, if he be an author especially.
        - Bronson Alcott

I chart a little first—lists of names, rough synopses of chapters, and so on. But one daren't over-plan; so many things are generated by the sheer act of writing.
        - Anthony Burgess, interview, *Writers at Work*

Run fast, stand still. This, the lesson from lizards. For all writers…Be a chameleon, ink-blend, chromosome change with the landscape. Be a pet rock, lie with the dust, rest in the rainwater in the filled barrel by the drain spout outside your grandparents' window long ago.
        - Ray Bradbury, "Run Fast…" *Zen in the Art of Writing*

When I write, I follow an image, a piece of music that can't get out of my mind. I let it lead me, like a clue to a mystery to be revealed.
        - E.L. Doctorow

I do a first draft as passionately and as quickly as I can. I believe a story is only valid when it is immediate and passionate: when it dances out of your subconscious. If you interfere in any way, you destroy it.

- Ray Bradbury

I always try to write on the principle of the iceberg. There is seven-eighths of it underwater for every part that shows.

- Ernest Hemingway

I might write four lines or I might write twenty. I subtract and I add until I really hit something I want to do. You don't always whittle down, sometimes you whittle up.

- Grace Paley

Think of and look at your work as though it were done by your enemy. If you look at it to admire it you are lost.

- Samuel Butler, *The Note-Books*

After all, writers are autodidacts. They have to teach themselves everything...It really is not a profession for the Wunderkind, even if it looks that way...It's incomprehensible that anyone engages in something which is so utterly impossible. Every word, every comma, every sentence is a problem. Nothing writes itself any more, every page I produce I regard with the very deepest suspicion.

- Jens Bjørneboe, Interview, *Aftenposten*, 1959

A writer is unfair to himself when he is unable to be hard on himself.

- Marianne Moore, *Writers at Work: The Paris Review Interviews*

Your letter is come; it came indeed twelve lines ago, but I could not stop to acknowledge it before, & I am glad it did not arrive till I had completed my first sentence, because the sentence had been made since yesterday, & I think forms a very good beginning.

- Jane Austen, letter

I became an afternoon writer when I had afternoons. When I was able to write full-time, I used to spend the morning procrastinating and worrying, then plunge into the manuscript in a frenzy of anxiety around 3:00 P.M. when it looked as though I might not get anything done.

- Margaret Atwood

Read carefully, then don't read; work hard, then forget about it; know your traditions, then liberate yourself from it; learn language, then free yourself from it. Finally, know at least one form of magic.
    - Gary Snyder

Everything comes to him who hustles while he waits.
    - Thomas Edison

All my major works have been written in prison…I would recommend prison not only to aspiring writers but to aspiring politicians too.
    - Jawaharlal Nehru

Few good writers come out of prison. Incarceration, I think, can destroy a man's ability to write. The noise in prison is tremendous. Plus the paranoia—you do have to fear or distrust too many of the people you are among…Only the best survive to be able to write once they get out.
    - Norman Mailer, *The Spooky Art*

I wrote the scenes…by using the same apprehensive imagination that occurs in the morning before an afternoon's appointment with my dentist.
    - John Marquand

You enter a state of controlled passivity, you relax your grip and accept that even if your declared intention is to justify the ways of God to man, you might end up interesting your readers rather more in Satan.
    - Ian McEwan

Writing a book is like rearing children—willpower has very little to do with it. If you have a little baby crying in the middle of the night, and if you depend only on willpower to get you out of bed to feed the baby, the baby will starve. You do it out of love. Willpower is a weak idea; love is strong. You don't have to scourge yourself with a cat-o' nine tails to go to the baby. You go to the baby out of love for that particular baby. That's the same way you go to your desk.
    - Annie Dillard, *The Art and Craft of Memoir*

It is much easier to sit at a desk, and read plans for a billion gallons of water a day, and look at maps and photographs; but you will write a better article if you heave yourself out of a comfortable chair and go down in tunnel 3 and get soaked.
    - Stuart Chase, in Ken Macrorie, *Telling Writing*

Don't expect to write well about the love affair that you are in the midst of, or have just mailed a letter to break off.
- Sidney Cox, *Indirections*

Talking is a hydrant in the yard and writing is a faucet upstairs in the house. Opening the first takes the pressure off the second.
- Robert Frost, *Vogue* 15 Mar '63

For a long time before I start to write a novel, anywhere from one year to two, I make it up. This is the happiest time I have with my books. The novel in my imagination travels with me like a small lavender moth making loopy circles around my head. It is a truly gorgeous thing, its unpredictable flight patterns, the amethyst light on its wings.
- Ann Patchett, *Writers [on Writing] Vol. II*

It is my design to render it ["The Raven"] manifest that no one point in its composition is referable either to accident or intuition—that the work proceeded, step by step, to its completion with the precision and rigid consequence of a mathematical problem.
- Edgar Allan Poe, "The Philosophy of Composition"

My method is one of continuous revision. While writing a long novel, every day I loop back to earlier sections to rewrite, in order to maintain a consistent, fluid voice. When I write the final two or three chapters of a novel, I write them simultaneously with the rewriting of the opening, so that ideally at least, the novel is like a river uniformly flowing, each passage concurrent with all the others.
- Joyce Carol Oates, *Writers [On Writing]*

I've never read any books on how to write. It's like reading books on how to play golf. There's only one way to play golf. You swing the club and clop the ball. The only way to learn to write is to write, and keep doing it until you get it damn right.
- Tom Clancy, in Richard Joseph, *Bestsellers: Top Writers Tell How*

What do you think of my becoming an author and relying for support on my pen? Indeed, I think the illegibility of my handwriting is very author-like.
- Nathanial Hawthorne, letter

For us there is only the trying. The rest is not our business.
- T. S. Eliot

John Cheever wrote some of his early stories in his underwear. Hemingway is said to have written some of his fiction standing up. Thomas Wolfe reportedly wrote parts of his voluminous novels while leaning over the top of a refrigerator…Eudora Welty has said that she straight-pinned pieces of her stories together on the dining room table, as though she were pinning together parts of a dress…I prefer a cool room in the basement…and I write my first drafts blind on an old manual typewriter…perhaps because writing fiction—this weird practice of telling lies, this peculiar habit of inventing imaginary people who talk and move and sleep and dream and wake up and kick and kiss one another—is so bizarre in itself is the reason why writers have to find bizarre ways to make it possible even to consider doing it.
    - Kent Haruf, *Writers [on Writing]*

I type in one place, but I write all over the house.
    - Toni Morrison

I compose sometimes with a pen and notebook, sometimes on the computer; it makes no difference. If all I had was a chisel and a rock I would write on the rock.
    - Ursula K. Le Guin

Between my finger and my thumb the squat pen rests. I'll dig with it.
    - Seamus Heaney

Give me a condor's quill! Give me Vesuvius' crater for an inkstand! Friends, hold my arms!
    - Herman Melville, *Moby Dick*

The devil himself gets in my inkstand.
    - Nathanial Hawthorne

A writer uses a pen instead of a scalpel or blowtorch…
    - Michael Ondaatje

I don't use a pen. I write with a goose quill dipped in venom.
    - Jay Dratler

Every drop of ink in my pen ran cold.
    - Horace Walpole

The pen is mightier than the sword, and considerably easier to write with.
    - Marty Feldman

I've always had a very comfortable relationship with No. 2 pencils.
    - William Styron

I believe more in the scissors than I do in the pencil.
    - Truman Capote

I think best with a pencil in my hand.
    - Anne Morrow Lindberg

This writing business. Pencils and what not. Overrated if you ask me. Silly stuff. Nothing to it.
    - A. Milne, *Winnie the Pooh* (Eeyore)

People on the outside think there's something magical about writing, that you go up to the attic at midnight and cast the bones and come down in the morning with a story, but it isn't like that. You sit in back of the typewriter and you work, and that's all there is to it.
    - Harlan Ellison

I feel it in me like a woman having a baby, all that life churning inside me. I feel it every day; it moves, stretches, yawns. It's getting ready to be born. I know exactly what it is.
    - Maurice Sendak

You have to protect your writing time. You have to protect it to the death.
    - William Goldman

My own experience has been that the tools I need for my trade are paper, tobacco, food, and a little whiskey.
    - William Faulkner

You must stay drunk on writing so reality cannot destroy you.
    - Ray Bradbury

Your work is to keep cranking the flywheel that turns the gears that spin the belt in the engine of belief that keeps you and your desk in midair.
    - Annie Dillard, *The Writing Life*

I'd say it [writing] occurs in the quiet, silent moments, while you're walking or shaving or playing a game, or whatever, or even talking to someone you're not vitally interested in.
    - Henry Miller

If I work toward an end, meantime I am confined to a process. The rainbow is more beautiful than the pot at the end of it, because the rainbow is now. And the pot never turns out to be quite what I expect.
- Hugh Prather

The Author continued for about three hours in a profound sleep, at least of the external senses...On awakening he appeared to himself to have a distinct recollection of the whole, and taking his pen, ink and paper, instantly and eagerly wrote down the lines that are here preserved.
- Samuel Taylor Coleridge, Prefatory Note to "Kubla Khan"

There are three general stages in the writing process...Some people believe that the only stage that really counts in the second—writing. This isn't so. You need thoughtful prewriting to develop something worth writing about. And you need careful rewriting to develop something worth reading.
- John B. Karls and Ronald Szymanski, *The Writer's Handbook*

No pen, no ink, no table, no room, no time, no quiet, no inclination.
- James Joyce

I think I did pretty well, considering I started out with nothing but a bunch of blank paper.
- Steve Martin

Paper is soft and ink is fluid; if might be better if some pages of this chronicle could be written on chips of granite at the point of steel.
- E. M. Almedingen

All I do is watch the human condition and write it down. It's like stealing.
- Erma Bombeck

Write a little every day, without hope and without despair.
- Isak Dinesen

As a writer I want uncertainty. It's part of life. I want something the reader is uncertain about. It is this uncertainty that produces drama.
- Bernard Malamud

As cows need milking and sweet peas need picking, so writers must continually exercise their mental muscles by a daily stint.
- Joan Aiken

A cow does not know how much milk it has until the milkman starts working on it. Then it looks round in surprise and sees the pail full to the brim. In the same way a writer has no idea how much he has to say till his pen draws it out of him.
     - Gerald Branan

Three hours a day will produce as much as a man ought to write.
     - Anthony Trollope, *An Autobiography*

It takes an awful lot of time for me to write anything. I have endless drafts, one after another, and I try out 50, 75, or a hundred variations on a single line sometimes. I work on the process of refining low-grade ore. I get maybe a couple of nuggets of gold out of 50 tons of dirt.
     - James Dickey

...between 8:36 and 2 p.m. I'm doing one of three things: I'm writing. I'm staring out the window. Or I'm writhing on the floor.
     - Thomas Harris

Agatha Christie...could finish a book in six weeks using three fingers on the typewriter. "A sausage machine," she called herself. "A perfect sausage machine."
     - Sophy Burnham, *For Writers Only*

I seat myself at the typewriter and hope, and lurk.
     - Mignon Eberhart

All the work a writer does in a day *can* be changed, and much of it *should* be changed.
     - Arthur Plotnik, *The Elements of Authorship*

The writer is either a practicing recluse or a delinquent, guilt-ridden one; or both. Usually both.
     - Susan Sontag

Every writer is limited by the constraints of the world in which he writes, be it the real world or a world he's created.
     - Michael A. Stackpole

A pathological business, writing, don't you think? Just look what a writer actually does: all that unnatural tense squatting and hunching, all those rituals: pathological!
     - Hans Magnus Enzensberger

My only ritual is to sit close enough to the typewriter so that my fingers touch the keys.
- Isaac Asimov

There's a time to go to the typewriter. It's like a dog—the way a dog before it craps wanders around in circles—a piece of earth, an area of grass, circles it for a long time before it squats. It's like that—figuratively circling the typewriter.
- James Thurber in Alice W. Flaherty, *The Midnight Disease*

When I'm writing, everything shuts down. I get up about five...I get in my car and drive off to a hotel room...and ask them to take everything off the walls so there's me, the Bible, Roget's Thesaurus and some good, dry sherry and I'm at work by 6:30...I write in longhand on yellow pads. Once into it, all disbelief is suspended...I've set for myself 12:30 as the time to leave, because after that it's an indulgence, it becomes stuff I am going to edit out anyway...then 8:00 at night is the cruelest hour because that's when I start to edit and all that pretty stuff I've written gets axed out. So if I've written ten or twelve pages in six hours, it'll end up as three or four if I'm lucky.
- Maya Angelou, [Donald McQuade, Robert Atwan, *The Writer's Presence*]

James Joyce, meanwhile, worked anywhere, everywhere, carting his voluminous notes, revisions, little scraps of paper and reference books around in a valise.
- Gail Sher, *The Intuitive Writer*

I worked on that book [*Presumed Innocent*] for eight years on the morning commuter train...
- Scott Turow, *Writers [on Writing]*

Get black on white.
- Guy de Maupassant

The faster I write the better my output. If I'm going slow I'm in trouble. It means I'm pushing the words instead of being pulled by them.
- Raymond Chandler

When genuine passion moves you, say what you've got to say, and say it hot.
- D.H. Lawrence

Don't trust deer trails; they meander and fade. Head downhill, where you'll come to a stream; follow it to town.
- Maxine Hong Kingston, *The Writer on Her Work*

I never find words right away. Poems for me always begin with images and rhythms, shapes, feelings, forms, dances in the back of my mind.
- Gary Snyder

The way a surgeon would prepare himself for a new operation was exactly the way I approached the task of writing, and since words were to be my new instruments, I had to learn them, learn how to use them, put them down in order, suture them together. It's [the pen]...about the same size as a scalpel, has the same circumference...it was an instrument so like the one I had used all my life that it was not a stranger, but a distant cousin of the knife. In the use of each, something is shed. When you use the scalpel, blood is shed; when you use the pen, ink is shed.
- Richard Selzer, interview, [Donald McQuade, Robert Atwan, *The Writer's Presence*]

The thing to do, of course, is to find out what people know and what they don't know, and then to write accordingly...Say what you have to say and then stop.
- Rudolph Flesch, *The Art of Readable Writing*

I am going to be the World Authority on Peafowl and I hope to be offered a chair some day at the Chicken College.
- Flannery O'Connor, letter to Robert Lowell

I write at high speed because boredom is bad for my health. It upsets my stomach more than anything else. I also avoid green vegetables. They're grossly overrated.
- Noel Coward

The best time for planning a book is while you're doing the dishes.
- Agatha Christie

If you are in difficulties with a book, try the element of surprise: attack it an hour when it isn't expecting it.
- H.G. Wells

When I stop [working] the rest of the day is posthumous. I'm only really alive when I'm writing.
- Tennessee Williams, *Pittsburgh Press,* 30 May '60

If you look at anything long enough, say just that wall in front of you—it will come out of that wall.
- Anton Chekhov

I sit at a desk. I face the wall. If you sit facing the wall, the only out is through the sentences.
    - E.L. Doctorow

The ideal view for daily writing, hour for hour, is the blank brick wall of a cold-storage warehouse. Failing this, a stretch of sky will do, cloudless if possible.
    - Edna Ferber

Appealing workplaces are to be avoided. One wants a room with no view, so imagination can meet memory in the dark.
    - Annie Dillard

It is by sitting down to write every morning that one becomes a writer. Those who do not do this remain amateurs.
    - Gerald Brenan

Flannery O'Connor, afflicted with lupus, could only write two hours a day—always at the same time, in the same place.
    - Sophy Burnham, *For Writers Only*

You write by sitting down and writing. There's no particular time or place—you suit yourself, your nature.
    - Bernard Malamud

Meditation has been a loyal friend to me…*The Color Purple* owes much of the humor and playfulness to the equanimity of my mind as I committed myself to a routine, daily practice.
    - Alice Walker, *Writers [on Writing]*

Once I have the idea for a story, I start collecting all kinds of helpful information and storing it in three-wring notebooks. For example, I may see a picture of a man in a magazine and say, "That's exactly what the father in my book looks like!"…I save everything that will help—maps, articles, hand-jotted notes, bits of dialogue from conversation I overheard.
    - Phyllis Reynolds Naylor

When you're writing, it's as if you're within a kind of closed world.
    - Michael Ondaatje

Most of the basic material a writer works with is acquired before the age of fifteen.
    - Willa Cather

I would get up every morning, go to my office and write without qualms until I felt it was time to go home. As I neared the end I was too frightened that I might lose the conclusion—which I did not know yet—and so I merely sat in the garden and wrote in a notebook. I suddenly felt an enormous tension; but my ending, when it came, surprised me into laughter. I felt like a spectator at my own game.

    - Anita Brookner

I write by hand as I have always done, and enjoy opening an empty notebook waiting to be filled in.

    - Muriel Spark

If you stuff yourself full of poems, essays, plays, stories, novels, films, comic strips, magazines, music, you automatically explode every morning like Old Faithful. I have never had a dry spell in my life, mainly because I feed myself well, to the point of bursting. I wake early and hear my morning voices leaping around in my head like jumping beans. I get out of bed to trap them before they escape.

    - Ray Bradbury

If I don't write to empty my mind, I go mad.

    - Lord Byron

You can only write what you need to write.

    - P. D. James

I like to get 10 pages a day, which amounts to 2,000 words.

    - Stephen King, *On Writing: A Memoir of the Craft*

Push your sentences until they say something interesting…Keep coming back to your work. Sneak up on it. You don't have to solve all the problems at once. The more sittings, the more likely you are to find unusual things to add.

    - David Long

I'm always working on the entire book at once, with a particular emphasis on one chapter. My bodily sense at the end of a day's work is that the whole thing has somehow shifted a little, not that I have written or edited X number of pages. It is anything but a linear way of working.

    - Virginia Woolf, *The Diary of Virginia Woolf, Volume Three*

Be obscure clearly.

    - E.B. White

Write when there is something that you know, and not before; and not too damned much after.
- Ernest Hemingway

At the age of thirty-one, a series of strokes left her [Carson McCullers] paralyzed on the left side; subsequent strokes and operations led to her having to type her novels with one finger, then to write in longhand, and finally to dictate...She kept writing until seven weeks before she died of a brain hemorrhage in 1967.
- Susan Cahill, *Women & Fiction*

I am content. I sit down at my desk, a bare kitchen table with a blotter, a bottle of ink, a sand dollar to weight down one corner, a clam shell for a pen tray, the broken tip of a conch, pink-tinged, to finger, and a row of shells to set my thoughts spinning.
- Anne Morrow Lindbergh, *Gift from the Sea*

Books don't happen in my mind. They happen somewhere in my belly. It's like a long elephant pregnancy that can last two years. And then, when I'm ready to give birth, I sit down. I wait for January 8th, which is my special date, and then that day, I begin the book that has been growing inside of me...I write the first sentence which usually is the first sentence of the book...by the time I finish the first draft I know what the book is about. Not before.
- Isabel Allende

Perhaps in order to write a really great book, you must be rather unaware of the fact. You can slave away at it and change every adjective to some other adjective, but perhaps you can write better if you leave the mistakes.
- Jorge Luis Borges

There is only one trait that marks the writer. He is always watching. It's a kind of trick of the mind and he is born with it.
- Morley Callaghan

There is no rule on how to write. Sometimes it comes easily and perfectly; sometimes it's like drilling rock and then blasting it out with charges.
- Ernest Hemingway

Just write very straight. Write so even a baby can understand.
- George Crane, *Bones of the Master*

I sit in bed with a big breakfast and then I write. I like that.
- Katharine Hepburn

I learned that you should feel when writing, not like Lord Byron on a mountain top, but like a child stringing beads in kindergarten—happy, absorbed and quietly putting one bead after another.
- Brenda Ueland

I read the essays George Plimpton had done for *Paris Review* about how Hemingway and other great ones got their paragraphs hung together, and I tried to diagnose my own talents, and lack of them. I decided I was adept at description, good at moving narration along, and dialogue was no problem. I had no ideas whether I could develop a plot or how I could shape characters.
- Tony Hillerman

It was a dreary night of November that I beheld the accomplishment of my toils.
- Mary Godwin Shelley, after creating the
character Victor Frankenstein

I write every morning as soon after the first light as possible. There is no one to disturb you and it is cool or cold and you…warm as you write.
- Ernest Hemmingway

Tennessee Williams wrote *Cat on a Hot Tin Roof* on an assortment of hotel stationery.
- Sophy Burnham, *For Writers Only*

I always write with a Ticonderoga #2 pencil. I started out with it, and I'll go to that Great Bookstore in the Sky with one of those in my hand.
- Robert Ludlum

I write when I'm inspired, and see to it that I'm inspired at nine o'clock every morning.
- Peter De Vries

If I have ten minutes I use them even if they bring only two lines, and it keeps the book alive.
- Rumer Godden

Niccolo Machiavelli would wash up, dress up before going to his writing room in the evening and there "hold conversation with the ancient worthies."
- James J. O'Connell, *Avatars of the Word*

I never write except with a writing board. I've never had a table in my life. And I use all sorts of things. Write on the sole of my shoe.
- Robert Frost, *Writers At Work*

When my horse is running good, I don't stop to give him sugar.
- William Faulkner

I can write with a crying child on my lap. I have. Often.
- David Baldacci

To me…writing is addictive. If I don't get to write three or four times a week, I start getting very angry with people, very annoyed.
- Laurence Yep

If you're trying to write, you have to let your attention drop. You can't maintain an interest in anything.
- Barbara Tuchman

I'm highly irritable and my senses bruise easily, and when they are bruised I write.
- S.J. Perelman

One can write out of love or hate. Hate tells one a great deal about a person. Love makes one become the person. Love, contrary to legend, is not half as blind, at least for writing purposes, as hate. Love can see the evil and not cease to be love. Hate cannot see the good and remain hate. The writer, writing out of hatred, will, thus, paint a far more partial picture than if he had written out of love.
- Jessamyn West

The perfect place for a writer is in the hideous roar of a city, with men making a new road under his window in competition with a barrel organ, and on the mat a man waiting for the rent.
- Henry Vollam Morton

Writing is an escape from a world that crowds me. I like being alone in a room It's almost always a form of meditation—an investigation of my own life.
- Neil Simon

You write by sitting down and writing. There's no particular time or place—you suit yourself, your nature.
- Bernard Malamud

A surprising number of writers belong to the Bathrobe School. When he first started writing, John McPhee not only worked in his bathrobe but tied its sash to the arms of his chair to keep from even thinking about leaving.
- Ralph Keyes

I even shower with my pen, in case any ideas drip out of the waterhead.
- Graycie Harmon

In order to really crank it up you need to get dressed and put on your shoes and act as if you're going to an office to work.
- Anne Bernays

No day without lines.
- Émile Zola

A writer should write with his eyes and a painter should paint with his ears... One of the pleasant things those of us who write or paint do is to have the daily miracle. It does come.
- Gertrude Stein

I write because I am driven to know, and writing for me is a wonderful way to learn. I also write because the discipline it takes is good for my mind; it keeps it in shape and youthful and alive...I write because of the joy involved in giving birth.
- Matthew Fox, *Creativity*

I talk out the lines as I write them.
- Tennessee Williams

I hear and I forget; I see and I remember; I write and I understand.
- Chinese Proverb

Most writers find they can write for three or four hours at a stretch when composing new material, though they can correct and edit for twice that long. Occasionally we read of an author—John Fowles, for example—who works twelve to fourteen hours in a kind of drunken trance.
- Sophy Burnham

I've written thirty to forty hours at a sitting.
- Richard Jones

Write about winter in summer. Describe Normandy as Ibsen did, from a desk in Italy; describe Dublin as James Joyce did, from a desk in Paris. Willa Cather wrote her prairie novels in New York City; Mark Twain wrote *Huckleberry Finn* in Hartford, Connecticut. Recently, scholars learned that Walt Whitman rarely left his room.

    - Annie Dillard, *The Writing Life*

I write in a quite deliberate way. I write three, four pages a day. I don't go too quickly.

    - Jane Smiley

Writers kid themselves—about themselves and other people. Take the talk about writing methods. Writing is just work—there's no secret. If you dictate or use a pen or type or type with your toes—it is just work.

    - Sinclair Lewis

Fill your paper with the breathings of your heart...

    - William Wordsworth

19.

What should I know about personal writing – journals, diaries, and memoirs?

What good is this journal? I cling to these pages as to something fixed among so many fugitive things.
- André Gide

Journals are a kind of deep planting. Some blossom into a whole garden; others, a single bloom…A journal is always a self-portrait, its narrative still evolving.
- Alexandra Johnson, *Leaving a Trace: On Keeping a Journal*

To keep a journal is to embark on a journey.
- Marlene A. Schiwy, *A Voice of Her Own*

In my journal, anyone can make a fool of himself.
- Rudolf Virchow, *Zeitschrift für Ethnologie*

To Nobody, then, will I write my journal! Since to Nobody can I be wholly unreserved—to Nobody can I reveal every thought, every wish of my heart, with the most unlimited confidence, the most unremitting sincerity to the end of my life!…No secret can I conceal from No-body, and to No-body can I be ever unreserved…Nobody will not reveal when the affair is doubtful. Nobody will not look towards the side least favourable.
- Frances Burney

The journal is the ideal place of refuge for the inner self because it constitutes a counterworld: a world to balance the other.
- Joyce Carol Oates

To awaken, to open up like a flower to the light of a fuller consciousness! I want to see and feel and expand, little book, you holder of my secrets.
- Emily Carr, *Hundreds and Thousands: the Journal of an Artist*

Writing a journal means that facing your ocean you are afraid to swim across it, so you attempt to drink it drop by drop.
- George Sand

The concept that underlies the Intensive Journal approach is that the potential for growth in a human being is as infinite as the universe.
- Ira Progoff, Thomas Mallon, *A Book of One's Own*

A journal-keeper is really the natural historian of his own life…But many of the great journals are marked by a dogged absence of self-consciousness, a willingness to suspend judgment of the journal itself.
- Verlyn Klinkenborg

All writers are observers, fascinated with human goings-on but journal writers are a special breed, I think, suspicious of their own memories, like tourists taking snapshots of everything they see.
- Robin Hemley

I knew as I wrote them [journals] that even though they provided an excellent place for brain (and heart, and psyche) dump, they were mainly a map of me.
- Colleen Wainwright

A writer uses a journal to try out the new step in front of the mirror.
- Mary Gordon

I went through a period once when I felt like I was dying. I wasn't writing any poetry, and I felt that if I couldn't write I would split. I was recording in my journal but no poems came…The next year I went back to my journal and here were these incredible poems, I could almost lift out…These poems came right out of the journal. But I didn't see them as poems then.
- Audre Lorde

I have decided to keep a full journal in the hope that my life will perhaps seem more interesting when it is written down.
- Sue Townsend, *Adrian Mole*

A journal is a leap of faith. You write without knowing what the next day's entry will be—or when the last."
- Violet Weingarten, *Intimations of Morality*

Journal writing is a voyage to the interior.
- Christina Baldwin

And now, O my journal! Art thou not highly dignified? Shalt thou not flourish tenfold?
- James Boswell

Leap—leap—remembering my journal that looks like a Beethoven manuscript—blots, blue ink, red, yellow and green, pages torn by an angry pen, smudged with tears, leaping with joy from exclamation marks to dashes that speak more than the words between, my journal that dances with the heartbeat of a process in motion.

   - Marion Woodman, *The Pregnant Virgin*

When the notebook was full, I began another. During the day I hid them under my mattress. When I shut myself into my room in the evening I retrieved them with the joy that might have been reserved for a handsome new lover. It happened simply, easily. I didn't think I was writing, even. With pencil and paper, I let my mind wander.

   - Marie Cardinal, *The Words to Say It*

The chief utility of the *journal in time* is to restore the integrity of the mind and the equilibrium of the conscience, that is, inner health.

   - H. F. Amiel

My Journal is that of me which would else spill over and run to waste, gleanings from the field which in action, I reap. I must not live for it, but in it for the gods…"Says I to myself" should be the motto of my journal. It is fatal to the writer to be too much possessed by his thought. Things must lie a little remote to be described…The charm of the journal must consist in a certain greenness, through freshness, and not in maturity.

   - Henry David Thoreau, *The Book of Concord*

The point of my keeping a notebook has never been…to have an accurate factual record of what I have been doing or thinking…At no point have I ever been able successfully to keep a diary; my approach to daily life ranges from the grossly negligent to the merely absent, and on those few occasions when I have tried dutifully to record a day's events, boredom has so overcome me that the results are mysterious at best…*How it felt to me*: that is getting closer to the truth about a notebook.

   - Joan Didion, "On Keeping a Notebook,"
   Slouching Towards Bethlehem

People who keep journals live life twice.

   - Jessamyn West

A journal is how memory and meaning finally meet, finding a core image that begins to unlock important connections in a life.

   - Alexandra Johnson, *Leaving a Trace: On Keeping a Journal*

…the habit of writing thus for my own eye only is good practice. It loosens the ligaments. Never mind the misses and the stumbles. Going at such a pace as I do I must make the most direct and instant shots at my object, and thus have to lay hand on words, choose them and shoot them with no more pause than is needed to put my pen in the ink.
 - Virginia Woolf, *A Writer's Diary*

I often reread old journals and make notes to my former selves in the margin.
 - Gail Godwin

It is a strangely pleasurable thing to read your own words from widely varying periods and phases of your life. You can hear not just how you thought but how you sounded at the moment you were thinking it. It's so much clearer and more specific than when your memory plays it back.
 - Merrill Markoe

We are drawn toward journals out of a craving for the authentic, for the uncensored word and thought.
 - Mark Rudman

What fun it is to generalize in the privacy of a notebook. It is as I imagine waltzing on ice might be. A great delicious sweep in one direction, taking you your full strength, and then with no trouble at all an equally delicious sweep in the opposite direction.
 - Florida Scott-Maxwell

Most people are conscious sometimes of strange and beautiful fancies swimming before their eyes: the pen is the want to arrest, and the journal is the mirror to detain and fix them.
 - Robert Willmott

They are loaded with opinion, moral thoughts, quick evaluations, youthful hopes and cares and sorrows. Occasionally, they manage to report something in exquisite honesty and accuracy.
 - E. B. White

Memoirs: The backstairs of history.
 - George Meredith

Memory and writing are intertwined. Writing tries to extend our memories infinitely.
 - Alice W. Flaherty, *The Midnight Disease*

…why the journal distresses me, but also fascinates: I'm required to use my own voice. And record only the truth. But not to record *all* the truth. There have been many things I've eliminated over the years…or hinted at so slantwise no one could guess…Still, what is recorded is always true. At least at the time it is recorded.
- Joyce Carol Oates

For any writer who wants to keep a journal, remember to be alive to everything, not just to what you're feeling, but also to your pets, to flowers, to what you are reading.
- May Sarton

It is often on days when I thought nothing happened that I'll start writing and go on for pages, a single sound or sight recalled from the afternoon suddenly loosing a chain of thoughts.
- Thomas Mallon

I'm finding now that some of the freest writing I do is in the journal because psychologically that feels like playtime. Once I get into the chapter itself it starts feeling too earnest. I think, this is a solemn piece of writing here and I had better not make a mistake, and so I start getting tense.
- Sue Grafton, Naomi Epel, *Writers Dreaming*

A writer is rarely so inspired as when he talks about himself.
- Anatole France

The chief danger memoirists face is starring in their own stories and becoming fascinated.
- Annie Dillard

Writing is conscience, scruple, and the farming of our ancestors.
- Edward Dahlberg

Too often memories die with their owner, and too often time surprises us by running out.
- William Zinsser

Anyone who believes you can't change history has never tried to write his memoirs.
- David Ben Gurion

The telling of your story is a revolutionary act.
>   - Sam Keen

Autobiography, however, does not suffer either liars or fibbers gladly...It has no materials beyond its own subject and no plot beyond its own already lived one.
>   - Phyllis Tickle, *The Shaping of a Life: A Spiritual Landscape*

Memoirs, like journals, often mimic the way memory works; shifting back and forth between past and present, trying to link event and meaning.
>   - Alexandra Johnson, *Leaving a Trace: On Keeping a Journal*

With my own memoirs, they are truthful, and I write everything fully expecting to some day end up television on Court TV, and I'm fully prepared to be challenged legally on it.
>   - Augusten Burroughs

I dislike modern memoirs. They are generally written by people who have either entirely lost their memories, or have never done anything worth remembering.
>   - Oscar Wilde

Perhaps writing opens up a parallel universe into which, one by one, we'll move all of our dearest memories and rearrange them as we please. Perhaps this is why all memoirists lie.
>   - André Aciman, *Writers on Writing*

20.

What do I need to know about writing for children and adolescents?

A good book for children is simply one which is a good book in its own right, and which should thus also be a source of pleasure, profit, or interest to any adult reader…The touchstone of truth is in the children themselves.
> - Mollie Hunter, *Talent is Not Enough*

Pretty much all the honest truth-telling there is in the world is done by children.
> - Oliver Wendell Holmes

Anyone who has survived his childhood has enough information about life to last him the rest of his days.
> - Flannery O'Connor

There is always one moment in childhood when the door opens and lets the future in.
> - Graham Greene

Childhood is the small town everyone came from.
> - Garrison Keillor

A kid is a guy I never wrote down to. He's interested in what I say if I make it interesting.
> - Theodore Geisel (Dr. Seuss)

A book worth reading only in childhood is not worth reading even then.
> - C.S. Lewis

Only as we give children the truth about life can we expect any improvement in it.
> - Mabel Louise Robinson

Anyone who knows the children's book field will tell you that a good story for children should be enjoyable to readers of any age. It should not for example, bore the mother who is reading it aloud, even though it is only the short text contained in a picture book.
- Phyllis A. Whitney

Children, like animals, use all their senses to discover the world. Then artists come along and discover it the same way, all over again.
- Eudora Welty

Our senses are indeed our doors and windows on this world, in a very real senses the key to the unlocking of meaning and the wellspring of creativity.
- Jean Houston

Children are a wonderful gift…They have an extraordinary capacity to see into the heart of things and to expose sham and humbug for what they are.
- Desmond Tutu

Children reinvent the world for you.
- Susan Sarandon

It is the so-called realistic stories which deceive children. The fairy tale, like the myth, on the one hand arouses longing for more ideal worlds, and on the other, gives the real world a new dimension of depth.
- Clyde S. Kilby

Children have a lot more to worry about from the parents who raised them than from the books they read.
- E.L. Doctorow

I don't believe in children's books. I think after you've read *Kidnapped, Treasure Island* and *Huckleberry Finn*, you're ready for anything.
- John Mortimer

The characters in a children's book must reach into the heart of the reader on page one. Emotional content is the main reason a child and a parent will go back to a book again and again.
- Rosemary Wells

A child can identify with adult characters—but only if they are sympathetically drawn and simple enough.
- E.W. Hildick, *Children and Fiction*

There's so much more to a book than just reading. I've seen children play with books, fondle books, smell books, and that's every reason why books should be lovingly produced.
- Maurice Sendak

When I was 8, I was reading a book in which it was snowing. When I looked outside, I expected there to be snow on the ground. I thought, "This is the most powerful thing I can do! I'm going to be a writer."
- Candace Bushnell

A child's story reading if it is rich lays open a world that lasts a lifetime; an impoverished, banal story world dulls the spirit forever.
- Angus Wilson

Children don't read to find their identity, to free themselves from guilt, to quench their thirst for rebellion or to get rid of alienation. They have no use for psychology...They still believe in God, the family, angels, devils, witches, goblins, logic, clarity, punctuation, and other such obsolete stuff...When a book is boring, they yawn openly. They don't expect their writer to redeem humanity, but leave to adults such childish illusions.
- Isaac Bashevis Singer

A children's story which is enjoyed only by children is a bad children's story. A waltz which you can like only when you are waltzing is a bad waltz.
- C.S. Lewis

I don't write for adults. I want to write for readers who can perform miracles. Only children perform miracles when they read.
- Astrid Lindgren

You must write for children the same way you write for adults, only better.
- Maxim Gorky

Adults are only obsolete children.
- Theodor S. Geisel (Dr. Seuss)

I'm not writing to make anyone's children feel safe.
- J.K. Rowling

You have to write whichever book it is that wants to be written. And then, if it's going to be too difficult for grown-ups, you write it for children.
- Madeleine L'Engle

He (C. S. Lewis) never wrote down to or for children except to use them as characters. He writes what he was passionate about.
- Adam Gopnik, "Prisoner of Narnia," New Yorker, Nov. 21, 2005

A good children's book strikes a vibration in the soul that lasts a lifetime.
- William Targ

It does not seem to me that I have the right to foist a story on people, most of whom are children who should be learning all the time, unless I am learning from it too.
- Diana Wynne Jones

The best children's book writers are not people who have kids, but people who write from the child within themselves.
- Andrea Brown

It is not necessary to have children of your own in order to write children's books. The only condition is that one was once a child oneself—and then try to remember what it was like.
- Astrid Lindgren

I conceive that the right way to write a story for boys is to write so that it will not only interest boys but strongly interest any man who has ever been a boy. That immensely enlarges the audience.
- Mark Twain, Letter

I believe that good questions are more important than answers, and the best children's books ask questions, and make the readers ask questions. And every new question is going to disturb someone's universe.
- Madeleine L'Engle

I found in my mother's dressing room some odd volumes of Shakespeare, nor can I easily forget the rapture with which I sat up in my shirt reading them by the light of the fire in her apartment, until the bustle of the family rising from supper warned me it was time to creep back to my bed where I was supposed to have been safely deposited since nine o'clock,
- Sir Walter Scott

The stories of childhood leave an indelible impression, and their author always has a niche in the temple of memory from which the image is never cast out to be thrown on the rubbish heap of things that are outgrown and outlived.
- Howard Pyle

I had just taken to reading. I had just discovered the art of leaving my body to sit impassive in a crumpled up attitude in a chair or sofa, while I wandered over the hills and far away in novel company and new scenes…the reading habit had got me securely.
  - H.G. Wells

Words were intoxicants. I tasted, smelled, touched them. They were unknown fruit, strange and delectable, fragrance floating across wide seas, moonlight on still water. They were as remote from my stupid halting speech as I was from my immediate and material surroundings. I never said them aloud, but I dwelt with them "in faery lands forlorn."
  - Mary Ellen Chase

As a child I felt that books were holy objects, to be caressed, rapturously sniffed, and devotedly provided for. I gave my life to them—I still do. I continue to do what I did as a child: dream of books, make books, and collect books.
  - Maurice Sendak

As a little girl my greatest joy was to lose myself in a book…Today, many years later and millions of words later, I still get a positively physical pleasure from a beautifully carved sentence or a powerfully expressed idea.
  - Arianna Huffington

I think a children's writer has a dual responsibility—you must entertain the child, it must be something they enjoy reading, but I think also because we're adult and we have had experiences we need to kind of show a way through what seems to be a hopeless tangle at times. I don't necessarily mean a happy ending, because happy endings aren't always right for a book, more often than not, but the possibility of a solution I think is important.
  - Berlie Doherty, *Talking Books* ed. James Carter

I will not take a young reader through a story and in the end abandon him. That is, I will not write a book that closes in despair. I cannot, will not, withhold from my young readers the harsh realities of human hunger and suffering and loss, but neither will I neglect to plant that stubborn seed of hope that has enabled our race to outlast wars and famines and the destruction of death.
  - Katherine Paterson, *A Sense of Wonder*

The imagination is an eye, a marvelous third eye that floats free. As children, that eye sees with 20/20 clarity. As we grow older, its vision begins to dim.
  - Stephen King, *Danse Macabre*

Children like to read about success, whether it's winning the hand of the best princess or prince, saving a life, helping people who need it, beating the other team in the game of the year, or discovering another universe.

> \- Janet Asimov and Isaac Asimov

Children long for models of effective action. "What could a kid really do?"… Really doing something is hard. It's just *because* children feel so little power that they need the hope that an individual—that they themselves—can act and accomplish.

> \- Judy K. Morris, *Writing Fiction for Children*

We can get away with things in children's books that nobody in the adult world ever can because the assumption is that the audience is too innocent to pick it up. And in truth they're the only audience that does pick it up.

> \- Maurice Sendak

Children's authors generally write in one of two ways, either to please children or to please themselves. The more numerous of them, those who write to please children, have traditionally been the purveyors of ephemera and dreck; those who write to please themselves have given us most of the best children's books we have…

> \- John Goldthwaite

The best way to make money in the children's-book business is to both write and illustrate…When I'm old and infirm and my fingers start to shake, I'll only write. But for now, I write out the stories first, get them the way I want them, and then illustrate them. I save the drawing for dessert.

> \- Arnold Lobel, *People Books, Book People* [David W. McCullough]

I never spent less than two years on the text of one of my picture books, even though each of them is approximately 380 words long. Only when the text is finished…do I begin the pictures.

> \- Maurice Sendak

All really good picture books are written to be read five hundred times.

> \- Rosemary Wells

I start drawing, and eventually the characters involve themselves in a situation. Then in the end, I go back and try to cut out most of the preachments.

> \- Theodor Seuss Geisel, (Dr. Seuss)

Childhood is the world of miracle and wonder, as if creation rose, bathed in light, out of the darkness, utterly fresh and astonishing. The end of childhood is when things cease to astonish us.
- Eugene Ionesco

Our responsibility to [children] is not to pretend that if we don't look, evil will go away, but to give them weapons against it…Laughter, a gift for fun, a sense of play.
- Madeleine L'Engle, *A Circle of Quiet*

The stories of childhood leave an indelible impression, and their author always has a niche in the temple of memory from which the image is never cast out.
- Howard Pyle

Sure, it's simple writing for kids…Just as simple as bringing them up.
- Ursula K. Le Guin

…I am reading a lot of books with names like *Conrad Cantaloupe Has a Sad Day*. As far as I can tell, modern children's books are written by people who (a) get paid by the page, (b) are hitting the bourbon pretty hard.
- Dave Barry

That adolescent me, the girl who was, as I remember her, insecure, unsure, dreaming, yearning, longing, that girl who was hard on herself, who was cowardly and brave, who was confused and determined—that girl who was me—still exists. I call on her when I write. I am the me of today—the person who has become a woman, a mother, a writer. Yet I am the me of all those other days as well. I believe in the reality of the past.
- Norma Fox Mazer

I think if what you're writing is realistic fiction for teens, then you need to reflect their lives. The one thing I have heard from teenagers is that they want honesty.
- Kathy Stinson

But what the young adult novel does that the adult novel doesn't is get into the heart and soul of the teenager as a teenager. Not as an adult reminiscing, not as the subject of a narrator, but as a teenager with teenage concerns that have nothing to do with adult memories because they are being lived at that moment.
- M. Rachel Plummer, "What Makes a Young Adult Novel A Young Adult Novel?"

Fantasy is the easiest thing to write badly.
>   - Phyllis A. Whitney, *Writing Juvenile Stories and Novels*

When I was little, the most thrilling words in the language were "Once upon a time."
>   - Mary Higgins Clark

Little Red Riding Hood was my first love. I felt that if I could have married Little Red Riding Hood I should have known perfect bliss.
>   - Charles Dickens

It [fantasy] implies the supernatural, but need not express it.
>   - E.M. Forster, *Aspects of the Novel*

Everyone's life is a fairy tale, written by God's fingers.
>   - Hans Christian Andersen

Fairy tales don't come from old wisdom, they come from old foolishness—just as potent.
>   - Eudora Welty, *The Eye of the Story*

I consider the dark side of fantasy to be a relief from the bright side of reality.
>   - Forrest J. Ackerman

The two basic stories of all times are *Cinderella* and *Jack the Giant Killer*—the charm of women and the courage of men.
>   - F. Scott Fitzgerald, *The Crack-up*

Fairy tales are more than true: not because they tell us that dragons exist, but because they tell us that dragons can be beaten.
>   - G.K. Chesterton

I like nonsense; it wakes up the brain cells. Fantasy is a necessary ingredient in living; it's a way of looking at life through the wrong end of a telescope. Which is what I do, and that enables you to laugh at life's realities.
>   - Theodor Seuss Geisel (Dr. Seuss)

Fantasy is to the human mind what salt is to the diet.
>   - Stephen King

I recall reading with such intensity that my mother forbade me to go to the 82nd St. Library because I was so inflamed with fairy stories that I couldn't sleep.
>   - Richard Stern

Far from dulling or emptying the actual world, [stories] give a new dimension or depth. The one who listens to stories does not despise real woods because he has read of enchanted woods. The reading makes all real woods a little enchanted.
- C. S. Lewis, *Of Other Worlds, Essays and Stories*

Fantasy is the richest source of human creativity...In fantasy no holds are barred...In fantasy we become not only our ideal selves, but totally different people. We abolish the limits of our powers and perceptions. We soar.
- Harvey Cox, *The Feast of Fools*

According to Tolkien the appeal of the fairy story lies in the fact that man there most fully exercises his function as a "sub-creator"; not, as they love to say now, making a "comment upon life" but making, so far as possible, a subordinate world of his own...For Jung, fairy tale liberates Archetypes which dwell in the collective unconscious, and when we read a good fairy tale we are obeying the old precept, "Know thyself."
- C.S. Lewis, *Of Other Worlds*

If it has horses and swords in it, it's a fantasy, unless it also has a rocket ship in it, in which case it becomes science fiction. The only thing that'll turn a story with a rocket ship in it back into fantasy is the Holy Grail.
- Debra Doyle

A fairy tale...demands of the reader total surrender; so long as he is in its world, there must be for him no other...The way, the only way, to read a fairy tale is to...throw yourself in. There is no other way.
- W.H. Auden

[A great author of fantasy] makes a Secondary World which your mind can enter. Inside it, what he relates is "true": it accords with the laws of that world. You therefore believe it, while you are, as it were, inside.
- J.R.R. Tolkien, *The Tolkien Reader*

The essence of fairy-stories is that they satisfy our heart's deepest desire: to know a world better than our own, a world that has not been flattened and shrunk and emptied of mystery.
- Ralph C. Wood, *The Gospel According to Tolkien*

Jung said that studying fairy tales is a good way to study the comparative anatomy of the collective unconscious, the deeper layers of the human psyche.
- Marie-Louise Von Franz, *Archetypal Patterns in Fairy Tales*

I am sure I read every book of fairy tales in our branch library, with one complaint—all that long golden hair. Never mind—my short brown hair became long and golden as I read and when I grew up I would write a book about a brown-haired girl to even things up.

    - Beverly Cleary

Fantasy can be an economical way of trying on alternative ways of feeling, acting, and being. In the safety of the imagination we can become Charles Manson and purge our murderous rage without shedding blood, or make love to anyone without the entanglement of an actual relationship, or play God without having to reckon with the Devil.

    - Sam Keen, Anne Valley Fox, *Telling Your Story*

At the deepest levels of consciousness, visionary work propels our beliefs into a larger, timeless dimension—one that honors archetypal power. Fairy tales, myths and stories from all history grow meaningful…We find personal meaning in everything from the Odyssey to the Song of Solomon to the tale of little Red Riding Hood…Through archetypes, we are shown the way…The more we write, the more we recognize how the truths we seek are evident everywhere, in every circumstance, whether negative or positive.

    - Laura Cerwinske, *Writing as a Healing Art*

Every creative individual whatsoever owes all that is greatest in his life to fantasy. The dynamic principle of fantasy is play, a characteristic also of the child…Without this playing with fantasy no creative work has ever yet come to birth.

    - Carl Jung

No such thing as fantasy exists. There is only a succession of folk memories filtered through the storyteller's imagination and since all mankind shares in these memories, they are the common store on which the modern storyteller must draw in his attempts to create fantasy.

    - Mollie Hunter, *Talent is Not Enough*

Am I in earnest? Oh dear no! Don't you know that this is a fairy tale, and all fun and pretense; and that you are not to believe one word of it, even if it is true?

    - Charles Kingsley, *The Water-Babies*

Fairy stories open a door on other time and if we pass through, though only for a moment, we stand outside our own time, outside time itself, perhaps.

    - J.R.R. Tolkien

These stories [folktales] are very old. In times past they have no doubt meant many different things to different people. Some meanings may well have disappeared forever, together with the vanished circumstances of lives gone by. Today some of us, in our turn, perceive meanings in terms of the unconscious and its symbolism. In centuries to come, the tales will still be there, but what they will then seem to mean we cannot tell.
  - Richard Adams, *The Unbroken Web*

The sort of fiction, commonly called "sword and sorcery" by its fans, is not fantasy at its lowest, but it still has a pretty tacky feel; mostly it's the Hardy Boys dressed up in animal skins and rated R…Horror fiction…is one circular area in the larger circle of fantasy, and what is fantasy fiction but tales of magic? And what are tales of magic, but stories of power?
  - Stephen King, *Secret Windows*

Every fairy tale offers the potential to surpass present limits, so in a sense the fairy tale offers you freedoms that reality denies…there is an affirmation of life against the transience of that life, an essential defiance…The perfection and beauty of form rebels against the ugliness and shabbiness of the subject matter.
  - Azar Nafisi, *Reading Lolita in Tehran*

I remember vaguely that I liked Hans Andersen better than Grimm because he was less homely, but even he never gave me the knights and dragons and beautiful ladies that I longed for.
  - William Butler Yeats, *Reveries Over Childhood and Youth*

No such thing as pure fantasy exists. There is only a succession of folk memories filtered through the storyteller's imagination and since all mankind shares in these memories, they are the common store on which the modern storyteller must draw in his attempts to create fantasy.
  - Mollie Hunter, *Talent is Not Enough*

When the legends die, the dreams end. When the dreams end, there is no more greatness.
  - Hal Borland, *When the Legends Die*

About the Author

Karen Speerstra's prolific publishing career spans twenty-seven years of publishing experience including nine of free lance writing and public relations, and eighteen in book acquisitions and management with two major college text book and national and international professional publishing companies. Since 2000 she has been living with her husband John in central Vermont, writing and helping other writers realize their own publishing dreams.

Her company, Sophia Serve (see www.sophiaserve.com) serves select clients with their various needs from thought partnering to creating the book plan and proposal, developmental editing, co-writing and helping sort through publishing options.

She has published eight books, in addition to numerous articles, ten years of weekly regional and national newspaper columns, booklets, card sets, children's religious curriculum, and poetry.

The Writer's Prayer

You know my passion. I'm a word-weaver, a thought-shaper.
I craft words that become vibrations and set loose powerful ideas.
Help me to choose words wisely and aim them with care.
May they find their mark.
And remind me, because I'm prone to forgetfulness,
that I'm only borrowing these words for a little while.
They're really yours—for "in the beginning was The Word."
I need your help to become the very best crafter I can be,
because thought-shifting is a big responsibility.
It's hard, and downright scary.
What if someone who reads my words thinks they're stupid or silly or simple?
Trite or contrite. Listless or clichéd. Too dense. Or just plain boring!
Or, worse, what if someone uses my powerful words to destroy or cause pain?
May my words cushion life—never debase, harm, or kill.
Help me find the discipline to meet deadlines,
the resilience to face rejection
and the endurance to start all over again.
Give me the patience and insight to hone and rewrite
until all the words dance and sparkle. And all sound true.
Then grant me the courage to share them, for without a reader,
a listener or a viewer, they form hollow shapes that hold no song.
As paper and pixels carry my words around the world,
I pray some editor will find them timely and worthy and send me a check.
It won't always be a big check, but payment of any kind—
including bartering—shows that someone values my crafting.
Then I will write more words, and more words after that.
Some will take poetic form, others will become stories, essays,
songs, articles, memoirs, scripts, marketing pieces.
Some quieter words will find their way into my journals, e-mails, letters, blogs
and I vow to treat them all with the same reverence.
And, finally, I ask that someone, somewhere, will read my words
and smile and say, "This is really good! I want to keep this and read it again.
I wonder what else this person has written."
Then I'll know I'm truly a writer. My words have made a difference
in someone's life, for however long—a few seconds or as long as it takes
to change the course of the stars.
Thank you. Stay close to my keyboard, Great Word-Smith.
Amen. May it be so.
© Karen Speerstra, 2009

**For The Writer's Prayer, go to www.writersprayer.com
and print out (for FREE) a copy that is suitable for framing.**

Other Books by Karen Speerstra

The Earthshapers, 1980, (still in print after numerous reprints) (Naturegraph Press).

Several children's books, including *Let's Go, Jesus* and *I Believe* (Concordia Press).

She published with her son, Joel Speerstra, *Hunab Ku: 77 Sacred Symbols for Balancing Body and Spirit* (Crossing Press) May, 2005.

Divine Sparks: Collected Wisdom of the Heart, October 2005, (Morning Light Press).

Our Day to End Poverty: 24 Practical Ways You Can Make a Difference (Berrett-Koehler, 2007). Her role in this team of five people was primarily editor, with some writing.

A Green Devotional: Active Prayers for a Healthy Planet (Conari/Weiser, is scheduled to publish late 2009.)

Deal a Story

101 cards ~ 1,000,001 Story Ideas

There are 6 different-colored sections, each containing 16 cards, plus 5 wild cards. Deal a Story combines characters with a variety of plots and genres, giving the writer unique ways to dream up new stories. The writer picks a card from each group and is automatically presented with the start of a story. This is an ideal teaching tool for almost any level of creative writing classes including adults, college and high school students, for screen writing and improv workshops, theater groups, and for critique groups.

No more writer's block!

WRITERS

An endless array of possibilities!

Robert D. Reed Publishers Order Form

Call in your order for fast service and quantity discounts!
(541) 347-9882

OR *order online at* **www.rdrpublishers.com** *using PayPal.*
Or *order by FAX at* **(541) 347-9883** OR *by mail:*
Make a copy of this form; enclose payment information:
Robert D. Reed Publishers, 1380 Face Rock Drive, Bandon, OR 97411

Send indicated books to:

Name _____

Address _____

City _____ State _____ Zip _____

Phone_____ Cell _____

E-mail_____

Payment by check /__/ or credit card /__/ *(All major credit cards are accepted.)*

Name on card _____

Card number _____

Exp. Date _____ Last 3-digit number on back of card_____

	Quantity	Total Amount
Questions Writers Ask by Karen Speerstra $16.95	_____	_____
Deal a Story (card set) by Sue Viders $19.95	_____	_____
Make Steady Money as a Travel Writer by Jack Adler $14.95	_____	_____
Fearless by Steve Chandler $12.95	_____	_____
The New American Prosperity by Darby Checketts. . $12.95	_____	_____
The Secret Sin of Opi by Peter Cimini $24.95	_____	_____
Buddha's Wife by Gabriel Constans $14.95	_____	_____
Gringa in a Strange Land by Linda Dahl $14.95	_____	_____
PickOne by Colin Ingram and Robert D. Reed $14.95	_____	_____
How Bad Do You Really Want It? by Tom Massey. . . $19.95	_____	_____

Quantity of books ordered: _____ Total amount for books: _____

Shipping is $3.50 1st book + $1 for each additional book: Plus postage: _____

FINAL TOTAL: _____